Thomas Griffith

**Fundamentals or Bases of Belief**

Concerning Man, God, and the Correlation of God and Men

Thomas Griffith

**Fundamentals or Bases of Belief**
*Concerning Man, God, and the Correlation of God and Men*

ISBN/EAN: 9783337071134

Printed in Europe, USA, Canada, Australia, Japan

Cover: Foto ©Lupo / pixelio.de

More available books at **www.hansebooks.com**

# MAN AND GOD.

'Concerning the bonds of unity, extremes are to be avoided; which will be done, if the league of Christians framed by our Saviour Himself were, in the two cross clauses thereof, soundly expounded: "He that is not with us is against us;" and again: "He that is not against us is with us;" i.e. if the points FUNDAMENTAL and of substance in religion were truly discerned, and distinguished from points not of faith, but of opinion only.'—BACON, *Essays*, iii.

# FUNDAMENTALS

OR

## BASES OF BELIEF

CONCERNING

MAN, GOD, AND THE CORRELATION OF GOD AND MEN.

A HANDBOOK

OF

MENTAL, MORAL, AND RELIGIOUS PHILOSOPHY.

BY

THOMAS GRIFFITH, A.M.

PREBENDARY OF ST. PAUL'S;

*Author of 'The Spiritual Life,' 'The Apostles' Creed,' 'The Fatherhood of God.'*

LONDON:
LONGMANS, GREEN, AND CO.
1871.

LONDON: PRINTED BY
SPOTTISWOODE AND CO., NEW-STREET SQUARE
AND PARLIAMENT STREET

# CONTENTS.

### I. OF THINKING.

|  | PAGE |
|---|---|
| All thinking must begin with FACTS; but it must complete itself by conclusions from these Facts . . | 3–10 |

### II. OF MAN.

The fundamental Fact with which I begin is, that I AM. I find myself existing as a Simple, Self-same, Substantial Being . . . . . . . . . . . 13–30

I find myself, moreover, existing with certain QUALITIES; in some of which I am like lower animals, but in others altogether unlike them . . . . 31–78

I am *like* lower animals in being Sensitive, Causative, Intellective . . . . . . . . . 31–46

I am altogether *unlike* them in being Moral, Religious, Progressive . . . . . . 47–78

And these Facts involve a conclusion that I am also a Permanent being . . . . . . . 79–100

### III. OF GOD.

The Facts of an organised world oblige the conclusion of an INTELLIGENT WILL as the Originator of this organisation . . . . . . . . . . 103–116

This Intelligent Will is a Person; unknowable in his essence, but knowable in his character, through his dealings with this world . . . . . . . . . 117–134

## IV. OF THE CORRELATION OF GOD AND MEN.

### i. *God's dealings with us.*

| | PAGE |
|---|---|
| The Facts of History oblige the conclusion that God is carrying on a process of Development for the human race | 137–145 |
| In order to this Development He has endowed us with a nature like his own | 145–152 |
| To this development He makes subservient even intermediate evil | 153–167 |
| This Development He commences by awakening men to their need of Himself, and sending gifted spirits to respond to this need | 168–197 |
| This Development He advances by means of an ascending series of religious communities, from a sacred Family in Abraham, through a sacred Nation by Moses, culminating in a sacred Brotherhood in Christ | 198–206 |
| And in this Brotherhood He dwells; to consecrate men to his service, commune with them by his Spirit, assimilate them to his image, and perfect them in his final kingdom | 206–212 |

### ii. *Our duties in return.*

| | |
|---|---|
| God is the universal Sovereign. Our corresponding duties therefore are, to this divine *King*, those of loyal subjects; to his *people*, those of faithful fellow-citizens; to our own *selves*, whatever will make us most efficient in these two relations | 213–230 |

## APPENDIX.

| | |
|---|---|
| Notes I. to XXV. | 233–281 |

# OF THINKING.

'L'homme est visiblement fait pour penser; c'est toute sa dignité et tout son mérite. Tout son devoir est de penser comme il faut; et l'ordre de la pensée est de *commencer par soi*, par son *auteur* et sa *fin*.'—PASCAL, *Pensées* (Paris, 1812), ii. 179.

'Never write on a subject without having first read yourself into it; and never read on a subject till you have *thought yourself* hungry on it.'—J. P. RICHTER.

'Faith is the reasoned-out conviction of things not seen.'—HEB xi. 3.

'La foi est la dernière démarche de la raison.'—PASCAL.

'Nicht jedes metaphysische System der Religion gleich gute Dienste leisten kann.

'Der religiöse Glaube **auf *dem Gegebenen*,** auf der Naturbetrachtung, als eine *theoretische nothwendige Ergänzung unseres Wissens, beruht*.'—HERBART, *Lehrbuch der Philosophie*, 2nd edit., p. 216.

Not every metaphysical system is equally favourable to religion; but religious faith rests on the *facts* which we observe in nature, and is the *necessary complement* of these facts and of our knowledge concerning them.

# LETTER I.

## *OF THINKING.*

My dear Friend,

You tell me that amidst the dust raised by the conflict of opinion in this unsettled age, you begin to lose sight of the landmarks which have hitherto been your guides. You are perplexed by the contradictions between reason and faith; between the novelties of science and the traditions of theology; and especially between the cheerless creed of a material philosophy and those beliefs of a spiritual world which are so precious to you. And you ask, 'How shall I attain to firm convictions on these points? Are there no foundation truths on which to plant my tottering feet?'

Now I think there are such truths; I seem to myself to have found them. And hence my present response to your complaint; hence the endeavour I am going to make to help you to grasp them for yourself. And I say emphatically, 'to *help* you to grasp them for *yourself*,' for no man can teach another; he can only help this other to be his own teacher. The loud voice of authority is here utterly vain. Only in the low, soft tones of sympathy can we reach the mind. In these tones, therefore, I would speak. Not unacquainted with the pains of thought myself, I know how to feel for every sufferer under such pains; and having discerned what seems to me the majestic form of Truth, I would gladly place you in my point of view that, thence looking, you may behold her too. Like Richard Baxter, I may say, 'One reason of this work is, *Quod cogitamus loquimur*; that which is most and deepest in our thoughts is aptest to break forth to others. Man is a communicative creature. Necessity, through perplexed thoughts, hath made this subject much of my meditations. It is the subject which I have found most necessary and most useful to myself; and I have reason enough to think that many others may be as weak as I; and I would fain have those partake of my satisfaction who have partaked of my difficulties.'[1]

My method will be to begin with *Man*; that through a well-grounded knowledge of ourselves we may reach a correlative conviction concerning God, and his relations towards us. And my object is to lead you through a realistic as opposed to a material psychology, a spontaneous as opposed to a calculated ethic, and a dynamic as opposed to a mechanical theism, to find your rest in a Christianity of eternal ideas instead of ephemeral notions; wherein the great facts of inspiration, revelation, and redemption take their true place, as moments in the ever-widening process of the divine education of the human race. And in pursuing this object, I shall not confine myself to laying before you the fruit of my own meditations, but shall illustrate, confirm, and adorn my subject by copious extracts from the deepest thinkers of the old world and the new. Thus, what I write to you will

---

[1] Baxter, Reasons of the Christian Religion; Preface.

furnish a text-book for students as well as an outline of
my own personal thought; and when you are wearied of
the dryness of *my* utterances, you will get refreshment
from the sparkling flow of theirs.

I begin, then, with those beautiful words of the philosophic emperor, in which he counsels for himself the
laying such foundation stones of truth as I am about to
lay for you. 'As physicians are always provided with
instruments ready for all emergencies, so do thou keep by
thee fixed determinations concerning things divine and
human. And whatsoever comes before thee, deal with it
in constant remembrance of the close connexion which
exists between these two; for never wilt thou do anything
well in human matters without reference to divine ones,
nor in divine matters without reference to human ones.'[1]
'And let these decisions be brief and *fundamental*, such
as shall at once suffice, when thou recurrest to them, to
purify thy soul from all its perturbations, and to send thee
back, no more disheartened, to the work which lies before
thee.'[2] With which compare what Seneca quotes from
Demetrius: 'A few precepts of wisdom, well remembered
and well used, are far more useful than a thousand things
which you may have read, but have not *ready at hand*.'[3]
To supply such *handy* wisdom is the object of my writing
to you.

But then all wisdom must be derived from careful observation of *facts*. With facts, in every department of
thought, must it begin; and yet not with these terminate.
'Those,' says Bacon, 'who have handled science have

---

[1] Antonini Comment. iii. 13. Compare Lactantius, Instit. i. 4. 'Neque religio ulla sine sapientia suscipienda est, nec ulla sine religione probanda sapientia.'
[2] Anton. Comment. iv. 3.  [3] Seneca, De Benef. vii. 1.

either been men of experiment or men of theory. The men of experiment are like the ant—they only collect and use. The theorists resemble spiders, who make cobwebs out of their own substance. But the bee takes a middle course; it gathers its material from the flowers of the garden and the field, but transforms and digests it by a power of its own. Not unlike this is the true business of philosophy.'[1]

We must then gather the material for our decisions from facts, yet not indolently rest in them. Facts have their meaning, and this meaning must be evolved from them. The relations which they bear must be noted. The suggestions which they furnish must be followed out. Newton indeed said, 'I invent not hypotheses.' Yet Newton refused not to admit the widest *inferences* from the simplest facts. He began with the falling apple, but he stopped not till he reached the universal law of gravitation.[2]

Nay, we must not only *accept* the suggestions which facts furnish, we must search out the intimations which may be involved in them. The process of philosophy is a putting nature to the question in order to extract from her the secrets of which her surface facts awaken some suspicion.

What's sought for may be found,
But truth unsearch'd for seldom comes to light.[3]

And yet Mr. Lewes praises Hume because 'probing deeper in the direction Berkeley had taken, he found that

---

[1] Bacon, Nov. Organum. Aph. 95.
[2] 'Will'st du ins Unendliche schreiten?
Geh im Endlichen nach allen Seiten.'—*Goethe.*
[3] Sophocl. Œd. Tyr. 110. τὸ δὲ ζητούμενον
Ἁλωτόν, ἐκφεύγει δὲ τἀμελούμενον.

not only was matter a figment, but mind was no less so. The substance *of* which our ideas are supposed to be impressions is occult, is a mere inference; the substance *in* which these impressions are supposed to be is equally occult, is a mere inference.' Observe : ' a *mere* inference.' Yet what is an ' inference' but a conclusion which facts not only suggest but require for their legitimate interpretation?[1] What is all thinking but a series of ' inferences'? Nay, whence comes our knowledge of facts themselves, but through our belief in the validity of ' inferences'? What certainty have we of anything that we call a fact, which does not rest upon the *inferences*, that our senses are to be relied on, that our powers of observation are to be relied on, that our power of memory is to be relied on, that the senses of others are to be relied on, that their testimony to what these senses report is to be relied on?[2]

And you know well, from your own experience, how vain it is to insist on shutting out all inferences from the facts which lie before us, how impossible it is to enforce the self-denying ordinance of positivism, ' Thus far shalt thou go and no further.'[3] The tide of thought

---

[1] ' Rationem quæ debitis modis *elicitur a rebus*, Interpretationem naturæ vocare consuevimus.'—Bacon, *Nov. Org. Aph.* 26. Similarly H. Ritter, *Unsterblichkeit*, p. 13 : 'Of what use is experience if it be not understood? All sciences which rise above the mere verification of facts undertake the *comprehension* of these facts, and speculate about their meaning.'

[2] So Herbert Spencer : ' Positive knowledge never can fill the whole region of thought. At the uttermost reach of discovery there must ever arise the question, What lies beyond? The human mind, throughout all time, must occupy itself, not only with ascertained phenomena and their relations, but also with that unascertained something which phenomena and their relations *imply*.'—*First Principles*, 16, 17. See further, Appendix, Note I.

[3] ' The term "positive," as implying a system of thought which assumes nothing beyond the content of observed facts, implies that which never did exist and never will.'—Huxley, *Lay Serm.* 178.

must rise. Its onward flow must sweep away the artificial dams which would confine it. Try to drive back from your mind every intimation which this school brands with that term 'occult.' Try to contract your thoughts within the narrow confines of the visible, to imprison them within the walls of sense. Try to conceive the possibility of there being nothing deeper than what appears; no substance, of which all show must be the manifestation; no inwardness, of which all outwardness can be nothing but the husk; no under side of which the upper side of the medal is but the obverse. You cannot accomplish this. The very words you use keep you back from this. For what if you call all facts 'phenomena' only? The very term includes a reference to *things* of which they are phenomena. 'Phenomenon' is an *adjective*, which cannot stand alone. It has no meaning but in relation to a *substantive* as its subject and support.[1] Just as the images you see in a mirror are reflections of *things* which throw these images upon it. Just as Mr. Pepper's ghosts bear witness to substances somewhere of which they are the apparitions. Just as all shadows testify to something which casts the shadows. The law is universal; if nothing *were*, then nothing could *appear*. Some appearances, it is true, are the product of other appearances, as the visible flower springs from its equally visible seed; but all these manifest antecedents have their ultimate ground in something *not* manifest, nay not manifestible.[2] This is what St. Paul means

---

[1] See Appendix, Note II.

[2] And therefore Socrates says, 'You ought never to think contemptuously of things invisible, but recognise from their manifestations the power they possess, and reverence the divine that is in them (τιμᾶν τὸ δαιμόνιον).'— Xenoph. *Mem.* iv. 3, 6. See further, Appendix, Note III.

when he says, 'the things which are seen' (the whole sphere of the visible, τὸ βλεπόμενον) 'are not made of things which do appear'; spring not, as to their *ultimate* ground, from anything observable in this sphere. That ground is non-apparent, transcendent.[1]

Besides, we must not forget that the very sciences which seem most exclusively occupied with facts, and the possessors of which most strenuously claim to keep entirely and solely within the domain of facts, cannot themselves be cultivated without the assumption of laws and principles, to which indeed the facts point, and which are legitimately inferred from the facts, but which, nevertheless, are something more and other than these facts. There is no such thing as a science purely experimental, any more than there is a science purely speculative. No science, for instance, seems so independent of experience as that of mathematics, yet it takes its first data from experience. Suppress the testimony of the senses touching extension, and you have no geometry. Suppress the testimony of consciousness concerning force, and you have no mechanics. So, equally, those sciences of observation which profess to consult nothing but facts cannot shape themselves into any system but by the aid of principles anterior to observation. Physics, chemistry, physiology could have no existence if their professors were not guided by the axioms, 'Every phenomenon implies a *cause* of its manifestation,' and 'Nature is subject to *laws* constant and universal.'[2]

Therefore it is not only allowable but indispensable for us, beginning with facts as our data, to proceed to such conclusions from these facts as they themselves

---

[1] Heb. xii. 3. [2] See De Margerie, Théodicée, i. 60.

point out. We must travel, warily yet hopefully, from the known to the unknown, assured that this unknown is contained within things known, as certainly as the corn in the husk, the kernel in the shell, the rich fruit in the hard rind. But the things known which are the most immediately before us, and of which we are best assured, are the facts of our consciousness as *Men*.[1] These facts include in themselves intimations of a Somewhat whose existence can alone explain them, and whom we recognise as *God*. And then arises the inquiry, what *correlation is there between God and Men?* So that we fall naturally into the course of thought prescribed to himself by Antoninus. Beginning with 'things human' we rise thence to 'things divine,' and end with 'the connexion between the two.' And thus we accomplish what St. Bernard prayed for, 'May I gather myself in from things outward to things inward, and then ascend from things inward to things upward!'[2]

---

[1] 'Of the two existences, that of mind as independent of matter is more certain than that of matter apart from mind.'—Lord Brougham, *Nat. Theol.* 57. 'As Descartes tells us, our knowledge of the soul is more intimate and certain than our knowledge of the body.'—Huxley in *Macmillan's Mag.*, May 1870.

[2] 'Ab exterioribus ad interiora redeam, et ab interioribus ad superiora ascendam.'—*S. Bernard.*

OF MAN.

Know then thyself, presume not God to scan,
The proper study of mankind is Man.'—POPE.

' On earth there is nothing great but man;
In man there is nothing great but mind.'—SIR W. HAMILTON.

'Deux choses instruisent l'homme de toute sa nature: l'instinct et l'expérience.'—PASCAL, *Pensées*, i. 191.

' It is not sufficient to have read the Delphic inscription, "Know thyself!" We must fix our attention upon it, and set earnestly to work to examine our own selves; for it will be difficult for us to know anything if we know not ourselves.'—XENOPH. *Mem.* iv. 2, 10.

## LETTER II.

### OF MAN'S PERSONALITY.

WE have seen that all well-grounded thought must have its foundation in facts; and that the first set of facts nearest and clearest to us are those which concern our nature as *Men*.

Now, of these facts, the most immediate and most certain is that we *are*. Of nothing can I ever be so sure as that I am. No one has taught me this, no one can prove it to me; yet no doubt can darken such a truth, no sophism can confute it. This is a certainty, if there be none other. This, therefore, is the basis of all science; and hence we make this certainty the measure of all other certainty. Our strongest possible form of asseveration is, 'As sure as I am!' or, 'As sure as thou art!' As the woman of Tekoah said to David, '*As thy soul liveth*, O king, none can turn to the right hand or to the left from aught that the king hath spoken!' And so Uriah to David, '*As thou livest*, and *as thy soul liveth*, I will not do this thing!'

It seems therefore, to me, a somewhat subtle distinction of Dr. Huxley's when he says that while we have an 'unquestionable and immediate certainty of the existence of mind, we have less certitude of the existence of ourself as the base of this mind.' For what is 'mind' according to his own definition?—'A state of consciousness.' But 'a state' must be a state of *something*; and 'consciousness' is not mere knowledge, but knowledge *to* and *by* something, of states pertaining to this something. It is *con-scio; mecum scio; mihimet ipse scio.* And the 'state of consciousness' which he recognises as 'an immediately observed fact' is a fact observed, not by somebody else, but by the Something, and observed by this something as a 'state' of its own self. So that, when he speaks of the certainty of 'mind,' he falls into that abstract language which he so justly censures. The 'mind' which I observe is no abstraction; it is *my* mind. It presents itself to *my* observation as a 'state' or modification of *my* self; and all the transformations of this 'mind,' in their various stages of sensation, perception, volition, action, are recognised by me as, not indeed my self but, affections and exertions of my self. That which I call my Self is not a mere congeries of thoughts, but a something which *has* these thoughts, *to* which they present themselves, *in* which they converge, and *from* which they emerge. Sensations and perceptions are but *im*pressions made on this something; volitions and actions are but *ex*pressions of this something. Always this something suggests itself, makes itself present to us as the ultimate subject and source of all that we are conscious of.

As surely, therefore, as we affirm our consciousness, so surely do we affirm therewith this Me, as inseparable from it; and this Me we affirm as a something *single* amidst the complexity of its manifestations, *selfsame* amidst their variety, and *substantial* amidst their merely phenomenal character.

1. In affirming that 'I am,' I affirm myself a something *single* amidst the complexity of my thoughts; a

central point on which all the influences which affect me converge, and from which all the effluences by which I affect other things diverge. That single word 'I' asserts emphatically Number One (No. I.) 'The student of history,' says Professor Maurice, 'finds himself amidst a world of I.s. And am I, then, to allow that this term is a mere abstraction? that it points to no substance? Every man who is most busy in the affairs of the world would raise his voice against me if I did that. "What! You put this slight upon Number One? You say that I am a nonentity! What then, pray, is not a nonentity?" A question which I should have much trouble in answering.'[1]

By this word 'I,' then, I mark myself as one and indivisible in contradistinction from *the world* with which I am mixed up, from the *body* which is so close to me, and even from the *mind* which is the object of my consciousness.

I am indeed mixed up with a surrounding *world*.[2] To this world I owe the particles which compose my frame, the breath I draw, the nourishment by which I am sustained. Nay, by this world I have been moulded into what I am. Through the parents from whom I sprang, the nurses who reared me, the teachers who

---

[1] Professor Maurice on the Conscience, p. 5, 15.

[2] 'Man's connexion with the great scheme of animated nature is intimate and inseparable. The physical conditions under which life exists are the same to him as to other animals. Air, land and water, heat, light, and moisture are as essential to him as to the other forms and grades of vitality. He originates like the other animals, embryologically passes through the same stages, and when launched on the field of independent being is subjected to the same functional round, and the same struggle for existence. Life, growth, reproduction, and decay are phases of being characteristic of all that lives. As a mere animal, man, like other animals, has his place in nature.'—Dr. Page, *Man*, p. 35.

trained me, the family in which I have grown up, the race to which I belong, the clime, the nation, the country, the department, the town, the circle in which I live, the temperament of my body, the texture of my nervous system; through all these agencies I am *what* I am. But yet I am distinct from them; I am not a mere particle and product of other things, but a separate indivisible thing.

Nor am I less separate from the *body* which is so close to me. This has been so thoroughly shown by Butler that I need not add a word. You know how he argues: 'The simplicity and oneness of the living agent which each man calls himself cannot indeed, from the nature of the thing, be properly *proved* by experimental observations, but as these fall in with the supposition of our unity, so they plainly lead us to conclude with certainty that our gross organised bodies are no more ourselves or part of ourselves than any other matter around us. For we see by experience that men may lose their limbs, their organs of sense, and even the greatest part of their bodies, and yet remain the same living agents.'[1] And you know the argument by which Plato distinguishes between the body, and the soul, or self: 'What is *the man*? Is it not that which makes use of the body as its instrument? But what makes use of the body as its instrument but the *soul*? And the user of a thing is assuredly distinct from the thing used. Besides, this user of the body is also master of the body, and there are only three suppositions we can make concerning the mastery of the body; this mastery must lie either in the body, or in the soul, or in a compound of both. But

[1] Butler, Anal. i. 1.

it cannot lie in the body, for we have seen already that the body is by no means master, but is mastered. Nor can it lie in a compound of body and soul, for one element of this compound is, as we have conceded, mastered. By what contrivance then can you make the two elements together become master? It remains therefore that the man, being neither the body by itself nor any compound of body and soul, must be either nothing at all, or that one thing in which the mastery resides, i.e. the soul. And therefore when I, Socrates, address myself to you, Alcibiades, I speak not to your bodily frame, but to your soul; my soul communing with your soul. And consequently, when we are admonished by the oracle to become acquainted with our self, it is plain that this self must mean our very self, our soul. For however thoroughly I may become acquainted with my body I thereby know only what *belongs* to me, not what is properly my self. Even a physician, as a physician, does not necessarily know himself.'[1] All which is in perfect consonance with the Scriptures, which represent the body as but the *scabbard* in which the soul is enclosed;[2] its earthly domicile;[3] its tabernacle or *tent*;[4] and its *clothing*, which it shall exchange for a better garment.[5] And this soul, thus distinct from the body and occupying it only as a temporary residence, is one and

[1] Plato, 1 Alcib. (Bipont, v. 58). See Appendix, Note IV.
[2] Daniel vii. 15, 'I was grieved in my spirit in the midst of its sheath.'
[3] Job iv. 19, 'We dwell in houses of clay.'
[4] 2 Cor. v. 1, 'Our earthly house, this tabernacle.' 2 Pet. i. 13, 'I must shortly put off this my tabernacle.'
[5] Job x. 11, 'Thou hast clothed me with skin and flesh;' xxx. 18, 'By the great force of my disease is my *garment* changed.' 2 Cor. v. 24, 'Desiring to be clothed upon with our house which is from heaven.'

the same with our very self. For whereas in Matt. xvi. 26, the question is, 'What is a man profited if he shall gain the whole world and lose his own *soul?*' this term is exchanged in Luke ix. 25, for 'What is a man advantaged if he lose *himself?*'

But further still, our soul or self is distinguished not only from the world at large, and from our own body in particular, but from even what we call our *mind*; that is, from the phenomena of consciousness. For we say in common parlance, not only 'my body,' 'my brain,' but 'my *mind*,' as a something not constituting our proper self but *belonging* to this self. 'A man is one thing,' says Professor Rolleston, 'his mind another, his body a third. Although they both *belong* to him they are no more the man himself than his horse or his dog. It is a mere blunder in natural history to confound these things.'[1] And so the sacred writers distinguish in like manner between the multiplied phenomena which make up the *mind* of a person—i.e. which he is conscious of—from the individual person himself to whom these phenomena present themselves. These last St. Paul calls 'the things of a man' ('What man knoweth the things of a man save the *spirit of man*,' the man himself, the spirit, 'which is in him?').[2] And the Psalmist says, 'The Lord knoweth the *thoughts* of man that they are but vanity.'[3] And again, 'In the multitude of my *thoughts* within me, thy comforts delight my *soul*.'[4] Whence St. Paul again distinguishes the *mind* as much as the flesh or body, from the man who possesses both; 'with the mind, I *myself*

---

[1] Lecture at the Royal Institution.
[2] 1 Corinth. ii. 11.
[3] Ps. xciv. 10.
[4] Ps. xxxiv. 19.

(the *same man*) 'serve the law of God, and with my flesh the law of sin.'[1]

All the most intimate phenomena of consciousness are therefore, as much as the world without us, and the body around us, affections, movements, manifestations of the simple self; but are not themselves this self. Whence we say, '*I* am thinking;' '*I* feel;' '*I* determine;' '*I* did this or that.' In no way can we rid ourselves of this ever present and efficient *me*.[2] And always do we recognise it, not as the *product* of the bodily or mental elements, but simply as in correspondence with them, their employer, and their regulator. 'Whatever I be,' says Antoninus, 'this is certain, that besides my flesh and my breath of life there is in me a *governing principle*.' 'I am more than a life,' says the author of Thorndale, 'I am the somewhat who *has life*.'[3] And so John Smith of Cambridge,—'because the soul feels itself,' as Tully declares, 'not moved by extraneous force but from itself alone,' it can say of all the assaults which are made against these sorry mud walls which enclose it, 'you are nothing to ME! I can live anywhere, without this feeble carcase; for *I* was not *that*, but had only a command over it while I dwelt in it!'[4] And you find this conviction mixed up inseparably with all men's views of each other as well as of their own selves. No one treats us, any more than we treat them, as other than *a person* and not an abstraction; a producer and not a product; a substantial reality and not a mere logical figment. 'Amidst all the insinuations of doubt, this Me stands up in native majesty and records her protest against the everlasting No. I am not No,

---

[1] Rom. vii. 25.  
[2] See Appendix, Note V.  
[3] Thorndale, 385.  
[4] Discourses, 91.

but Yea, and free! In *me* is vital fire, spirit, invisible force!'[1]

2. But the same consciousness which recognises my self as one, equally testifies to my being, under all changes of manifestation, the *selfsame* one. Not only do I find myself, amidst the *complexity* of the thoughts *concomitant* in my mind, a *simple, incomplex*, being; but I find myself also, amidst the *variety* of the thoughts *consecutive* in my mind, *the same unchanging* being. That is, I possess not only personal *individuality*, but personal *identity*.

It is true indeed that we are conscious of many *concomitant* thoughts filling together our field of vision at one and the same moment, and we speak of them in their entirety as constituting the 'self' of this moment. And it is also true that we are conscious of many *consecutive* thoughts replacing each other in this field, and constituting, each group, the self of successive moments; as Job, for instance, exclaims, 'O that *I* were as in months past, when by God's light *I* walked through darkness,' distinguishing thus his present self involved in sorrow from a past self suffused with joy; and as we say in common parlance, '*I* was at such a time so and so, and *I* am not

---

[1] Carlyle, Sartor Resartus, ch. 7 & 9. Compare Mr. J. A. Froude in his Address at St. Andrew's: 'What the thing is which we call ourselves we know not. It may be true, and I for one care not if it be, that the descent of our mortal bodies may be traced through an ascending series to some glutinous jelly formed on the rocks of the primeval ocean. It is nothing to me how the Maker of me has been pleased to construct the organised substance which I call my body. It is mine, but it is not *me*. The intellectual spirit, being an essence, I believe to be an imperishable something engendered in us from a higher source.

> "The soul that rises in us, our life's star
> Hath elsewhere had its setting,
> And cometh from afar."'

what *I* was.'[1] But still, though we thus gather up the consciousness of each successive moment into the formal centre of an ideal self as the seat of it, we seldom contemplate these successive groups of thought, with their conventional centres, as other than merely changing representatives of an unchanging self, a real selfsame 'I,' underlying all these phenomenal transformations.

Sometimes indeed it is otherwise. Sometimes we lose this conviction of a real identity underlying all apparent diversity, because the strangeness of the manifestations makes it difficult for us to recognise under them the sameness of the manifester. Hence the poet, in his moments of inspiration, seems to himself (or once *did* seem when poetry was real) 'carried out of himself;' actuated by a personality different from his own, and pouring forth his unpremeditated lay at the suggestion of some Muse within him. Hence the Seer, 'beside himself,' seems to be only the mouthpiece of an overmastering Deity. Hence the miserable slave of passion imputes to sin as a personality distinct from himself the aberrations of his own disordered individuality. Hence the madman fancies himself taken possession of by a demon; nay, a legion of demons. Hence the mystic distinguishes from himself what he believes to be the voice of the Spirit of God within him. And even common speech inclines continually to this multiplication of persons within us, when people say, 'Reason assures me of this!' 'Imagination suggested to you that!' 'You are indebted to fancy for your facts,

---

[1] 'People are not only their present selves, but all their old selves at the same time. Sometimes one and sometimes another comes uppermost.'— *Cornhill Mag.*, April 1870.

and to memory for your fancies!' 'Queen Mab has been with you!'

But, that we are invariably the selfsame person, amidst all the variations of our mind, is attested by many proofs. And first by the intimate *unity of all thought* within us. The association of ideas shows the sameness of the base into which they all converge. The chain of reasoning shows that the reasoner is, throughout each successive link, the same. The phrase, indeed, 'Discourse of reason' acknowledges the *running on* (discurro) from one thought to another. Yet still this running on must be accomplished by one and the same thinker. For no one imagines that one person within him has supplied the major of a syllogism; a second the minor; and a third the conclusion.[1]

But next, the phenomena of *Memory* prove our personal identity. For memory is the emergence above the horizon of my consciousness, of conceptions already formed in me, but kept down for a season out of sight by other thoughts. To remember a thing is to call up

---

[1] Janet, Materialisme contemporain, 122; see also 129, 130: 'L'unité du Moi est un fait indubitable. Toute la question est de savoir si cette unité est une résultante ou un fait indivisible. Mais, si l'unité du Moi est une résultante, la *conscience* qui nous atteste cette unité est aussi une résultante. Mais comment admettre que deux parties distinctes puissent avoir une conscience commune? L'unité perçue par le dehors peut être le résultat d'une composition; mais elle ne le peut pas quand elle se perçoit elle-même au dedans.' And so John Smith (Discourses, 82): 'We find such a faculty within us as *collects* and *unites* all the perceptions of our several senses, and is able to *compare* them together; something in which they all meet as in one centre. And Plotinus well says, "That in which all our several sensations meet, as so many lines drawn from several points in the circumference, and which comprehends them all, must needs be *one*. For should *that* be various and consisting of several parts, which thus receives all these various impressions, then must the *sentence and judgment* upon them be various too." Aristotle says, "That must be *one* which judges things to be diverse," and which too must thus judge *setting all before* it at once.'

my own previously existing conceptions of this thing.
It is the waking up a past act of my self, to become again
a present act of my self. And 'if our souls were nothing
but a complex of fluid atoms we should be continually
roving and sliding from ourselves, and soon forget what
we were. The new matter that would come in to fill up
that vacuity which the old had made by its departure,
would never know what the old was. Heraclitus truly
said, "You cannot bathe twice in the same stream."'[1]

Nor, thirdly, could we feel ourselves *responsible* persons,
or treat others as responsible, if we were not instinctively
conscious that all the variations in every man's mind and
will must have their centre and source in one and the
same thinker and actor. 'It is a fallacy to charge our
present selves with anything we did yesterday, if our
present self is not in reality the same with the self of
yesterday, but another self or person coming into its
room and mistaken for it.'[2] And this explains why
persons, striving to throw off from themselves the responsibility of their doings, attempt this by suppressing their
sense of personal identity and attribute these doings to
other centres than their own self. They plead, for instance, 'The furies possessed me!' 'It was drink that did
it!' 'The devil put it into my mind!' But St. Paul,
though he, too, sometimes pushes distinction of *states* of
mind into difference of the *subject* in which these states
inhere (as when he says, 'It is no more I that do it, but
*sin* that dwelleth in me'), yet soon returns to the full
assertion of personal identity. 'I, the selfsame man
(αὐτὸς ἐγώ), with my mind indeed' (when in a rational

[1] Smith, Discourses, 83.  [2] Butler, Analogy, 380.

state) 'serve the law of God, but with my flesh' (when in an animal mood) 'the law of sin.'[1]

3. But now to one more fact to which our observation of ourselves and others bears abundant testimony. I find myself, in actual experience, not only a something *simple*, amidst the complexity of my *concomitant* conceptions, and also *selfsame* amidst the ever-changing variety of my *consecutive* conceptions, but *substantial* amidst the merely *phenomenal* character of all these my conceptions.[2]

This last fact is indeed denied by materialists. They ascribe all the phenomena of consciousness simply to the bodily organism. Thought is only the molecular action of the brain;[3] or a secretion from its substance;[4] or a function of its constitution;[5] or a resultant of its vibrations.[6]

But, grant that the *occasion* of innumerable thoughts is furnished by the state of the cerebral matter; grant even that many movements take place in our frame by

---

[1] Romans vii. 17, 25.

[2] Where note well that by 'substantial' I do not mean (what is so often confounded with it) *material*. Matter is no substance; it is only the *form* in which substances manifest themselves, and this with continual flux and variation; as, e.g. from the hardest iron to the most volatile vapour of iron. Substance is that which *stands under* matter (or extended phenomena) as their base. It has none of the qualities of matter, neither extension nor weight. See Appendix, Note VI.

[3] 'Thoughts result from the movements of matter.'—*Moleschott*.

[4] 'La pensée est une sécrétion du cerveau.'—*Cabanis*. 'Thought bears the same relation to the brain as the bile to the liver.'—*Vogt*.

[5] 'Nous avons dit, M. Robin et moi, que l'âme est une fonction du cerveau. Le physicien reconnaît que la matière pèse; le physiologiste que la substance nerveuse pense.'—*Littré*. See Le Blais, Matérialisme et Spiritualisme, xix. And Janet, Le Matérialisme contemporain, 32.

[6] 'Thought is not a secretion which the brain throws out, but it is the action itself of the brain, the resultant of all the forces which make up the composition of the brain; the effect of the nervous electricity'—*Büchner*.

simple reflex action; still, there is another fact which these writers always ignore. This namely, that in all conscious presentment there is the sense of a Something *to* which the presentment is made; a something distinct from the ultimate cerebral vibration which is in correspondence with this vibration, nay co-operates with it, and is a coefficient in the generation of thought. Not nervous vibrations *per se* make thought; but you yourself, in correspondence with these vibrations, make thought.

Nay, more than this, you find this something not only making thought out of cerebral vibrations (which in themselves are not thought), but itself in return *generating* cerebral vibrations. And this something, which is not merely receptive of movements but creative of movements, you cannot merge in the movements. Produce these movements, if you please, by a galvanic battery, you cannot thereby produce the something which observes these movements, is conscious to itself of these movements, responds to these movements, uses these movements, and originates counter movements in return. This something therefore must *be*, independently of the movements which converge on it or emerge from it. This is what Descartes meant by his formula, 'I think, therefore I am.' He did not mean, 'I *am* thinking, therefore I am.' Such a surreptitious begging of the question, which Huxley among others imputes to him, was far from him. But his argument is, 'Thoughts are present. Every one allows this. But thoughts, to *be present*, must be in relation to a something *to which* they are present. The existence of sensations, perceptions, volitions, proves the being of a something sentient, percipient, willing. In short, you must apply to this particular case of mental phenomena the universal axiom which is true of all phenomena, "Where there is show there must be substance. If there were no substance there could be no show."[1] On this axiom Herbart insists as the foundation of all belief in real being.[2] This axiom Herbert Spencer has laid down in these words: "The relative is conceivable as such only by opposition to the irrelative or absolute. The momentum of thought inevitably carries us beyond conditional existence to unconditional existence; and this unconditional existence ever persists in us as the body of thought to which we give no shape. Hence our firm belief in objective reality. Though we can *know* only of certain impressions produced in us, we are yet by the relativity of thought compelled to *think* of these impressions *in relation to a positive* cause; and so the notion of a *real* existence which generates these impressions becomes nascent."[3] And this axiom Spencer himself applies to the particular case of proving the reality of the human soul. I give you an outline only of his argument.[4] 'Belief in the reality of self is a belief which no hypothesis enables us to escape. What shall we say of those successive impressions and ideas which constitute consciousness? Are they *affections* of the mind which is the subject of them? Then, this

---

[1] Cf. Giordano Bruno—'God would never deceive us, and, therefore, things that appear must exist; they are in a certain sense shadows, but even as shadows imply the presence of a sun' (De Umbris Idearum).—*Macmillan's Mag.*, Feb. 1871.

[2] See his Hauptpunkte der Metaphysik, 19, 20. And Allgemeine Metaphysik, ii. 78, 79, 351. Compare also Hegel, in Stirling's Schwegler, 327: 'Manifestation is not essenceless appearance, but appearance which is filled up, implemented by essence. *There is no appearance without an essence,* as there is no essence that passes not into manifestation. Every essence is unity of matter [i.e. of material] and form; i.e. it Exists. Existence is not immediate being, but *grounded* being, traced back to an antecedent source.'

[3] First Principles, 89.  [4] Ibid. 64–66.

mind must be an entity capable of such affections. Are they *modified forms* of thinking substance? Then, modifications involve the notion of a something modified. Are they *impressions*? Then, an impression implies a something impressed. And you cannot consider them as *your* impressions if there be no *you* of which they are the impressions. You must admit therefore the reality of the individual mind. And if you urge that this reality cannot be comprehended, this is the fate of all ultimate scientific ideas. They are all representatives of realities which cannot be comprehended. So that the personality of which the existence is to us a fact beyond all others most certain, is yet a thing which cannot be truly *known* at all.'

And yet, though not strictly known, this personality we cannot but be certain of from the simple principle that all things known, without us or within us, must have a somewhat unknown for their base. 'The notion of the ATOM, the indivisible, the *thing* that has place, *being*, and power; this' (says Sir John Herschel) 'is an absolute necessity of the human thinking mind, and is of all ages and nations. It underlies all our notions of being, and starts up *per se* whenever we come to look closely at the objective nature of things.'[1] And for the full validity of such application of the law of causation to facts, Professor Tyndall pleads when he urges the use of imagination (by which he means, of soaring from the actual into the ideal) in science; for 'without this power, which lightens the darkness that surrounds the world of the senses, our knowledge of nature would be a mere tabulation of coexistences and sequences. We should still believe in the

[1] Herschel, Lectures on Scientific Subjects, 454.

succession of day and night, summer and winter; but the soul of *force* would be dislodged from our universe; *causal relations would disappear*, and with them that *science* which is now binding the parts of nature to an organic whole.'[1]

And therefore these 'causal relations,' which science assumes in all phenomena, we may with full confidence apply to the phenomena of consciousness also. What says Ritter on this point? 'As all predicates imply a subject, of which they are predicated, so all attributes imply a substance, to which they are attributed. Wherever, therefore, you observe the attributes of thought, there you must recognise a *thinking substance*, of which they are attributes. And let no one be shy of this word substance when it indicates the base of actual phenomena, for we are obliged by an universal irresistible law of thought to regard every phenomenon as the manifestation of a thing, a base, a substance to which it refers.'[2] And how does Mr. Grote apply this argument, in words which seem the very echo of Herbart? 'What we have as the two things to be contradistinguished are not matter and mind, but *fact and seeming*. And seeming is nothing in contrast with truth, but the *presentation to something* of things as being; for this seeming of things implies more than the existence of things; it implies *something to which* they seem as they do. However it may be a fact that the phenomenal world *is*, it is at least as much a fact that it *seems* (i.e. presents itself as an object of thought) TO something which, *in virtue of this fact, we must consider as different from itself*. And this something, we come to

[1] Tyndall, Use and Limit of the Imagination, 16, 17.
[2] Ritter, Unsterblichkeit, 24, 25.

find, is *we*; and it is only in virtue of this seeming of the universe to *us* that we have all along been talking of "being." All that we call "being" we can only call so as "seeming" to *us* to be, as thought of by *us* as being.'[1]

Here, then, we have reached the solid conviction of a *real substance* as the base of all our phenomenal consciousness. When we affirm a soul or self as the unit of this consciousness, we do so not in the sense in which we speak of 'a tree' or 'a river' as the merely *formal* unity of its constituent parts. We affirm for the phenomena of thought a substance non-phenomenal as their base, in precisely the same sense and with precisely the same right and validity as we affirm for the phenomena of the bodily frame various 'elementary substances' as their base; as we affirm for each kind of these phenomena their *distinct* base. No one ascribes the phenomena of acidity (for instance) to hydrogen, or the phenomena of water to oxygen. Nor can any one with any more reason ascribe the phenomena of mind to chemical or electric bases; but by the same necessity and the same authority with which we conclude from the phenomena of acidity to a peculiar 'elementary substance' *generative* of acidity, and call this substance oxygen, and from the phenomena of water to a peculiar 'elementary substance' *generative* of water, and therefore call it hydrogen, with just the same authority, from just the same necessity, are we entitled and obliged to conclude from the phenomena of thought to a peculiar 'elementary substance' *generative* of thought, which therefore I propose, by parity of nomenclature, to call Noerogen. Cicero tells us that Aristotle recognised, besides the four elements then

---

[1] Grote, in Macmillan's Magazine for March 1867.

accepted, a fifth, as the base of mind, 'Because to think, to foresee, to learn, to teach, to invent, and so many other things, such as remembering, loving, hating, desiring, fearing, being distressed, and being joyful, could not possibly have their seat in any of those usually accepted elements, therefore did he add a fifth, which completes humanity, though he gave to it no name.'[1] This element, therefore, which (Cicero adds) 'is easier understood than named,' is what I would call Noerogen. Each man is a particle, an atom of noerogen; and this atom of noerogen, working in correspondence with the other atoms which lie at the base of the chemical and vital phenomena of body, is the seat and source of the specially mental phenomena. *What* it is, remains, indeed, as thoroughly unknown to us as do the other 'elementary substances' of nature; but that it *is*, and that it is essentially distinct from them, is sufficiently indicated by its manifestations.'[2]

[1] Cicero, Tusc. Disp. 1–10.     [2] See further, Appendix, Note VII.

## LETTER III.

*OF MAN'S GENERAL QUALITIES.*

In trying to lay down some stepping-stones on which you may pass securely over the shifting sands of doubt, I have seized first those immediate facts which underlie the conviction of all men when they affirm '*I am.*'

For in this affirmation there is involved the assurance of my simplicity, as the individual base of all the phenomena of my mind; my selfsameness as the identical base of these phenomena; and my substantiality as their real base.

But then I find myself not only existing, but existing in ever varying *forms* of consciousness. My mind is constantly assuming new states, though my self, as the base of this mind, remains the same. And the description and classification of these states of consciousness is the business of mental philosophy.

Now these facts of consciousness tell us that, as included in the animal kingdom, we have certain *general* qualities (though in much higher degrees) in common with other members of this kingdom; but that we have also other *special* qualities, which altogether contradistinguish us from them.

As to our *general* qualities, we find ourselves sensitive, causative, and intellective beings.

1. As *Sensitive* beings we are incessantly susceptive of impressions, sensations, feelings, and affections produced by the influence of persons and things external to ourselves.

Of *Impressions* there is a vast number made through the nervous system of our body, of which we do not take any cognisance, but which, nevertheless, move in us correspondent reflex actions. But another and larger class do produce changes in our consciousness, and bring thereby to our cognisance objects of various kinds.[1] These objects, thus brought before us, are what Locke calls, though incorrectly, 'ideas.' And they are simple or complex. *Simple*, such as when the eye presents to us colours, red, blue, and so on; or when the ear makes us sensible of sounds, loud, low, and so on; or when the touch renders us aware of bodies, hard, soft, and so on. And *complex*, when by means of several senses these simple impressions are combined into wholes, and make us sensible of the presence of complex objects, such as a tree, a house, a man.

Next to impressions, and generally roused in us by them, come *Sensations*. As when, by means of the nerves of *taste*, we become sensible of things as sweet or bitter; and, through the nerves of *smell*, as fragrant or offensive. Or when, in a much more extensive way, the general condition of our frame renders us sensible of various degrees of bodily ease or disease; deepening from

---

[1] These Shakespeare calls 'pressures':—

'Yea, from the table of my memory
I'll wipe away all trivial fond records,
All saws of books, all forms, all *pressures* past,
That youth and observation copied there.'

*Hamlet*, i. 5.

a vague sense of *comfort* or of discomfort, to definite *pleasure* or pain, and prolonged *enjoyment* or misery. All these experiences are termed (not from their *seat*, for this is ever the incorporeal self, but from the *source* whence they arise) *bodily sensations.* [1]

But above these come experiences which have their source not in the body, but solely in the mind, and which result from the various relations of harmony or discord into which our *thoughts* fall. And these we call distinctively *Feelings*, mental feelings. Such are our feelings of *elevation*, when our thoughts move freely and harmoniously, and 'our bosom's queen sits lightly on her throne.' And feelings of *depression*, when the web of thought is entangled, clogged, perplexed. The intensification of such feelings raises them up to *joy*, or casts them down to *sorrow*. And their prolongation constitutes a condition of *happiness* or **unhappiness**.

Nor are these all the feelings which result from modifications of our thoughts. There are others which spring from the satisfaction or dissatisfaction of our sense of *proportion*, whether in thoughts, forms, colours, sounds; or in words, dispositions, and acts. Thus, in objects of *nature and art*, the well-proportioned, the beautiful, the harmonious, produce in us a feeling of *complacency*, and their contraries a feeling of *displacency*. And these may be intensified, on the one hand, into *relish* and 'gusto;' on the other, into *disrelish* and disgust. And so in thoughts and *words*; when we observe them to be accurate, well adapted, and logically ordered, there arises in us a recognition of *truth*

---

[1] 'Qu'est-ce qui sent du plaisir en nous? Est-ce la main? Est-ce le bras? Est-ce la chair? Est-ce le sang? On verra qu'il faut que ce soit quelque chose d'immatériel.'—*Pascal*, i. 187.

bringing with it a feeling of *complacency*, and when we see their contraries, a recognition of falsehood, accompanied by a feeling of displacency.[1] Still more when we observe, or even only imagine to ourselves, the proper, the correct, the well-proportioned, in *disposition and character*, there awakes in us a feeling towards these of *complacency*, similar to that with which we look on natural and artistic beauty. We call them lovely, charming. We derive from them a relish, a sweet savour; while for the opposites of such sentiments and acts we have a feeling of *displacency* and disgust. Hence such feelings, from their similarity to the sensations of touch and taste, and to the sense of what is lovely or deformed, are called the Æsthetic sentiments. And they are considered as the offspring of a certain natural '*taste*,' because they rise in us as spontaneously, in presence of their appropriate objects, as do our sensations of *savour*. Their verdict comes forth as instinctively and as quickly as do the judgments of the palate concerning what is bitter or sweet. 'Taste,' says Voltaire, 'is a quick discernment, a sudden perception, which, like the sensations of the palate, anticipates reflection.'

But, as our impressions and sensations result from states of body, and our feelings from modifications of mind, there is a fourth class of movements which spring from our relations of *social* life. These are the *Affections*, whether benevolent or malevolent. Affections of *agreement* with others, of sympathy, and of concord. And

---

[1] This logical complacency Herbart distinguishes from æsthetical complacency as consisting simply in a pleased *recognition* of the object before us. And yet he himself allows that there is combined therewith a *feeling* made up of the force with which the evidence strikes us, and the gratification of finding what we have been seeking.—Lehrbuch der Psychologie, 41.

affections of *disagreement* with others, of antipathy, of discord. Affections of *trust* in them, or mistrust of them. Affections of *love* for them, or hatred of them.

2. As sensitive beings we are mainly passive, receptive of influences from things without us. But as *Causative* beings we are active, productive of influences on these things;[1] and such causative acts take place in us either consciously or unconsciously.

The causative acts which work in us, at least in their first movements, without our consciousness, rise in the scale of intensity from *instincts*, through *propensities* and *appetites*, to *passions*.

Those which spring from consciousness, and are mixed up with consciousness, of the object towards which we move, proceed in an ascending scale from *desires*, through *determinations*, to *doings*. Desire is a movement within us towards something seen to be 'desirable' (Ignoti nulla cupido); and it contains in it the commencement of corresponding determinations for the attainment of the object desired, and doings for the accomplishment of these determinations; whence it is that our Lord treats desire as incipient doing, and would have us nip in the bud whatever ought not to flower into fruit.[2] And St. James gives the genealogy of sin when he declares that 'each man is tempted when he is drawn away by his own desire and enticed, so that desire when it has conceived brings forth, as its natural offspring, sin;

---

[1] For as a unit of force the self within us has, like other centres of force (as the heart), its systole and diastole; its movements of self-contraction and self-expansion. In self-contraction it retires into the abyss of self, with intensification of the *self-preserving* power. In self-expansion it issues into sympathy and intercommunication with other forces, putting forth its *self-assertive* power.

[2] Matt. v. 22, 28.

and sin, when it comes to maturity, brings forth, as *its* offspring, death.'[1]

3. But we are not simply sensitive beings, the subject of *impressions* from things without us; and *causative* beings, the source of *expressions* bearing on these things; but we are *Intellective* beings, *taking notice* of these impressions and expressions, and forming in ourselves an extensive range of *thoughts* or presentments to our mental eye concerning them.

These thoughts ascend along the scale of intelligence from perceptions to conceptions, to notions, to imaginations, and to conclusions or judgments. But the one mark stamped upon them all is that they are *intellective*; that is, that they are formed by a process of distinguishing and *selecting* (inter-lego) the phenomena which, through our senses and our consciousness present themselves to our notice. All thought is essentially differentiation.[2]

(1.) This differentiation commences at its lowest stage with the raising mere sensations of outward things into *perceptions*, or recognitions of the objects whence the sensations flow. And herein, therefore, we do not merely *receive* impressions, as wax receives the impress of a seal, or prepared paper takes the rays of light, but we are active as well as passive, formative as well as receptive. 'We may often' (as Mrs. Somerville well says) '*see* an object without *perceiving* it, and we may hear a sound without attending to it. So that we must *look* in order to see, *listen* in order to hear, and *handle* in order to feel; that is, we must adjust the muscular apparatus of all our senses, if we would have a distinct

---

[1] James i. 14, 15.   [2] See Appendix, Note VIII.

perception of external exciting objects.' Perception is in fact, according to its literal meaning, the taking up *wholly* (*per*-capio) what presents itself to us. And it varies, therefore, according to the force and the fulness of our *attention* to this présentment. 'In every object,' says Carlyle, 'the eye sees what the eye brings the means of seeing. To Newton, and to Newton's dog, Diamond, what a different pair of universes; while the painting on the optical retina of both was most likely the same.'[1]

(2.) A second stage in thought is that of *conceptions*. These are formed when we *take together* different objects that we perceive, and arrange them into wholes. For to conceive is con-capere; to take up this *along with* that, so as to form, by the combination a whole, distinct from other wholes. Look at your conception of a table, as a something distinct from the objects surrounding it. An infant regards the table and the floor on which it stands as *one* thing, as much as you regard the table top and its legs as one thing. But when it comes to observe this table removed from its place on the floor, a separation takes place in its mind between the perceptions hitherto combined there. It *distinguishes*, differentiates, the table from the floor, and parts them asunder as two separate things. It has grasped the one *along with* the other (concepit), as related indeed but yet distinct. It has distinguished in order to combine and unify. It has separated off one set of perceptions from another neighbouring set, in order to grasp each as a whole. It has formed a conception of a table, and *along with this* of the floor on which it ordinarily stands, as another whole. So the first perception of the Spanish cavalry by the South Americans

---

[1] Carlyle, French Revolution, i. 8.

was that of horse and man as *one person*. But when they afterwards saw the Spaniards dismount, and remain separated from their steeds, then they learned to conceive of man and horse as two things. They took together, not all their perceptions of man and horse as *one* object, but their perceptions of the man combined into one whole, and their perceptions of the horse combined into another whole, as two objects. And in this way, by a continuous process of 'discernment' or differentiation into new wholes, we discriminate things from things, and the parts of things from each other, almost without end. And such differentiation is as much a fundamental law of *growth*, for our mind, as a similar differentiation is for the cellular tissues of our body. In our first general perceptions of objects we see little more than a sort of Turner picture, with masses of reds, whites, blues. Next, we discern, or separate off, amidst these masses, 'things' such as houses, roads, trees. Next, we discriminate from this 'still life,' men, 'like trees walking.' Next, men as altogether different from trees. Next, one man as distinguishable from another. And next, the particular parts and features of each single man by himself.[1]

(3.) And this process of differentiation, carried further still, brings us to form another and more abstract class of thoughts which we call *Notions*. Beyond the first simple impressions made on us through the senses, the perceptions which we form out of them, and the conceptions into which we separate and combine them, the mind passes on, by its power of abstraction, to arrange and classify these conceptions among themselves according to their common and their specific marks. And thus we have no

---

[1] See Appendix, Note IX.

longer 'regard to *things as they are* as horse, ship, tree, but to things as they are *understood* by us,' i.e. as known and cognised by us (notio from nosco) ' under the relations of genus, species, attribute, subject,' whence we are said to ' understand ' things (have a *notion* of them) in proportion as we find for them a class under which to ' stand ' them. For ' to stand ' was formerly not only a neuter but an active verb, and remains so still in popular speech. 'He *stood* the candle on the table.' 'She *stood* the child down.' And 'the understanding' therefore is the faculty by which we ' stand ' (or place) things ' under ' or among their several classes. And 'notions' are the product of this ' understanding.' They are *clear* or obscure, and *distinct* or confused. *Clear*, when we discriminate a notion as a whole from others; obscure when not so. *Distinct*, when we discriminate the several marks in each notion from each other; and confused when not so. Thus we have a *clear* notion of a triangle when we discriminate it from other figures. We have a *distinct* notion of it when we think of it as a figure whose three angles taken together are equal to two right angles.[1]

Now, this process and clarification and distinction may be carried on through successive stages, from *particular* notions, up to *special, general*, and *universal* notions. And it is the highest class, that of *universal* notions, which Plato terms ' Ideas,' and to which this much-abused word

[1] See Herbart, Einleit. in d. Philosophie, 3: 'Die *Deutlichkeit* besteht in der Unterscheidung der Merkmale eines Begriffs, sowie die *Klarheit* in der Unterscheidung mehrerer Begriffe unter einander.' And so Crabbe (Synonyms): 'A notion is *clear* when we know what it *is not*; *distinct* when we know what it *is*. *Clearness* discerns between two or more notions; *distinctness* discerns all the characteristics of any one notion.' And Coleridge (Aids to Reflection, 138): 'This every human being *knows* with equal *clearness*, though different minds may *reflect* on it with different degrees of *distinctness*.'

ought to be limited. 'Ideas,' because he regarded them as the *patterns* (ἰδέαι), or prototypes, of which all general, special, and individual existences are more or less imperfect copies.[1]

Notions, therefore, as abstractions of the mind, as (to use Sir W. Hamilton's language) [2] 'concepts of concepts, formal, mediate, reflex,' in distinction from conceptions, which are 'concepts of things real, immediate, direct,' are of immense importance and extent; since out of them the whole system of logical reasoning is constructed. For 'a logician has nothing to do with ascertaining whether a horse, or a ship, or a tree *exists*, but whether one of these things can be regarded as a genus or species; whether it can be called a subject or an attribute; whether from the conjunction of many notions a proportion, a definition, or a syllogism can be formed.'[3]

(4.) But beyond the sphere of things *observed* by us as they are, and *thought* of by us under the relations in which we 'stand' them to each other, there is a fourth stage of the intellective process in which it passes from the acceptance of things actually existing, into the creation, out of them, of new forms of thought, analogous indeed to what observation has supplied us with, but yet transcending it. These new forms are *imaginations*. And they are the product of that 'daring' activity[4] of the mind which

---

[1] See Appendix, Note X.

[2] Discussions, p. 137: 'Conceptions' he calls 'first notions' (intellecta prima). Notions he terms 'second notions' (intellecta secunda). And thus defines them: 'A first notion is the concept of a thing as it *exists of itself*, as man, John, animal. A second notion is the concept, not of an object as it is in reality, but of the mode *under which it is thought* by the mind, as individual species, genus.' See J. S. Mill on the Nature of the Copula, Logic, i. 194.

[3] Abp. Thomson, Laws of Thought, 39, 40, in Fleming's Vocabulary, 348.

[4]                 'Pictoribus atque poetis
  Quidlibet audendi semper fuit æqua potestas.'—Horace, Ars Poet. 9.

constitutes its poietic (creative) and plastic (formative) power. This Mr. Bain well describes when he says, 'While the understanding has to do only with the literal resuscitation, revival, or reinstatement of former sensations, images, emotions and trains of thought, the operation known by the names of imagination, creation, constructiveness, origination, puts together new forms or constructs images, pictures, and modes of working such as we have never before had any experience of. It includes the genius of the painter, poet, musician, and inventor in arts and sciences.' To this, therefore, Coleridge gives the name of 'the esemplastic power, dissolving, diffusing, dissipating, in order to recreate.' But when he goes on to call it 'the tendency to *expand* infinitely,' and 'the struggle to *idealise* and unify,' he confounds it with the very different power of *ideality*, of passing, through the several stages of abstraction, into the region of universals, or *ideas*. For imagination, so far from raising notions into their highest sublimation, tends to *concrete* them into definite forms and figures. It reduces them into 'images.' It is in fact, by its very name, *image-making*. And Ferrier truly affirms that 'the idea, or universal, cannot be *pictured* in the imagination. We must be satisfied with *thinking* it as a fact of intellect, which cannot be apprehended either by the senses or by the imagination, which derives all its data from the senses, and copies their impressions. An idea is thus diametrically opposed to an image, although in ordinary language the two terms are frequently regarded as synonymous. You can form no sort of representation of the ideal, or universal, or paradeigma. It cannot be pictured to the imagination without being reduced to the particular. And then it is destroyed as an idea and converted into an instance.'[1] With which agrees what Coleridge had already said, 'No idea can be rendered by a conception. An idea is essentially inconceivable.'[2] And yet he goes on to speak of the Trinity as 'the only *form* in which an idea of God is possible,' which seems like saying, 'It is the only way in which it is *conceivable.*'

Mr. Dallas, indeed, contends that imagination includes ideality. For 'it is but a name for the free play of thought, the spontaneous action of the whole mind. It is the love of likeness and of wholeness. It is the discovery of resemblance advancing to the perception of unity. It *leaps from the particular* to the universal; from the accidental to the necessary; from the temporary to the eternal.'[3] Which last features are precisely those of the ideas, and of those *alone.* And Dr. Tyndall has clearly *ideality* in view when he writes 'concerning the scientific use of the *imagination.*' For he says, 'Newton's passage from a falling apple to a falling moon was, at the outset, a *leap of the imagination*' (say rather of the reason discerning beforehand consequences). But then he adds, 'Not, however, an imagination which catches its creations from the air, but one informed and inspired by facts *capable of discerning consequences*, and of devising means whereby these *forecasts* of thought may be brought to an experimental test.' And again, 'Imagination broods upon facts, and *by the aid of reason* tries to discern their interdependence.'[4] More simply, therefore, we may say that it *is* reason brooding on facts, and so discerning their interdependence.

[1] Ferrier's Lectures, i. 338, 339.  [2] Notes on English Divines, i. 12.
[3] Dallas, The Gay Science, i. 262, 292.
[4] Tyndall, Use and Limit of the Imagination, 4, 16. See my 'Faith grounded on Reason.'

Now, all this is true of the power of *idealisation*. This is found only in the highest minds. It is what Coleridge calls 'the fortunate *anticipation* and instructive *foretact* of truth.'[1] It is reasoning per saltum. It is the divining, guessing, and forecasting new thoughts in connection with those already before us; included in them, and flowing out of them. It is what the Germans call 'Ahnung,' Anticipation; and some English writers, 'Invention.' And it works mightily in the *discoverer*, whether in science or art. Shakespeare calls this quick apprehensiveness, 'the prophetic soul.'

But imagination, on the contrary, tends, not to 'idealise,' but to *sensualise* our conceptions; not to 'expand' but to contract them, and thus debase them. From this came all the 'endless genealogies' of the Gnostic theology. From this all the gross anthropomorphisms of Deity among the heathen, and their counterparts among heathenising Christians. The 'idea,' or abstract notion, of a One, supreme, all powerful, everywhere present, is true and sublime; but the 'images' of such a Being, whether material or verbal, carved in stone or moulded by the fancy, are necessarily false, low, and gross. See this in the sculptures of Hinduism; in the pictures and idols of Romanism, in the poetry of Pollock, and even of Milton. And the efforts of many poets and divines to *image* the unseen world, its pleasures and its pains, are another proof of the essential contrariety of imagination, which cleaves to the concrete and the sensuous, from reason which soars into the abstract and ideal. See this contrast in the inspired John. Full as his Apocalypse is of the boldest imagery, he carefully abstains from depicting

---

[1] Coleridge, Notes on English Divines, i. 4.

any sensuous form of the Great Supreme. All he can say of Him is that He was 'dazzling to the sight as are a jasper and a sardine stone.'

(5.) The last product of our intellective nature deals with all these previous ones, whether perceptions, conceptions, notions, or imaginations, and pronounces on them *judgments* concerning their truth or falsehood, their beauty or deformity, their being right or wrong.

Such judgments are of two kinds, mediate or immediate.

*Mediate* judgments result from comparing a notion with other notions so as to determine the relation which it bears to them, the class under which we are to 'stand' it. As when, for instance, we assume that we know all men to be mortal, and placing under this universal notion the particular one that John is a man, thence conclude that John therefore is mortal. Our final judgment concerning John is reached by means of the middle term, which connects John with the class of beings who are mortal. It is therefore a *mediate* judgment. And its decision is that the notion of John as *mortal* is a *true* one.

But then there are also *immediate* judgments; so called because on the presentation of their objects we pronounce concerning them (or seem to do so) without any intermediate reasoning. We need no process of proof, but see the truth concerning them *at once*, as the eye sees light by being only turned towards it. 'Thus the mind perceives that white is not black; that a circle is not a triangle; that three are more than two, and equal to one and two.'[1] Such judgments are called by Aris-

---

[1] Locke, iv. 2.

totle 'intuitive,' or self-evident, and are accepted by him as grounds of all knowledge. For 'all demonstrated knowledge,' he says, 'must rest on principles which are true and primary and *immediate* (ἄμεσοι); better known than the conclusions to be drawn from them, prior to these conclusions, and causative of these conclusions. . . And such principles *must* be primary and indemonstrable, because we should need a previous demonstration for them also, if they were not in their very nature intuitive and self-evident. Hence the principle of all *demonstration* (or *mediate* proof) must be an *immediate* proposition (πρότασις ἄμεσος); and by an immediate proposition I mean that to which there is nothing prior.'[1]

Thus, then, we arrive at judgments concerning what is *true* or *false*.[2]

But our judgments pronounce themselves with equal or greater immediateness concerning what is *beautiful* or *deformed*, and concerning what is *right* or *wrong*. For these decisions also are judgments. They arise from observation, not of any one thing by itself but of the *relations* of things; though their verdict is generally so immediate, at the first glance of their objects, that it resembles our bodily sensations, such as taste and touch. Whence we call our judgment of the beautiful, *taste*, and

---

[1] Aristotle, Analyt. Post. i. 2.

[2] It remains, however, to be considered whether many judgments which *seem* immediate are not the results of latent reasoning, or have been accepted simply through external teaching and authority. Axioms are different to different minds. That is 'self-evident' to one which is not to another. Even that 'three are more than two' becomes first manifest through the ocular demonstration of the fingers or of a ball frame. Mill reduces all 'first principles' to two: 'that things equal to the same are equal to each other,' and the converse (i. 241). And these are none other than the two old principles of 'identity and contradiction;' that A is A, and that A is not B, which Aristotle calls 'intuitive' judgments.

our judgment of the right, the moral *sense*. And Aristotle terms such judgments 'assertive,' because we are fully persuaded of them without requiring any grounds for this persuasion, and because they so commend themselves to our moral nature as to warrant our expectation that all whose æsthetic taste or moral sense is sound and normal, will of themselves, from simple sympathy with us, respond to and endorse them.

## LETTER IV.

### OF MAN'S SPECIAL QUALITIES.

Much thought has been expended on the question wherein man differs from the lower animals, for they have many qualities similar to ours. They exhibit not only a sensitive, but an intellective nature, of the same kind though not of the same degree as our own. And this through almost all the stages which I have already pointed out to you; from impressions, perceptions, conceptions, imaginations, up even to judgments. It is in our ability to form *notions,* especially notions of high abstraction, that our distinction from them becomes manifest. 'This I think,' says Locke, ' that the power of abstracting is not at all' (?) 'in brutes, and that the having of *general ideas* is that which puts a perfect distinction between man and brutes.'[1]

But I call your attention now to a class of attributes in which there is no question merely of degree but of kind. Man is distinguished from all other animals, essentially, by the possession of a nature *moral, religious,* and *progressive.*

And first I would beg you to consider how essentially Man is a *moral* being.[2] By which I mean a being

---

[1] Locke, ii. 11, 10.

[2] 'Nec vero illa parva vis naturæ est rationisque quod *unum hoc animal* sentit quid sit ordo; quid sit quod deceat; in factis dictisque quid sit modus. Itaque eorum ipsorum quæ *aspectu* sentiuntur nullum aliud

capable of being affected by beauty or deformity of character and conduct; of contemplating himself in the light of such affections; of pronouncing on himself a verdict of approval or disapproval according to his conformity or nonconformity with them, and of moulding himself into fuller correspondence with them. In other words, *this* constitutes our first distinctive feature as *Men*, that we are capable of *moral sentiments*, and of self-observation, self-judgment, self-control, and self-culture with reference to such sentiments.

1. These moral sentiments are of the same nature with those 'immediate' æsthetic judgments which pronounce at once concerning what is beautiful and deformed. 'The beautiful and the ugly,' says Herbart,[1] 'and still more the praiseworthy and the shameful, possess a primitive evidence, in the light of which they show themselves out clearly, without instruction or proof.'[2] Not that this evidence can always of itself break through the accessory conceptions in which the objects of these judgments are often entangled; they need to be helped out into dis-

---

animal pulchritudinem, venustatem, convenientiam partium sentit. Quam similitudinem natura ratioque ab oculis ad animum transferens, multo etiam magis pulchritudinem, constantiam, ordinem *in consiliis factisque* conservandum putat, cavetque ne quid *indecore* faciat.'—Cicero, *De Offic.* i. 4.

[1] Lehrbuch der Philosophie, 76.

[2] This 'naturalness' of the moral sentiments is finely urged by Cicero: 'Nos legem bonam a mala nulla alia nisi *naturæ* norma dividere possumus. Nec solum jus et injuria natura dijudicantur, sed omnino omnia honesta ac turpia; nam et communis intelligentia nobis notas res efficit, easque in animis nostris inchoat, ut honesta in virtute ponantur, in vitiis turpia. Ea autem *in opinione* existumare, *non in natura* posita, *dementis est.* Nam nec arboris nec equi virtus quæ dicitur in opinione sita est sed in natura, quod si est, honesta quoque et turpia *natura* dijudicanda sunt. Est enim virtus perfecta ratio; quod certe in natura est; igitur omnis honestas eodem modo. Nam ut vera et falsa ut consequentia et contraria *sua sponte* judicantur, sic constans et perpetua ratio vitæ, quæ est virtus, itemque inconstantia, quod est vitium, *sua natura* probatur.'—*De Legg.* i. 16.

tinctness by a clear exhibition of the pattern ideas on which these judgments are grounded. And such help is what the science of æsthetics, including that of ethics, has to supply.'

And so also Mr. Lecky: 'The close connection between the good and the beautiful has been always felt; so much so, that both are, in Greek, expressed by the same word, and in the philosophy of Plato moral beauty was regarded as the archetype of which all visible beauty is only the shadow or the image. We all feel that there is a strict propriety in the term moral *beauty*. We feel that there are different forms of beauty which have a natural correspondence to different moral qualities; and much of the charm of poetry and eloquence rests upon this harmony. We feel that we have a direct, immediate, intuitive perception that some objects, such as the sky above us, are beautiful; that this perception of beauty is totally different, and could not possibly be derived, from a perception of their utility; and that it bears a very striking resemblance to the instantaneous and unreasoning admiration that is elicited by a generous or heroic action. We perceive too, if we examine with care the operations of our own mind, that an æsthetic judgment includes an *intuition* or intellectual perception, and an *emotion* of attraction or admiration very similar to those which compose a moral judgment. The very idea of beauty, again, implies that it should be admired, as the idea of duty implies that it should be performed. There is also a striking correspondence between the degree and kind of uniformity we can in each case discover. That there is a difference between right and wrong and between beauty and ugliness are both propositions which are universally felt; that right is better than wrong, and beauty than ugliness, are equally unquestioned. When we go further and attempt to define the nature of these qualities, we are met, indeed, with great varieties of detail, but by a far larger amount of substantial unity. Poems like the Iliad or the Psalms, springing in the most dissimilar quarters, have commanded the admiration of men through all the changes of some 3,000 years. The charm of music, the harmony of the female countenance, the majesty of the starry sky, of the ocean, or of the mountain, the gentler beauties of the murmuring stream or of the twilight shades, were felt as they are felt now when the imagination of the infant world first embodied itself in written words. And in the same way, types of heroism and of virtue descending from the remotest ages command the admiration of mankind. We can sympathise with the emotions of praise or blame revealed in the earliest historians; and the most ancient moralists strike a responsive chord in every heart. The broad lines remain unchanged. No one ever contended that justice was a vice, or injustice a virtue; or that a summer sunset was a repulsive object, or that the sores upon a human body were beautiful. Always, too, the objects of æsthetical admiration were divided into two great classes, the sublime and the beautiful, which in ethics have their manifest counterparts in the heroic and the amiable.'[1]

---

[1] Lecky on European Morals. Judgments of this kind are called *moral*, because they are pronounced on the *mores*, or manners, i.e. modes of conduct, of mankind. And they are comprised under the phrase, the moral *sense*, because they come forth with a *spontaneity* equal to the judgments of taste and touch. And how instinctive such judgments are is well expressed by Seneca (Ep. 94): 'Quis autem negaverit feriri quibusdam præceptis etiam imperitissimos? Hæc cum ictu quodam audimus, nec ulli licet dubitare, aut interrogare Quare?' Whence St. Chrysostom attributes them to the inspiration of God Himself in us. See his twelfth Homily. 'It cannot be

And hence it is that the primary judgments of the moral taste have ever been recognised as part of the nature with which man is endowed, as universal for all men, and eternal for all time. Sophocles calls them

> Laws descended from above,
> Which, not like those by feeble mortals given,
> Buried in dark oblivion lie,
> Or worn by time, decay and die,
> But bloom eternal like their native heaven.[1]

And again,

> The firm unwritten laws
> Of the just gods. These are not of to-day
> Or yesterday, but through all ages live,
> And none knows whence they sprang.[2]

Socrates says of them, 'There are laws unwritten, yet universally in force, which no human legislation has established, for men cannot all have come together in one place with one tongue for this purpose; and such laws, therefore, I ascribe to God.'[3] Seneca extols them as 'laws not written, indeed, but far more valid than all that have

---

said that the heathen legislators held communication with Moses, or that they heard the prophets. It is evident, therefore, that their moral judgments came from the law which God placed in man when he formed him.'

[1] Sophocles, *Œd. Tyr.* 865:—

> ὧν νόμοι πρόκεινται,
> Ὑψίποδες, οὐρανίαν
> Δι' αἰθέρα τεκνωθέντες, ὧν Ὄλυμπος
> Πατὴρ μόνος, οὐδέ νιν
> Θνατὰ φύσις ἀνέρων
> Ἔτικτεν, οὐδὲ μήποτε λάθα κατακοιμάσῃ.
> Μέγας ἐν τούτοις Θεός, οὐδὲ γηράσκει.

[2] Antig. 454:—

> ἄγραπτα κἀσφαλῆ θεῶν
> Νόμιμα . . . . .
> Οὐ γάρ τι νῦν γε κἀχθές, ἀλλ' ἀεί ποτε
> Ζῇ ταῦτα, κοὐδεὶς οἶδεν ἐξ ὅτου 'φάνη.

[3] Xenophon, Mem. Soc. iv. 4, 7.

been written.'[1] And Cicero describes them as forming a
code of wisdom, 'eternal, and valid for the rule of the
whole world; whose authority is not simply older than
the age of peoples and states, but equal to that of
Him who watches over and governs heaven and earth.'[2]
For 'the dictates of our nature,' he says again, 'constitute
a perfect law, diffusing itself through all men, unchangeable, eternal, which calls us to duty and scares us from
wrong. No one may abrogate this law, no one lessen its
authority, no one explain it away. Nor is it a law prescribing one thing at Rome, another at Athens; one
thing to-day, another thing to-morrow; but in every
nation and through every age it constitutes one and the
same eternal and immutable code, and reigns as the one
common teacher, sovereign, nay, god of all things; for
none but God has conceived it, has put it forth, and enforces it. Whosoever, therefore, refuses to obey this
law, flies from the control of his own self, and spurning
the very nature of man must by such outrage severely
punish himself, even if he escape that outward vengeance
which men count punishment.'[3]

---

[1] Seneca, Controv. 1: 'Jura non scripta sed omnibus scriptis certiora.'

[2] Cicero, De Legg. ii. 4: 'Legem neque hominum ingeniis excogitatum
neque scitum aliquod esse populorum, sed æternum quiddam, quod univer-
sum mundum regeret imperandi prohibendique sapientia. . . . Quæ vis non
modo senior est quam ætas populorum et civitatum sed æqualis illius cœlum
et terras tuentis et regentis Dei.'

Add Saisset, Phil. rel. ii. 192: 'Il y a un certain nombre de vérités qui
ne meurent point. Je les trouve partout répandues, au moins en germe.
Elles vont s'épanouissant, s'épurant, se fortifiant d'âge en âge, toujours
jeunes, toujours vivantes, et dans leur évolution progressive elles maintien-
nent et consacrent la fraternité religieuse des nations.'

[3] Cicero, De Republ. iii. 22: 'Est vera lex recta ratio, naturæ congruens,
diffusa in omnes, constans, sempiterna, quæ vocet ad officium jubendo, a
fraude deterreat. . . . Huic legi nec abrogare fas est, neque derogari ex hac
aliquid licet, neque tota abrogari potest . . . neque est quærendus explanator

And I beg you to note well that the *existence* of such
moral judgments is denied by no school of moralists, whatever their divergence of opinion as to the *origin* of these
judgments. 'The *existence* of moral distinctions,' says
the 'Westminster Review,' 'is the one *fact* on which
utilitarianism and all other theories of morality are
based; so that to deny this existence would be equivalent to founding a system of geometry on the assumption that space does not exist.' And again, they are 'the
spontaneous and immediate promptings of the conscience,
or the moral sense.' And again, 'The derivative moralists are at one with the intuitional in their recognition of *the existence of moral sentiments*, and in their
anxiety to strengthen and refine them.'[1] So that we
may well conclude with Bishop Butler concerning their
verdict: 'This moral approving and disapproving faculty
is *certain*, from our experiencing it in ourselves, and
recognising it in others.'[2]

aut interpres ejus alius; nec erit alia lex Romæ, alia Athenis, alia nunc,
alia posthac, sed et omnes gentes et omni tempore una lex et sempiterna
et immutabilis continebit; unusque erit communis quasi magister et impe-
rator omnium deus, ille legis hujus inventor, disceptator, lator; cui qui non
parebit ipse se fugiet, ac *naturam hominis* aspernatus *hoc ipso* luet maximas
poenas, etiamsi cetera supplicia, quæ putantur, effugerit.'

[1] West. Rev. Oct. 1869, p. 519.

[2] Compare A. Helps in Cont. Rev. Jan. 1871: 'The *utile*, even when
brought home to a man's self, has much less to do with peoples' opinions
and desires than might be supposed. Men are prone to make light of and
postpone their nearest interests to sentiment and feeling. Indeed, I would
venture to maintain that *no great change has ever been produced in the world
by motives of self-interest*. Sentiment, that thing which many wise people
affect to despise, is the commanding thing as regards popular impulses and
popular action.'

Add Ibid. 237 (Calderwood). 'Mr. Wallace argues that the *practice* of
virtues on the ground of their utility cannot account for the *sanctity* which
attaches to them even among savage tribes.' And he adds: 'The utilitarian
hypothesis (which is the theory of natural selection applied to mind) seems
inadequate to account for the development of the moral sense. It is difficult

But then I do not mean to say that this 'certainty' is independent of the clearness with which we perceive the objects on which the moral judgments give their verdict. There is the same variation here as in the judgments of the *palate*, from which the very name of moral *taste* is by analogy derived. These judgments also depend for their force and purity on the way in which the objects to be tasted are brought into contact with the gustatory nerve; and, moreover, on the refinement to which this nerve has been raised. And just so the delicacy of our moral taste depends upon its culture. As wide, for instance, as the difference between your vinous taste and that of the experienced wine merchant, or your taste for food and that of the refined epicure, or your delicacy of touch and that of the tea-dealer, or the picture-dealer,[1] so wide may be the interval between the *moral* taste of the uncultured clown and that of the well-trained conscience. But still the tastes, however different in *degree*, exist in *kind*. The capacity for the full perception of their proper objects, and the full discrimination of these objects, is, however latent and uncultured, *there*. And in both classes of taste, the sensuous and the moral, the justness of the verdicts given will depend on the clearness

---

to conceive that such an intense and mystical feeling of right and wrong (so intense as to overcome all ideas of personal advantage and utility) can have been developed out of accumulated ancestral experiences, of utility.' —Wallace on *Theory of Nat. Sel.* 352–355.

'Quæ autem natio non comitatem, non benignitatem, non gratum animum et beneficii memorem diligit? Quæ superbos, quæ maleficos, quæ crudeles, quæ ingratos non aspernatur, non odit?'—Cicero, *De Legg.* 1.

[1] I knew a tea-dealer who gained a large fortune by the facility with which he could distinguish, by the touch, pure teas from adulterations. And Emerson (English tracts) tells of a picture-dealer who, at first glance, supposed a painting of Allston's to be an antique, but on feeling it exclaimed, 'It is not two years old!' So delicate was the man's touch.

of perception, and the sensitiveness of the discriminating tact. The expert in morals, like the expert in other matters of judgment, is *made* by exercise and use. Of Charles the Second, Macaulay says, 'Honour and shame were scarcely more to him than light and darkness to the blind.'¹ Of the mature Christian, St. Paul declares, 'Strong meat belongeth to them who have come to man's estate, and by reason of use have their senses *exercised* to discern both good and evil.'² And Job says concerning the moral judgment, 'Cannot my taste discern perverse things?'³

Thus, in the sphere of *truth*, the judgments which seem the most intuitive are due to a process, however latent, of ratiocination. When Newton saw at a glance the truths in Euclid, without requiring any conscious development of the proofs presented for them, the demonstration must nevertheless have gone on, as it were *per saltum*, beneath his consciousness. In the sphere of *beauty* our discrimination of this quality, whether in forms, in tones, in colours, or in proportions, depends on the clearness with which the objects to be appreciated are disentangled from perplexing accessories, and on the extent to which the *sense* of beauty has been given by nature, or acquired through culture, exercise and habit. For the beauties of nature are often least appreciated by those who are most among the forms of nature, if these forms are from infancy mixed up in their minds with poverty and hardship, and discoloured by association with what is low, and sordid, and selfish in their daily life. And the beauties of art, as displayed by a Titian, a Michael Angelo, a Mendelssohn,

---

¹ Macaulay, Hist. of England, i. 168.
² Hebrews v. 14.   ³ Job vi. 30.

are appreciated by those alone in whom the *sense* for art, in its threefold domain of colour, of form, and of tone, has been developed. Proficiency depends on culture. The sense must be 'exercised by reason of use.' But yet, in all these cases equally, the sense is *there*. It must be there, or it could never by any training be called forth. It must be there, in certain primitive universal principles of judgment and feeling, or when called forth its verdicts would not command such general acceptance as they do. What are concords, and what discords? What is proportion, and what disproportion? What is harmony of colour, and what disharmony? To these questions there may be many answers from untrained ears and eyes, but with all whose tastes have been refined by culture there will be substantial unanimity. For what is this *refinement* but the taste being *clarified* from the accretions with which the pure ore of truth is to the unpractised eye overlaid and hidden? And hence all taste, throughout all its departments, is in its essence *discrimination*. Feelings of complacency or displacency *accompany* its decisions, but the decisions themselves are acts of *judgment*, which pronounces with varying rapidity and justness, according to the clearness of its *perception* and the delicacy of its *tact*.[1]

And these decisions, in all their spheres of nature, of art, or of human disposition and conduct, have this special characteristic, that they are based on purely OBJECTIVE grounds, with no admixture of personal subjective bias. They are judgments formed, as it were, *in vacuo*. They contemplate their objects in that 'dry light' which belongs to an atmosphere unmixed with baser matter. And they pronounce on these objects, not from any consideration of

[1] See Appendix, Note XI.

their being *pleasurable* or painful to our individual sensations, or their being *profitable* or unprofitable to our individual advantage, but solely on the ground of their being *proper* or improper in the relation brought before us; whence it follows that they are of universal validity, and constitute the law for all persons, at all times, in all places, who may occupy the relation which they contemplate.

And I say emphatically, 'the relation which they contemplate;' for what is commendable in disposition or conduct cannot be laid down abstractedly, without limitation by the facts of each particular case. Nor can the whole system of morals be deduced from one leading principle branching out in all directions, as some moralists have attempted to do. The proper thing must be learned, in each particular case, from the facts of this case; whence the comprehensive rule of the Church Catechism, that we are ' to do our duty in *that state of life* to which God has called us.' As our relations, so are our duties; that is, literally, the disposition and conduct *due* from us in those relations. As Professor Maurice says: 'We are in an *order*; *relations* abide whether we be faithful to them or neglect them. And the conscience in each of us affirms, " I am in this order, I *ought* to act consistently with it, let my fancies say what they will."' And again: ' A man asks himself if he *ought* to do this, if he *ought not* to do that. Why? Because he fears he has been following a way of his own, *not consistent with his position* as lawyer, physician, clergyman; not consistent with that which was *due* from him to his clients, his patients, his flock.'[1]

And it is to such moral *positions*; to the *relations* in which we stand, whether inwardly to our own mind, or

[1] Maurice on the Conscience, 57, 91.

outwardly to our fellow-men, that our Lord adapts those promises with which he cheers his followers in his Sermon on the Mount. He assumes that they are lovers of *self-possession*, and therefore labouring after inward integrity ('purity of heart'); and of *self-perfectionment*, and therefore 'hungering and thirsting after righteousness.' And He assumes that they are lovers of *social order* ('men of peace'), and therefore wounded by every kind and degree of strife; lovers of *social welfare* ('merciful'), and therefore desiring the good of all sentient being; and lovers of *social equity*, and therefore longing for the triumph of retributive justice throughout the universe ('Count yourselves happy when men persecute you, for great is your *reward* in heaven).'[1]

Observe, then, how the first thing which everyone instinctively approves in himself and others is *self-possession*. By this I mean that mastery over all the movements of our mind by which there is maintained a thorough harmony between preference and performance; between what commends itself to the moral sense as right, and what comes out in purpose and act. It is that quality which, by saving us from the domination of passion, brings conduct into correspondence with conviction. And the extent to which we naturally admire this quality may be appreciated by observing the extent to which we detest its opposite—self-contradiction. This all men so hate

---

[1] Matthew v. 6-12. The object of the so-called 'Beatitudes' is to cheer the followers of Christ, amidst their experience of *personal sorrow* (3-5), of *moral imperfection* (6-9), and of *social injustice* (10-12), with the promise of a state in which all these evils shall be removed. And in our Lord's assumptions as to men's moral instincts, He has remarkably anticipated just those principles of personal and social ethics at which Herbart has arrived by his own independent investigations. See Herbart's Allgemeine practische Philosophie, a work to which I am deeply indebted.

that Schiller ventures to say, 'Self-contradiction is the only wrong.' And Milton exclaims, 'To be weak is to be miserable, doing or suffering.' And of such self-contradiction you have the most life-like picture in St. Paul's delineation of the slavery and the misery of one who, seeing what is right, does wrong; who, when to will is present with him, yet finds not how to perform that which is good; who finds a law in his members warring against the law of his mind, and bringing him into captivity to the law of sin which is in his members; and with whom therefore the result of his self-knowledge is a bitter sense of moral bondage, forcing out the despairing cry, 'Who shall emancipate me from this body of death?'[1]

Now just the reverse of this slavery is self-possession. It is the being a cubical man; foursquare; *à plomb*; the maintaining a harmony of the several elements of our mind; so that they shall not thwart and thereby weaken each other, but work in perfect fulness towards one end. It constitutes the liberty on which the Stoics insist so much—the maintaining our moral preference which God has implanted in us (τὴν ἡμῶν αὐτῶν προαίρεσιν κατὰ φύσιν).[2] It is that concerning which Mr. Gladstone says, 'τὸ μέσον of Aristotle is not a mean between extremes of mere quantity, but an *inward equipoise* of the mind and in the composition of mental qualities; abhorring excess in any one of them, because it mars the combination as a whole and throws the rest into deficiency.'[3] It is that which Clement of Alexandria terms 'the symphony of all the parts of the soul;' that which Shakespeare prescribes attention to when he says, 'Give no *unproportioned*

---

[1] Rom. vii. 14-24.  [2] Epictet. Man. 13.
[3] Gladstone, Juventus Mundi, 303.

thought his act;' that which Hobbes describes as 'an absence of the lets and hindrances of motion, so that the more ways a man can move himself the more liberty he hath;' and yet that which in the midst of all this liberty of movement, nay because of it, maintains and accomplishes perfect unity of purpose, and makes us *whole* men to whatever we undertake. And therefore, it is just what our Lord extols when he pronounces his benediction on 'the pure in heart.' For 'purity of heart' is unmixedness, wholeness; the opposite of double-mindedness, of having 'a heart and a heart,' of being false to oneself.[1] It is the quality of those happy natures, or those ransomed souls, whose will, like a well-poised needle, 'traverses freely' the whole circumference of the compass, and settles with quick fidelity to the pole; and with whom therefore to will and to do are one and the same act. For

> If our souls but poise and swing,
> Like the compass in its brazen ring,
> Ever level, and ever true
> To the toil and the task we have to do,
> We shall sail securely, and safely reach
> The fortunate isles, on whose shining beach
> The sights we see and the sounds we hear
> Will be those of joy and not of fear.[2]

---

[1] See James iv. 8: 'Purify your hearts, ye double-minded.' So that 'purity of heart' in Matt. v. 8, is synonymous with 'singleness of heart' in Eph. vi. 5, and with 'simplicity and godly sincerity' in 2 Cor. i. 12. Compare Matt. vi. 22, 'If thine eye be *single*.' Compare Silas Marner, 'Sincerity *clear* as the new-born dew;' and Longfellow, Voices of the Night:

> The star of the unconquered will,
> It rises on my breast,
> *Serene* and resolute and still,
> And calm and *self-possessed*.

[2] Longfellow, ibid.

You will see, therefore, at once how for such self-possession there is needed an element of *force* in full activity—such force as, by *keeping up* our purposes, shall help them on to performance, and by *keeping down* their contraries shall maintain the equilibrium of our mind. This force is so indispensable that, even without reference to the *sort* of purpose which it keeps up and makes successful, it draws from us involuntary admiration. Even where not linked with goodness it deludes us into praise. We bow down before strength for strength's sake. 'All force,' says Canon Liddon, 'whether moral or mental or physical, is of itself beautiful. It commands admiration in proportion to its intensity.' And hence Carlyle's worship of force; and his tendency to make right identical with might. Weak vice exposes itself naked to our detestation, bold vice covers its blackness with the shining armour of valorous force.

Nor can there be any virtue without such force. Virtue is not the innocence of a child, but the vigorous goodness of a man. The very word means manliness. And only where this manliness is aroused, to help our good desires against outward enemies and inward weakness, have we the *liberty* to do the things that we would. 'In whatever befalls you,' says Epictetus, 'examine what faculty you possess to meet it. If toil, for instance, be thrown upon you, bring forth against it such *inward force* (καρτερίαν) as you have.' Hence the Bhuddists say: 'He is a more noble warrior who *subdues himself* than he who conquers thousands;' and Solomon declares: 'He that is slow to anger is better than the mighty; and he that ruleth his spirit than he that taketh a city.'[1] Such force it was which formed the ground of Hezekiah's

---

[1] Proverbs xvi. 32.

greatness. 'In every work that he began, he did it with *all his heart*' (with the whole amount of force that was in him), ' and prospered.'[1] To the stirring up of such force we are so often called in Holy Scripture. 'Be thou *strong* and very courageous that thou **mayest** observe to do all the law, and **turn** not from it to the right hand or to the left, that thou mayest prosper whithersoever thou goest.'[2] 'Quit yourselves like *men.* Be strong.'[3] The successes of such force Wordsworth well describes in his 'Happy Warrior.'

> This generous spirit who, when brought
> Among the tasks of real life, hath wrought
> Upon the plan that pleased his childish thought;
> Whose high endeavours are an inward light
> That makes the path before him always bright.

And to the putting forth such force Thomson exhorts slaves of indolence, when he cries,

> Resolve, resolve, and to be *men* aspire!
> Exert that noblest privilege, alone
> Here to *mankind* indulged ; control desire!
> Let god-like reason from her sovereign throne
> Speak the commanding word, I will, and it is done!

But looking at a man with respect to the internal relations of his will, **you will feel** that self-possession at any given moment is not sufficient to satisfy your moral sense. You look further for *self-perfectionment.* The dull **man,** indifferent to **progress,** however punctilious in his little sphere, disappoints you. It is not enough that his mind be self-balanced ; you require that it be also self-expanding, ever taking in new views of duty, and

---

[1] 2 Chron. xxxi. 21.   [2] Joshua i. 7.   [3] 1 Cor. xvi. 13.

stretching onward to new conquests over evil; advancing steadily from one stage to another of that *completeness* which lies in the ideal of man. The smallest circle indeed, if fully rounded, 'satisfies;' but in the circle of the human character no present roundness is sufficient. We look to its enlarging its dimensions. 'No man,' says Theodore Parker, 'has yet had a complete, total, and permanent enjoyment of every part of his nature. This indeed is the ideal to which we tend, but one not capable of complete attainment in a progressive being: for if the ideal of yesterday has become the actual of to-day, to-morrow we are seized with manly disquiet and unrest, and soar upwards towards another ideal.'[1] Hence Wordsworth describes his 'Happy Warrior' as one,

> Who, not content that former worth stand fast,
> Looks forward, persevering to the last,
> From well to better, *daily self-surpast*.

Hence, too, Longfellow says,

> Not enjoyment and not sorrow
>   Is our destined end and way;
> But to act that each to-morrow
>   Finds us farther than to-day.
>
> Let us then be up and doing,
>   With a heart for any fate;
> Still achieving, still pursuing,
>   Learn to labour and to wait.

---

[1] See Herbart, Pract. Phil. 89: 'Ohne Frage, gefällt das Stärkere neben dem Schwächeren, missfällt das Schwächere neben dem Stärkeren. Möchte das Schwächere gleich geworden sein dem Stärkeren; wofern alsdann noch eins von beyden wüchse, so erzeugte sich das Verhältniss von neuem. So ins Unendliche.'

See Fraser's Mag., Feb. 1871: 'In Dryden there was nothing of that restless and unsatisfied yearning after perfection by which the loftiest souls are known. The painful process of correction, the Horatian *limæ labor*, were unknown to him.'

And hence the feeling of St. Paul: 'I count not myself to have apprehended, but forgetting those things which are behind, and reaching forth to those which are before, I press toward the mark to grasp the prize to which I have been called from on high.'[1] Hence, too, his exhortation to the Hebrews, 'Leaving the mere elements of the doctrine of Christ, let us go on unto perfection.'[2] And hence the benediction of our Lord, 'Blessed are they that hunger and thirst after righteousness' (are ever longing for a greater fulness of moral character), 'for they shall at last be filled.'[3]

Now let us pass from the moral sentiments which are roused in us when we contemplate the *internal* relations of our will in itself, to those which are produced when we contemplate our *external* relations to other persons. Here we pass from moral judgments on ourselves as standing alone, to moral judgments of ourselves as members of society. We find ourselves mixed up with the *rights* of others as constituted by the laws of this society; with the *claims* which equity makes as flowing from their character and position in relation to us; and with the *wants* under which they labour. And we instinctively pronounce ourselves blameworthy if we do not respect these rights, respond to these claims, and regard with active sympathy these wants. It is some dim feeling of the demands of moral feeling in these several respects which lies at the base of the famous formula of the French revolution, liberty, equality, fraternity; for liberty is the conceding to all their rights, equality recognises the claims they have on us according to their social worth ('*la carrière ouverte aux talents*'), and fraternity

---

[1] Philipp. iii. 13, 14.    [2] Hebrews vi. 1.    [3] Matt. v. 6.

sympathises with their wants. And a similar classification of the elements of all social duty is made by St. Paul when he says to the Ephesians, 'The fruit of the light (the product of an enlightened conscience) consists in perfect goodness, righteousness, and truth.' For 'righteousness' here is respect for the rights of others, 'truth' is responsiveness to their claims on us, and 'goodness' is practical regard to their wants.[1]

First then let me remind you how universal is the requirement that we should *respect the rights* of all with whom we have to do. All society depends on some degree of confidence and concord between man and man. To define the terms of this confidence and concord, and to secure their maintenance, law is introduced. Law assigns to each member of the society his position and rights in relation to all others. And everyone feels that violation of law, as tending to a violation of the confidence and concord on which society depends (to a 'breach of the peace,' as it is technically called), deserves censure and punishment; while he who reverences law, and

---

[1] For 'truth,' in a moral sense, is 'conformity to equity;' 'responsiveness to the claims which equity enforces.' See the phrase of Thucydides, iii. 56, 'Not being true' (i.e. equitable) 'judges.' And of Josephus, 'Their judgments were not according to *truth*;' not in accordance with the truth of the relation and its claims, on which they pronounced. So similarly Shakespeare:—

'Be to thine own self *true*,
And then it follows, as the day the night,
Thou never canst prove *false* to any man.'

That is, respond to the claims of your own conscience, then will you never be faithless to the claims which others have on you. The same principle of equitable recompense will run through your social as your personal life. It is usual to derive ἀλήθης from ά and λήθω, to conceal, q. d. open, frank. But is it not rather from λήθω (λανθάνομαι), to forget, to let slip, to pass over? (Compare λήθη, forgetfulness;) q. d. not forgetting, not letting slip, any facts that deserve our notice, but being *faithful* to them; being *true* to all the particulars which go to make up an equitable judgment.

reverences the rights which are set up and protected by law, is counted righteous and just. Peace is the first indispensable condition of social life; and to establish and maintain this peace the voice of the many, expressed in law, is called in to restrain the violence of the few. Distinctions are set up of *meum* and *tuum*; statutes are passed to enforce these distinctions; and penalties are agreed upon to punish the breach of these statutes. And thus the voice of law is the echo of that primary principle of all social life: 'Live peaceably with all men;' 'Be at peace among yourselves;' 'Blessed are the peaceful.'[1] And its admonition is, Do nothing which by infraction of law will stir up strife. Hence the rule laid down by Isocrates: 'Whatever things you are angry at when inflicted on you by others, these things abstain from inflicting on them.' Or as the book of Tobit puts it, 'What you hate to have done to you, this do not to anyone else.' But this admonition has its positive side, as

---

[1] It is this peacefulness which our Lord demands in Matt. v. 21-26, in the repression of violent *words*, bitter *feelings*, and a stubborn *will*. There is *word* murder and *heart* murder, as well as *hand* murder. See Helps in Cont. Rev., Jan. 1871. 'Most quarrels depend on words. These form the main substratum of all contentiousness. You may do a man a substantial injury and be easily forgiven; but utter only one injurious word, and there is a fine opening for a quarrel. Also, in the conduct of the quarrel there is nothing so much to beware of as the use of injurious words. Exaggeration is always punished, and never more speedily than when employed in the transaction of a quarrel. When in presence of your adversary understate your case to him (not your own *claim* but his neglect of it), and as regards the nicety of your expressions, talk as you would have talked if both of you were wearing swords.'

Hence our Lord's laying so much stress on evil *words* as well as deeds. (Matt. xii. 37.)

Hence the Spanish proverb, 'The man who says the *third* thing (who makes the rejoinder) is the man on whose shoulder the quarrel rests.' (Cont. Rev. ut supra, 257.) See Prov. xv. 1: 'A soft answer turneth away wrath, but grievous *words* stir up anger.'

well as its negative. It calls on us to do to others whatever would be grateful to ourselves, and increase our confidence in them. And so it takes the more general form of, 'Do as you would be done by;' 'Put yourself in another's place.' As Isocrates says, again, 'Behave towards your parents as you would wish your children to behave to you.' Whence Aristotle, being asked how we should demean ourselves towards our friends, replied, 'As we would wish our friends to demean themselves towards us.' And our Lord has set forth this principle in all its compass, negative and positive, in his golden rule: 'Whatsoever ye would that men should do to you' (whatsoever you would consider it right for them to do to you) 'that do ye also unto them.'

But besides the obligations which are bound upon us by social law—the neglect of which is odious to us, because such neglect disturbs the peace of the community—there are others, more extensive and more delicate, to which our sense of *equity* gives force. Beyond the rights established by written statute there are claims unwritten which result from the position in which men stand related to us, the disposition which in these relations they manifest towards us, and the services which they render us. And if we do not respond to such claims, the principle of retribution or recompense is felt to be violated by us, and we become censurable in the judgment of others and in our own. We equally disapprove and condemn the *defrauding* others of what they may *equitably expect* from us, as the *robbing* others of what they *legally possess*. And it is allegiance to this principle of *due return* which Scripture enforces by the injunction, 'Render unto all their *dues*;' i.e. whatever is *owing* to them by you on account of the several relations, natural civil, or social, in which you stand to them. Not only, therefore, 'tribute to whom tribute is due, and custom to whom custom,' but the finer and more undetermined debts of 'fear to whom fear is due, and honour to whom honour.' Whence the all-comprehending admonition, 'Owe no man anything;' neglect not to pay anyone the return which he may equitably look for at your hands, for his disposition and demeanour towards you, or from his connection with you. Whence, for instance, St. Paul's requirement, in the conjugal relation, of what *law* cannot compel, but *equity* enjoins : 'Let the husband render (ἀποδιδότω) to the wife all due benevolence' (τὴν ὀφειλὴν), the debt which from her relation to him he owes her.[1]

Yet neither of these spheres of obligation takes in that wider range of duties which are bound upon us by the universal relation in which we stand to others, as partakers of the same nature and sharers in the same wants, whether material or mental, which to this nature pertain. Whatever *needs* of our common humanity we ourselves yearn to have supplied to us, these we cannot overlook in others without making ourselves objects, both to their judgment and our own, of moral displacency. For we show ourselves thereby deficient in that *humanity*, good-will, sympathy, and love, which a common nature demands from every human being to his kindred. This good-will is what Cicero calls the '*caritas generis humani*,'

---

[1] And so, again, the same Apostle's deduction of the recompense owing by gentile converts to their Jewish brethren : 'Their debtors they are (ὀφειλέται αὐτῶν εἰσιν); for if the gentiles have been made partakers of their spiritual things, that which is due from them in return (the recompense which the mutual relation requires, ὀφείλουσι) is also to minister to them in carnal things.'—Rom. xv. 27.

and the expression of which drew forth such universal plaudits when the actor said 'I am a man, and therefore touched with sympathy for everything that pertains to man!'

Hence, the first impulse of the early Christians was to carry out this principle with reference to the *material* wants of their brethren : 'All that believed were together and had all things common, and sold their possessions and goods, and parted them to all men as every man had need.'[1] 'And the multitude of them that believed were of one heart and one soul, neither said any of them that aught of the things which he possessed was his own, but they had all things common; neither was there any among them that lacked, for as many as were possessors of lands or houses sold them, and brought the prices of the things sold and laid them down at the apostles' feet, and distribution was made to every man according as he had need.'[2] And although the abuse of this procedure soon obliged a departure from it, yet the principle itself, to be carried out so far as to produce equality of bodily comfort, was insisted on by St. Paul: 'I mean not indeed that others should be eased and you burdened, but by an equality' (ἐξ ἰσότητος, in order to an equitable adjustment), 'that your abundance' (περίσσευμα, overplus) 'may be a supply for their want' (ὑστέρημα, deficiency), 'that their abundance also may be a supply for your want, that there may be equality' (ὅπως γένηται ἰσότης, that by this adjustment all may have an equitable distribution); 'as it is written, He that gathered much had nothing over, and he that gathered little had no lack.'[3] And the

[1] Acts ii. 44.     [2] Acts iv. 32—35.     [3] 2 Cor. viii. 13-15.

same principle is applied to the mental as well as physical wants of our brethren. All gifts that we have are vouchsafed to us for *equitable distribution* among all less favoured. 'The manifestation of the Spirit is given to each man for the good of all;'[1] 'As each man therefore hath received the gift, even so minister the same one to another, as good stewards of the manifold grace of God.'[2] 'Have ye understood all these things? Then every scribe instructed concerning the kingdom of heaven is to be like a householder who *bringeth forth* out of his treasure things new and old.'[3] 'For there is nothing covered but in order to be revealed, nor hid, but in order to be made known. What I tell you in darkness that speak ye in light, and what ye hear in the ear, that preach ye upon the housetops.'[4] In short this principle is enforced to its full extent in the universal law, 'Thou shalt love thy neighbour as thyself,' and in the universal benediction, 'Blessed are the merciful,' i.e. those who sympathise with others in their various wants, and therefore bestir themselves to supply these wants. The type of which disposition is given us in the parable of the good Samaritan, who, instead of passing by the man in want, 'had compassion on him and took care of him;' or, as our Lord adds, '*exercised* mercy towards him' (ποιήσας τὸ ἔλεος μετ' αὐτοῦ), carried out the loving disposition to its practical results. With this compare the exhortations of St. Paul, 'Look not each man on his own interests, but on the interests of others also,' which enforces just the 'Altruisme' of Comte, in contradiction to our native 'Egoisme.' And again, 'Let no one seek his own

---

[1] 1 Cor. xii. 7.  
[2] 1 Peter iv. 10.  
[3] Matt. xiii. 52.  
[4] Matt. x. 26, 27.

welfare exclusively, but every one the welfare of others also.' And again, 'Charity seeketh not her own.'[1]

2. But as moral beings we are not only thus capable of being affected by sentiments of complacency or displacency when we contemplate human character, but further, of *pronouncing judgment* on ourselves with reference to such sentiments, and of practically *moulding ourselves* into increasing conformity with them.[2]

For though such sentiments arise at first impersonally, irrespective of their bearing on ourselves, yet they call up a demand for corresponding action, both in others and in ourselves. And this demand we find re-echoed by the moral judgment of the common conscience as well as our own. And a want of compliance with this demand exposes us to social blame and self-reproach. And thus we are impelled to take such steps of self-restraint and self-improvement as may remove or mitigate this blame and self-reproach. Our experience of responsibility urges us to reformation. Just as surrounding nature makes us responsible for our behaviour towards it by re-acting on our violation or even negligence of its laws, just so society makes us responsible for our

---

[1] 1 Cor. xiii. 5.

[2] This self-judgment is what Mr. Gladstone understands by the Homeric *Nemesis*. 'To this Nemesis, self-judgment, or sense of the moral law, often inaccurately rendered revenge, Menelaus appeals when exciting the Greeks to defend the body of Patroclus from insult (Iliad, xvii. 254: ἀλλά τις αὐτὸς ἴτω, νεμεσιζέσθω δ' ἐνὶ θυμῷ). But the whole matter is best learned from the address of Telemachus to the suitors, when he says, " Rouse within you, of yourselves, a nemesis (or moral sense) and an αἰδώς (or sense of honour or regard to the opinion of your fellow-citizens), and fear the wrath of the gods" (Odyss. ii. 64–67). These three principles were the three great pillars of morality. *Nemesis*, or self-judgment by our own inward law; αἰδώς, or self-judgment according to the standard supplied by the ideas of others; and *fear*, or anticipation of judgment by the divine law.'—Gladstone, *Juventus Mundi*, 383.

behaviour towards it by recompensing our insurrection against its judgment with dislike, disrepute, disfranchisement; and our submission to this judgment with approbation and advantage. It re-acts upon us by its feelings of esteem or disesteem; by its expressions of praise or blame; by its deeds of reward or punishment, social and civil; deeds sometimes summary, as in lynch law and its cognates, sometimes deliberate, as in criminal law. And in like manner, our own conscience (or consciousness of ourself as an object of moral approval or disapproval) makes us responsible. It smites us or it cheers us. It throws us into states of pleasure or pain. And thus it goads us to amend our character, if we would escape such pain or hope such pleasure. It was thus it wrought with David. The prophet excites in him, first of all, a purely impersonal moral judgment on an imagined case, and he gains from him the instantaneous verdict, 'As the Lord liveth the man that hath done this thing shall surely die.' But then, he throws back the monarch on his own consciousness, to find therein the image of himself, as answering to the one depicted. 'Thou art the man!' And thus the verdict which has been won from David against another, is turned inward on himself; and he exclaims, with shame and sorrow, 'I have sinned!'[1] And in the same way did our Lord bring out the slumbering conscience of the Pharisees. By a suitable story He roused their moral indignation against wrong-doers, and brought them to the verdict, 'He will miserably destroy those wicked men;' and then He left them to apply this verdict to themselves. 'They perceived that he spake of them.'[2]

---

[1] 2 Samuel xii. 1-13.     [2] Matt. xxi. 33-45.

And hence results all reformation. An adverse verdict works upon us; it calls up a new determination of ourselves, in order to free ourselves from its intolerable pressure; and in consonance with this determination we re-mould our conduct. As a burnt child dreads the fire, so the sufferer from social or self-blame shrinks from its repetition. As the acrobat, to avoid a fall, adjusts himself to the pressure of gravity; so we, to escape further censure, adjust ourselves to the pressure of public opinion and private conscience. And so we labour to become to ourselves and others a different kind of men.[1]

II. But another distinctive fact of our nature as men is that we are *religious* beings. The capacity of man for religion, his bias towards religion, his necessary development into some form or other of religion, is a fact as indisputable as that of his moral nature. Franck forcibly affirms: 'L'homme est diversement religieux, il l'est *incorrigiblement.*'[2] And Dr. Huxley beautifully says: 'When we find that on our brief gladness there follows a certain sorrow, and that the little light of awakened human intelligence shines so mere a speck amidst the abyss of the unknown and unknowable, seems so insufficient to do more than illuminate the imperfections that cannot be remedied, the aspirations that cannot be

---

[1] See Herbart, *Pract. Phil.* 20, 21 : 'Das Bild des Willens ist gebunden, nach Art der Bilder, an das willenlose Urtheil, das in dem Auffassenden hervortritt. Und der Wollende ist ausgesetzt dem *eignen* Anblick, worin mit seinem Bilde das *Selbsturtheil* zugleich erzeugt wird. Das Urtheil ist kein Wille, und kann nicht gebieten. Tadelnd aber mag es fort und fort vernommen werden, bis vielleicht den Willen ihm gemäss zu ändern ein neu erzeugter Wille sich entschliesst.' So that while we *admire* virtue, involuntarily, because it is *beautiful*, we pursue virtue, voluntarily, because it is *beneficial*.

[2] Tissandier, Théodicée, 25.

realised, of man's nature; then, in this sadness, this consciousness of the limitation of man, this sense of an open secret which he cannot penetrate, lies the essence of all religion.'[1] For religion arrived at by this line of thought is just the yearning of Elihu in the Book of Job, 'That which I see not, teach thou me!'[2] It is just that last resort of the baffled understanding which Max Müller describes: 'When we say that it is religion which distinguishes man from the animal, we mean that faculty which independent of, nay, in spite of, sense and reason' (?) 'enables man to apprehend the Infinite; that groaning of the spirit to conceive the inconceivable, to utter the unutterable; the longing after the Infinite. Whether the etymology which the ancients gave of the Greek word ἄνθρωπος be true or not, from ὁ ἄνω ἀθρῶν, "he who looks upward," certain it is that what makes man to be man is that he alone can turn his face to heaven, he alone yearns for something that neither sense nor reason can supply.'[3] And this bias towards religion being as essential a part of the human constitution as our intelligence or our moral sense, claims equally to be taken into account in the education of man. 'A culture therefore which ignores religion is essentially defective. It forgets that our powers must culminate in worship ere they bear their noblest fruit. Wordsworth used to say that the man who despised anything in nature had "faculties which he had never used." And the same may be said of those who omit the faculty of worship from their inventory of the powers of the soul. They are to that extent *defective as men*, and a singular Nemesis attends them. The very

---

[1] Huxley, Lay Sermons, 15.   [2] Job xxxiv. 32.
[3] Max Müller, Lect. on Religion, in Fraser's Mag., April, 1870.

faculty in course of time vanishes; the repressed instinct ceases to exert itself' (like the eye becoming effaced in animals secluded from the light); 'they become accustomed to the want of it, and ultimately deny the existence of it.' [1]

Now this bias towards religion is part of our tendency to idealise, i.e. to ascend from particular, special, and general, up to universal notions; to rise from all the *forms* of being which experience presents to us or imagination can invent, up to the *formless* essence of being. This tendency differences us altogether from brute animals. 'Religion is the seeing in nature a somewhat transcending nature.' [2] And whenever this 'somewhat transcending nature' is recognised, then we are moved with feelings of reverence, dependence, submissiveness to its sway, and to acts of worship by which to propitiate this supreme Force; to deprecate its harmful or supplicate its beneficial action towards us; to bring it into friendly relations with us. Whence the best derivation of the word religion is that from *religare*, to bind back, restrain: for religion is the *restraint* which we impose upon ourselves in presence of superior might.[3] Where such restraint is exercised from dread and with reluctance, there religion takes the form of superstition. But where it is the result of acquiescence, trust, and self-surrender to the power above us as good, there religion becomes filial piety. And it is then first *pure religion.* 'Religion is indeed submission, but that is not all, it is submission *with homage.* Submission with

---

[1] North Brit. Rev., March, 1869.
[2] Renan. 'Man, as soon as he comes to distinguish himself from animals becomes religious; that is to say, he begins to see in nature a somewhat transcending nature.'
[3] See Fleck's Dogmatik, 3–8; and Appendix, Note XII.

fear, submission to power simply as power, is nothing but superstitious baseness.'[1] 'Superstition is the fear of a spirit whose passions are those of a man, whose acts are the acts of a man; who is present in some places and not in others; who is kind to one person, not to another; who is pleased or angry according to the degree of attention you pay to him; who is hostile generally to human pleasure, but may be bribed by sacrifice of a part of that pleasure into permitting the rest. This, whatever form of faith it colours, is the hue of superstition. But religion, on the contrary, is the belief in a Spirit whose mercies are over all his works, who is kind even to the unthankful and the evil; who is everywhere present, and therefore is in no place to be sought and in no place to be evaded; a Spirit therefore whose eternal benevolence cannot be angered, whose laws are everlasting and inexorable, so that heaven and earth must indeed pass away if one jot of them failed—laws which attach to every wrong and error a measured inevitable penalty; to every rightness and prudence an assured reward—penalty of which the remittance cannot be purchased, and reward of which the promise cannot be broken.'[2]

And hence it follows that the presence of the superstitious or of the religious element in our notions, feelings, and worship, depends on the idea we have formed to ourselves of the transcendent Power before which we bow. Life eternal depends on our knowing the one true God in his real character, as it is now revealed to us in his Son. Where this transcendent Power is known only as capricious *wilfulness*, the result is Feticism. Where

---

[1] Henry Holbeach, Vol. I.
[2] Ruskin, as quoted in Fortnightly Rev., Oct. 1, 1865.

it is known only as *fate*, i.e. determination of all things without purpose, there you have simply the worship of nature and impersonal law. Where it is recognised as intelligent moral purpose, or *will*, it rises into pure theism. And only where it is not simply recognised, but accepted as *Fatherly goodness*, does religion become filial trust—that trust which breathes in Antoninus when he says: 'Everything is music to me which is music to thee, O Universe! Nothing is for me too early or too late which thou accountest well-timed! Everything to me is fruit which thy seasons bring, O Nature! From thee are all things, in thee are all things, and to thee all things return!'[1] The trust of the Psalmist, 'The Lord is good to all, and his tender mercies are over all his works.'[2] The trust of the Apostle, 'All things work together for good!'[3] The trust of Jesus, 'Even so Father, for so it seemeth good in thy sight!'[4]

III. But there is yet another quality by which we are differenced from animals—our *progressive* nature. There is in us a potentiality for indefinite advancement. Even our physical conformation announces this. For 'the brain of savage man is much larger than the requirements of his mode of life demand. And the idea is thus suggested of a surplusage of power; of an instrument beyond the needs of its possessor.'[5] And the facts of human

---

[1] Anton. iv. 23, where mark the similarity, not only of thought, but words, with St. Paul, Rom. xi. 36.

Anton. has ἐκ σοῦ πάντα, ἐν σοὶ πάντα, εἰς σὲ πάντα·
Paul has ἐξ αὐτοῦ καὶ δι' αὐτοῦ καὶ εἰς αὐτὸν τὰ πάντα.

And this εἰς αὐτὸν Fritzsche renders, 'ad eum omnia conversa sunt, i. q. ab eo suspensa sunt. (1 Cor. viii. 6.)'

[2] Psalm cxlv. 9.  [3] Romans viii. 28.  [4] Matt. xi. 26.

[5] Wallace on Natural Selection, as quoted by Calderwood in Cont. Rev., Jan. 1871.

development confirm this. From the cradle to the grave in individuals, and from the cradle of the race up to its present age and stature, we see *progression*—physical, mental, moral, social, religious. Man has a capacity for 'intellectual and moral ascension.'[1] And hence 'the essence of spirit has been rightly placed by Kant in *freedom*, if by freedom we understand that spontaneity of thought and act which originates changes not transmitted by the mere traditional habits of the race. The whole activity of animals is mere persistency. The bee constructs her cells in accordance simply with her bee nature. She does but copy the traditions of her race. But man has power to originate new thoughts, new devices, new contrivances, new modes of action. He is emphatically an author, not a transcriber; an original, not a plagiarist. And in this sense it is that Hegel calls him a real *subject*, not merely a substance but a subject; i.e. not merely a foundation but a founder; not merely mediately causative but immediately originative; not merely an imitator but an inventor; not merely a *thing* conditioning other things but a *person* giving birth to them. So that Lichtenberg justly defines man "an originative animal."'[2]

[1] Page on Man. See the whole chapter on Man's *Progressive Relations*, 163–181.
[2] Erdmann, Psychologische Briefe, 48, 49.

## LETTER V.

### *MAN'S PERMANENCE.*

IN laying for you some stable foundations on which to build up firm convictions concerning Man, I have begun with admitted facts. First that we assuredly *are*, and next that we are endowed with certain qualities some of which we share with lower animals, by others of which we are essentially distinguished from them. We are, like them, sensative, causative, and intellective beings. But we are also, unlike them, moral, religious, and progressive beings.

These are facts furnished us by observation. But these facts include in themselves an intimation which we have no right to put away, for it is by every one of them forced upon us as a legitimate result; this namely, that being what we are, we cannot conceive ourselves as ceasing thus to be. The *permanence* of our existence seems guaranteed by the fact and the nature of this existence. This may be called an inference only, but it is that kind of inference which, far from being mere conjecture or hypothesis, flows by direct legitimate deduction from the premises supplied by observation. 'He who infers,' says Archbishop Whately, 'proves.'[1] 'To infer,' says Locke, 'is nothing but by virtue of one proposition laid down as true to *draw in* another as true.'[2]

[1] Whately, Logic, iv. 3, 1.     [2] Locke, Essay iv. 17.

Take then the first fact which we have received, not only as admitted, but as held for the most certain of all facts, the fact of our present *existence*. This fact includes in it the certainty that if existing at all in any proper sense, as simple, selfsame, substantial beings, we exist as 'elementary atoms'; similar, in this fact of existence, to the other elementary atoms to which are traced up all the forms of phenomenal life. If I am an indivisible atom, I must be an indestructible atom. For 'what is essentially incomplex and without admixture of parts, and having nothing unequal and dissimilar in itself, cannot be susceptible of division, and therefore cannot be susceptible of destruction.'[1] The soul, therefore, having no commixture of parts, cannot be severed, divided, disintegrated, or diffused, and therefore cannot perish; for to perish is to undergo separation and disintegration.'[2]

And further, if I am a *substantial* atom, I must therefore also be a permanent one. For 'all observation supplies us with this one invariable law, that what once exists always exists.' 'To the man of science, matter' (meaning by this term the elementary *material* of nature, the sixty ponderables, and the three imponderables) 'with trumpet tongue declares, "I change but still I am!"' that which to the ignorant seems destruction is but a

---

[1] Cicero, De Senect. 21 : 'Cum simplex animi natura esset, neque haberet in se quicquid admixtum dispar sui atque dissimile, non posse eum dividi; quod si non possit, non posse interire.'

[2] Cicero, Tuscul. i. 29 : 'In animi autem cognitione dubitare non possumus, nisi plane in Physicis plumbei sumus, quin nihil sit animis admixtum, nihil concretum, nihil copulatum, nihil coagmentatum, nihil duplex. Quod cum ita sit, certe nec secerni, nec dividi, nec discerpi, nec distrahi potest; nec interire igitur. Est enim interitus quasi discessus et secretio ac diremptus earum partium quæ ante interitum junctione aliqua tenebantur.'

change into a newer state of being, or into a newer form of life.'[1] Now, if this be true of the 'elementary substances' which lie at the base of physical phenomena, it must be equally true of that other distinct but similar 'elementary substance' which lies at the base of mental phenomena. What is certain concerning oxygen, hydrogen, and the rest; what is certain concerning all force in the universe—that it is susceptible neither of extinction nor diminution; this must be equally certain of that force, that elementary substance, which we have agreed to call noerogen. It is acknowledged that 'nature does not destroy the smallest atom of matter,' i.e. of the material of physical phenomena; 'therefore, reasoning from analogy, we must conclude that if we had the power to trace the principle whose characteristic is consciousness, we should find that when it leaves the body it plays its part elsewhere.'[2]

To *be*, therefore is to be *always*. Whatever merely comes and goes, appears and disappears, is not true being. That only *is*, which is always the same. 'No substantial and indivisible thing ever perisheth. As Plotinus says, "Nothing of real being can ever perish." For even matter, though Proteus-like it may perpetually change its shape, yet will constantly appear under one form or other.'[3] 'Only the time shadows have perished and are perishable. The real being of whatever was, and whatever is, and whatever will be, is even now and for ever. Believe this thou must, understand it thou canst not.'[4]   All that is at all
Lasts ever past recal![5]

[1] Cooper on Indestructibility, 52 and 21.
[2] Ibid. 52.
[3] Jno. Smith, Discourses, 66, 67.
[4] Carlyle, Sartor Res. 100.
[5] Browning.

But we have seen that we *are*; we have true being. The soul is no phenomenon, but the seat and base of all phenomena; it is simple, selfsame, substantial; therefore it is permanent, it must continue to be. 'Thomas Aquinas says: "God created things in order that they might *be*." These words when I first met them seemed somewhat childish, but on further consideration I divined their depth of meaning. I saw in them the best rendering of the thought of Christ, " God is not the God of the dead but of the living." God created things that they might *be*. But the acts of God are without repentance; He has not raised us out of nothingness to plunge us again into that abyss; He has not given us life, then to thrust us down to death. What He has done He has done for ever; we are not the ephemeral spawn of the ever-tossing spray of life; we are not a momentary manifestation of the forces of nature. We are realities, and God has willed that realities should be enduring; He has created them that they might be.'[1]

Such are the convictions of the deepest thinkers concerning real being as involving in its essence permanency of such being. And they are countersigned and sealed as true convictions by Holy Scripture. 'The things which are seen are for a time only, but the things which are not seen are out of all time.'[2] 'Yet once I will shake' (will move from their place as by an earthquake, σείσω) 'both earth and heaven. And that phrase "yet once" implies the removing of those things that are shaken' (the transitory phenomena of earth and heaven) · in order that the things which *cannot be shaken*' (the permanent elements, of which those phenomena are but the tem-

---

[1] Naville, La Vie éternelle, 223.   [2] 2 Cor. iv. 18.

porary forms) 'may remain undisturbed. So that we' (who shall endure through these changes) 'shall then receive a kingdom' (survive into a state of things) 'that cannot be shaken.'[1] 'God is not a God of dead persons but of living ones' (when He says 'I *am* the God of Abraham, Isaac, and Jacob,' He must be contemplating those persons as not mere shadows that have passed away, but as substances still before Him), " for all are living in his sight.'[2] Though unseen by men they must be seen by God. 'Nor can they die any more, being like the angels,' i.e. in this quality of permanent existence.[3] And the same truth follows from the declaration of St. Paul, 'In God we live, and move, and have our being.'[4] For if our being be 'in God,' if our life be wrapped up in God's life, then it can no more pass away than the life of God can pass away.

But now, again, the permanency of our being is guaranteed not only by the fact of our present existence, but by

---

[1] Heb. xii. 26–28, where the βασιλεία ἀσάλευτος is the same as the βασιλεία αἰώνιος of 2 Pet. i. 11.

[2] πάντες γὰρ αὐτῷ ζῶσιν· 'All men, dead as well as alive to us, are living in God's sight. The stress is on *all*. No one is really dead before him.'—*Meyer*. Those dead to us are alive before God. Compare what Philo says, 'No one is dead in the sight of Me the judge of men, but lives on through the eternal ages, never growing old, in that immortality which the soul enjoys when it has cast off the robes of the body.'

'It is certain from this scripture that souls departed out of these terrestrial bodies are neither dead nor asleep, but still alive and awake, our Saviour affirming that "they all live unto God;" the meaning whereof seems to be this: that they who are said to be dead are dead only unto men here upon earth, but neither dead unto themselves nor yet unto God, their life being not extinct but only disappearing to us and withdrawn from off our sight; forasmuch as they are gone off this stage which we still continue to act upon. And thus it is said also of Christ, that "He liveth unto God." (Rom. vi. 10.) Whence it is evident that they who are said to live to God, are not less alive than they were when they lived unto men.'—*Cudworth*, iii. 318.

[3] Luke xx. 36, 38.   [4] Acts xvii. 28.

the *qualities* which we possess in this existence. For none of these reach their proper development and satisfaction here. They are only pregnant with future fruit; prophetic of future maturity. As *sensitive* beings, made for happiness, this happiness we have still to seek. As *causative* beings there is force in us still to come out. As *intellective* beings we are as yet but children. As *moral* beings we have not yet realised either harmony with ourselves or peace with others. As *religious* beings we are far from unity with the universe. As *progressive* beings we are only in the earlier stages of our possible development.

(1.) Consult your own experience. Regard yourself as a *sensitive* being, made for happiness. Has this happiness been yet reached by you? Is there nothing more to seek? Have you found, like the animals beneath you, your point of rest? Are you enjoying the contentment which would thence result? On the contrary, 'Man never is, but always to be, blest!' You are made for well-being, you long and labour for well-being; but this well-being has never yet come to you, and you know it never will come to you in your present life. And what follows? What is the conclusion you must draw from these facts? Is it not that of Archbishop Leighton? 'If there be assigned to man a certain satisfying and permanent good, pertaining to his nature as man, and yet this good is never reached by him in earthly things, no, nor on earth in anything, then we must look further for this good in something beyond this earth. Therefore, it cannot be that in death we are extinguished, but only that we migrate to another country.'[1]

[1] Leighton, Prælectiones, 32. Add also 35: 'Nisi daretur verior et vita et felicitas, quis est qui non videat inter omnia animantia hominem, et inter

(2.) Take next the fact that we are *causative* beings. The very notion of causation is that of originative force, and the amount of force in the universe is confessedly insusceptible of diminution. And this must be true, as of the whole sum of force so equally of the particles of which this force is made up. It must be true, therefore, as of the particles of so-called physical force, so of the particles of mental force. It must be true, as of all existing atoms of oxygen and hydrogen, so of all existing atoms of noerogen. It must be true therefore of that force, that elementary particle of noerogen which constitutes the individual soul of each man in the universe. For this soul is an atom of force. Let me remind you of Plato's argument on this point : ' We must learn the nature of the soul by observing not only its passive but its active states.' But in its active states (its expressions as distinguished from its impressions) the soul is essentially causative, self-motive, not merely transmitting motion like a billiard ball, but originating motion from within itself. And what follows? 'Whatever is self-motive, with no loss of motive power when communicating motion to other things, this must have in itself a *principle* of motion. But a principle cannot be a product of other things, seeing that all products, on the contrary, proceed from a principle, while a principle can proceed

omnes homines optimos quosque miserrimos fore?' Which is just the argument of Paul: 'If in this life only we have hope in Christ, we are of all men most miserable.'—1 Cor. xv. 9. Again, 38: ' Egregius est ille divinioris auræ character, *inexplebilis* (scil.) *animæ sitis*, omnimode simul terreni boni laticibus nunquam sedanda. Secundum illud Psalmi, "Quemadmodum ad aquarum rivos glocitat cervus;" invisibile, incorporeum, immortale bonum sitit, quo ut fruatur non solum corporis ministerio tanquam prorsus necessario non indiget, sed et eo, quale nunc est, sese velut intergerino pariete interclusam ac præpeditam sentit, et ingemiscit.'

from nothing, or a principle (i.e. literally a beginning) it would not be. Therefore, whatever has in itself a principle of motion, this, being by nothing produced, can by nothing be destroyed. Else, all the heavens and all the earth, collapsing together, would stand still, and there would be no source whence motion could begin in them again. Well then, since it is thus manifest that whatever is self-motive is immortal, let no one be ashamed to maintain that this constitutes the essence and true notion of the soul. For every body to which motion comes from without itself has no soul. But that to which motion comes from within itself must have a soul, seeing that motion from within constitutes the very essence of soul. And then it follows that soul, as having motion from within itself, must be both unproduced and indestructible.'[1]

(3.) And now look at man as an *intellective* being. Here again, in this quality of our nature, we have a prophecy and pledge of continuous existence.

i. For remember the *peculiarity* of this quality. It is a something utterly unlike all material phenomena, though

---

[1] Plato, Phædrus (Bipont, x. 318). This whole passage Cicero has translated in Tusc. i. 23. And the sum of it is, All forces are indestructible. For their movement being set a-going by nothing without themselves, can be stopped by nothing without themselves. But the soul is a force, for motion from within itself is its specific mark. Therefore the soul is indestructible. πᾶσα ψυχὴ ἀθάνατος· τὸ γὰρ ἀεὶ κινητὸν ἀθάνατον. Where τὸ ἀεὶ κινητὸν is not (as Ficinus renders it) 'quod semper *movetur*;' and Cary, 'whatever is continually moved;' but (as Whewell), 'that which ever *moves*.' See Liddell and Scott, 'ἀεικίνητος, ever moving, in perpetual motion.' It is the same, therefore, as the ἀεὶ κινουμένη of Alcmæon quoted by Aristotle (De Anima): 'The soul must be immortal because it is in perpetual motion' (ὡς ἀεὶ κινουμένη). Or as Cicero has it: 'Animum ἐνδελέχειαν appellat Aristoteles quasi quondam *continuatam motionem*.'—Tusc. i. 10. And again, Ibid. 23, 'quod *se ipsum movet*.' And De Senect. 21: 'Cum animus se ipse moveat ne finem quidem habiturum esse motus, quia nunquam se ipse sit relicturus.'

so intimately associated with these phenomena. 'Suppose you could ascertain the last fact in the nervous system, in the order of impressions, and the first fact in the nervous system, in the will. Suppose that long and patient study shall at last have led to the knowledge that to a particular sentiment, a particular thought, a particular act of the will, there corresponds such a vibration of the fibres, such a discharge of electricity, such a combination of phosphorus. What follows? All that you have done will be only to have established in detail (what we know already in the general) the *intimate union* of two orders of phenomena, in their nature absolutely unlike. And the conclusion of materialism nevertheless will be, "These phenomena are linked together, therefore they are of the same nature!" "Thought, feeling, will, are always in harmony with a given condition of the material organs, therefore thought, feeling and will are properties or products of matter!" The sophism is always the same. It consists in saying, "These facts correspond to one another, they are closely united, therefore there are not two facts, there is only one!" It is like saying, "the magnetic force is always found in the loadstone, therefore the magnetic force is the product of the loadstone."'[1]

And as decidedly writes Professor Tyndall: 'Associated with this wonderful mechanism of the animal body we have phenomena no less certain than those of physics, but between which and the mechanism we discern no necessary connection. A man, e.g. can say, "I feel, I think, I love;" but how does *consciousness* infuse itself into the problem? Were our minds and senses so expanded as to be capable of following all the motions of the molecules of

[1] Perowne on Immortality, p. 10. Compare Naville, La Vie éternelle, p. 63.

the brain, all their grouping, all their electric discharges, if such there be, and were we intimately acquainted with the corresponding states of thought and feeling, we should probably be as far as ever from the solution of the problem, "How are these physical processes connected with the facts of consciousness?" The chasm between the two classes of phenomena would still remain intellectually impassable. The materialist is not entitled to say that his molecular grouping and his molecular motions explain everything. In reality they explain nothing. The problem of the connection between soul and body is as insoluble in its modern form as it was in the pre-scientific ages.'[1]

But now, if the nature of thought is thus essentially different from all material phenomena; if we ourselves, as thinkers, are contradistinguished from all merely physical or vital forces by this peculiarity of self-consciousness; it follows that no amount of evidence before us touching the dissolution of material phenomena can carry with it any proof of the dissolution of phenomena essentially non-material. On the contrary, we must be as certain of the continuous being of that somewhat which forms the base of thought, which constitutes intellective force (τὸ νοερόν), as we are certain of the continuous being, amidst all phenomenal changes, of the somewhats which form the bases of physical phenomena and of vital phenomena; of the various imponderable and etherial forces of the universe. And we must, moreover, be certain not only of the continuous existence of this intellectual force, but of its continuous existence *as* intellectual force, *as* conscious force,

---

[1] Tyndall, Norwich Address, in *Athenæum*, Aug. 29, 1868, as quoted by Perowne, 121.

*as* force which must ever put itself forth, whatever new relations it may enter on, in the forms of thought, feeling, and will. Pfleiderer, indeed, thinks that this force, by entering into new combinations, must become entirely new, and therefore that you cannot argue from the permanence of the force to the permanence of the phenomena associated with it here; to the permanence of the *personal* life we now possess. But Herbart has shown that though we first *acquire* our personal consciousness from our surroundings here, this personal consciousness once gained must remain as permanent as that which forms its seat and base, the intelligent atom or soul. For no internal states which any entity has once acquired can of themselves cease to be. Therefore, into the new state of the future we must carry along with us the personality which has been built up in our present state.[1]

ii. But our nature as intellective beings is distinguished not only by its *peculiarity* as a something altogether different from material phenomena, but also by its *purity*, its separation from all the concretions of these phenomena. And in this purity we see another prophecy and proof of our continuous existence beyond the sphere of these phenomena. For this purity of thought is such that, however dependent we may be on an external world for the first formation in our mind of sensations, conceptions, and imaginations, we find in ourselves a wondrous capacity of filtering the soul clear from the sensuous accretions with which these are encumbered, and emancipating ourselves into the pure serene of abstract truth, till we reach to the height of universal notions, or ideas. How then

---

[1] Herbart Ency. der Phil. 220: 'Von selbst können innere Zustände, die irgend ein Wesen einmal erlangt hat, nicht aufhören.'

can an entity which is able thus to free itself from material incrustations, even while still in the body, be swept away in the ruin and rubbish of this body? How can that whose distinctive mark it is to form ideas which transcend the limits of earthly time and space be otherwise than independent of these limits? This argument is urged by Plato, and I give it you in the summary of Whewell: ' While the *phenomena* of the universe are objects of mere sensation and opinion, there are *realities* behind these phenomena which are objects of true knowledge. The former is a world of transient appearances, the latter a world of eternal truths. These eternal truths are the real constituent principles of the universe, the fundamental types in the divine mind of all that exists in nature. But our human mind, by the aid of philosophy, can rise to a knowledge of these realities. That is, it has so far a community of nature with the divine mind. And if so, how can the soul be otherwise than divine? If it can possess within itself truths which are eternal, how can it be otherwise than eternal? If it can take hold of indestructible realities, how can it be otherwise than itself indestructible?'[1]

iii. 'Turn now to a third striking feature of our intellective nature, its *potentiality*, and you find in this another presage and pledge of continuous existence. For an essential quality of mind is its expansiveness; its power of endless development; its unceasing activity; and to suppose all this cut short before it has reached its maturity is to suppose a break of continuity not observable in any other department of being. There is in mind as well as in vital force what Mr. Murphy calls ' a potential

---

[1] Plato, De Rep. vii. Whewell, Platonic Dialogues, i. 439.

energy' stored up beyond the needs of ordinary action, and requiring for its development higher stimulants and a wider sphere than this present limited area of being affords. 'Then first,' says Plato, 'when we shall depart this life, can we attain that wisdom for which there is an incipient passion awakened in us here.'[1] Whence Cicero argues, 'When we look at the agility of mental life, at its vast remembrances of the past, its previsions of the future, its skill, its apprehensiveness, its power of invention; how can you imagine a substance capable of such things to be merely for a moment?'[2] 'And whatsoever, therefore, that may be which is thus sentient, and intelligent, and vivacious and progressive, it must be celestial and divine, and therefore eternal.'[3] 'Take the human intellect. Think of its grasp ever widening, its conceptions ever deepening, its capacity ever enlarging, and yet its aims ever in advance of its grasp, surpassing its present capacities and transcending its present conceptions. Think of what it has already achieved through the power given to it by God: it has penetrated far back into the womb of earthly time, almost into the genesis of a world; and it peers onward into space immeasurable, weighing and analysing the substance of the stars. It extracts from nature her choicest secrets, and then, as the trophy of its conquests, it compels the very mechanism of her own laws to do its bidding. And yet, amidst this grandeur of its conquests, how little after all has it achieved, compared with its insatiable aims and the infinite expanse of things at present surpassing its scrutiny. It feels as a giant entangled in the swaddling clothes of its infancy.'[4]

[1] Plato, Phædo. [2] Cicero, De Senect. 21. [3] Id. Tusc. i. 24.
[4] Pritchard on the Continuity of the Human with the Divine, 16.

(4.) So much for the conclusions which are forced upon us by the consideration of our intellective nature. If we go on now to our *moral* nature, we shall find the indications of our permanent existence increase upon us a thousandfold.

i. Look first at the *peculiar character* of our moral sentiments. Remember how they constitute our specific difference from all inferior animals, how they spring from other sources than the impressions of sense. Does not this assure us that we belong to a sphere not bounded by sense? 'Every divine thing,' argues Plotinus, 'is immortal. For, if a purified soul reflects upon itself, how shall it not appear to itself to be of such a nature as divine and therefore eternal essences are? Wisdom and virtue, being divine effluxes, can never enter into any unhallowed and mortal thing; that therefore into which they enter must be divine, seeing that it is filled with a divine nature through its consanguinity with the divine. And this consanguinity manifests itself in this: that the soul does not travel out of itself in order to behold justice and temperance in things foreign to itself' (i.e. does not fetch its notions of virtue from the impressions of sense, or from the calculations of understanding, but from its own immediate intuitions), 'but its own light sees them in the contemplation of its own being and of that divine essence which was before enshrined within itself.'[1] On which John Smith remarks, 'Though every good man is not so logically subtle as to be able by fit mediums to *demonstrate* his own immortality, yet he *sees* it in a higher light. His soul, being purged and enlightened by true sanctity, is more capable of those divine irradiations

[1] Jno. Smith, Discourses, 104.

whereby it feels itself in conjunction with God, and, by the light of the divine goodness mixing itself with the light of its own reason, sees more clearly, not only that it *may* exist eternally but that it *shall* do so. It knows that it shall never be deserted by that free goodness that always embraceth it. It knows the Almighty love which it lives by to be stronger than death and more powerful than the grave. It knows that God will never forsake his own life which He hath quickened in it; He will never deny those ardent desires of a blissful fruition of Himself which the lively sense of his own goodness hath excited in it. Those breathings and gaspings after an eternal participation of Him are but the energy of his own breath within us. If He had any mind to destroy it He would never show it such things as He hath done; He would not raise it up to such mounts of vision, to show it all the glory of the heavenly Canaan flowing with unbounded and eternal pleasures, and then tumble it down again into that deep and darkest abyss of death and nonentity. Divine goodness cannot and will not be so cruel to holy souls that are such ambitious suitors of his love. The more they contemplate the blissful effluxes of his divine love upon themselves, the more they find themselves strengthened with an undaunted confidence in Him, and look not upon themselves in these poor bodily relations and dependencies, but in their eternal alliances as the sons of Him who is the Father of souls, and therefore able to live anywhere in this spacious universe.'[1]

ii. Nor must we overlook the *strong anticipations* of continuous existence which are mixed up with the very experiences of moral sentiment. As these sentiments are

---

[1] Jno. Smith, Discourses, 102.

themselves unlimited, of universal validity, they form mute prophecies of a sphere of action as unlimited. 'The great hope of immortality developes itself out of our moral aspirations. To live in felt harmony with the good of the whole is our highest morality, and the desire for this perfect life brings and justifies a faith in immortality. As men grow better they will be more confident in their immortality.' [1]

> Fear not for them, my brother; they do well
> Having done well; and in their love they live,
> Because love dies not. For the past is made
> One with the future in the life of man,
> From age to age, by every deed that adds
> The love of each man to the life of all!
> Verily those that rest, as those that rise,
> They also that be dead as they that live,
> Living or dying, loyal to the light
> Of what is best and loveliest in themselves,
> Abide not in the darkness. But in them
> Is what makes all men's lives and all men's deaths
> Lovelier and better. And the men themselves
> Abide in God, for God is light, and light
> Is love, and love is everlasting life. [2]

iii. Nor must we omit the argument that our moral nature contains within itself a *moral demand* for continuous existence. For one essential element of this nature is that of equity, retribution, the giving to all things their due. But if our existence be cut short within the narrow sphere of earthly life, this sentiment is

---

[1] Thorndale, 46, 57. See also Martineau's 'Great Hopes for Great Souls.' And Wisdom, vi. 18-20: 'Love is the keeping of wisdom's laws; and our giving heed to wisdom's laws is the assurance to us of incorruption; and incorruption places us on the right hand of God.'

[2] R. Lytton, from Krasinski, in *Cornhill Mag.* Jan. 60.

not satisfied, is outraged. We find ourselves endowed with noble aspirations; these are thwarted now; and yet there remains no hope of justice being ever done to them. Here there is no proportionateness between our ideal of right and our actual attainment of right. Always we find the one hovering like a heavenly phantom above the other; attracting, stirring, inflaming our admiration, but ever escaping our embrace. Surely, then, this very fact, that such divine phantasms flit before us, that we cannot but sigh for them, strive to clasp them; that we must be lonely, incomplete, unsatisfied without them — this of itself contains in it a prophecy and pledge of some higher stage of being in which our moral longings shall be responded to. We cannot have moral peace without moral completeness; without that coincidence of conduct with conscience which Clement of Alexandria terms 'the symphony of all the chords of our being;' which Plato calls 'a wholeness of mind, like the harmony of musical accords;' and which he describes as 'a certain symmetry of mind resulting from our bringing into order all disorderly movements.' But such moral peace is never by anyone attained to in this life. What, then, are we, if there be no other life, but discords in the universe? notes that 'jar in the grand chorus, and complain?' This is well urged by Rückert: 'The body and the soul (or *vital* force) fulfil their destiny here; the *spirit* (or *mental* force) does not. As surely, therefore, as we believe in man's high destiny, so surely must we believe in another life for us wherein to accomplish this destiny.'[1] And so Mr. Perowne: 'All

---

[1] Rückert, Theologie, ii. 235. And again: 'Der Glaube glaubt ein ewiges Leben, weil es den Gedanken nicht ertragen kann, dass die Menschheit ihre heilige Bestimmung nicht erfüllen sollte.'

our honest, broken, imperfect struggles, ever baffled, ever disappointed, are they all without meaning and without aim? If the very fragmentariness of human efforts and aspirations may be taken as any indication that the heart and the intellect shall ultimately find their completeness, much more may we argue that the highest part of our nature is not intended to be always stunted and deformed.'[1] Whence the encouragements vouchsafed by our Lord to men of moral dispositions: 'Cheer up, ye who hunger and thirst after righteousness, who are merciful, pure in heart, peaceable, for to you pertains a kingdom wherein such dispositions shall be satisfied.'[2]

(5.) But this argument from our nature as moral beings is strengthened by the consideration that we are unavoidably *religious* beings also. For it is of the essence of religiousness to recognise a Somewhat not only transcending all limited existence, but ruling it by unchanging law. And all law divides itself into law regulative and law retributive. If, therefore, there be law regulative, there must also be law retributive in all things. Nay, we actually find this law retributive at work in the several spheres of nature, of society, and of conscience; and yet at work with respect to these latter, only incompletely, partially, variably. Consequently, law retributive must be reserving the full accomplishment of its operation in these spheres to another stage of being. This is the argument which Dionysius puts into the mouth of Coriolanus: 'If indeed when our body is dissolved our soul (whatever this may be) partakes this dissolution, how can we esteem those blessed who gain no sort of benefit from

---

[1] Perowne on Immortality, 26.
[2] Matt. v. 6-9. See further on this moral argument, Appendix, Note XIII.

virtue, nay, are on account of this very virtue destroyed?'[1] And so says Bishop Jeremy Taylor: 'Cicero had reason on his side to conclude that there is a time and place after this life wherein the wicked shall be punished and the virtuous rewarded, when he considered that Orpheus and Socrates, and many others, were either slain or oppressed to death by evil men. For when virtue made men poor, and free speaking of brave truths made the wise to lose their liberty; when an excellent life hastened an opprobrious death, and the obeying reason and conscience cost us our lives, or at least all the means and conditions of enjoying them; it was but time to look about for another state of things, where justice should rule and virtue find her own portion. And therefore men cast out every line, and turned every stone, and tried every argument, and sometimes proved it well; and when they did not, yet they believed strongly, and they were sure of the thing even when they were not sure of the argument.'[2] And it is to the demands of this same principle of retributive law that are addressed the parables and the promises of our Lord: 'Thou in thy lifetime receivedst thy good things, and likewise Lazarus evil things; but *now* he is comforted and thou art tormented.'[3] 'Verily I say to you, there is no one that hath left house and lands for my sake but he shall receive an hundredfold more even in this time, and in the world to come eternal life.'[4] 'Cheer up, ye dispirited, ye mourners, ye oppressed ones, for yours is the kingdom of heaven; ye shall be comforted; ye shall inherit the earth.'[5]

(6.) But beyond all these arguments for man's per-

---

[1] Dionys. Halic. vii. 530.   [2] Bishop J. Taylor, Sermons, ii. 536.
[3] Luke xvi. 25.   [4] Matt. xix. 29.   [5] Matt. v. 3-5.

manency stretches a final one, which is derivable from the fact that we are *progressive* beings, formed for 'continuous ascension' from one stage to another of perfection. This fact, of itself alone, demands our survival of the present unfinished stages of our growth. For here we have within us but the germ of that development to which our nature tends. This life at best is but the bud of being; our most 'ascensive' qualities are only flowering here; they never reach, as those of lower animals do, their destined ripeness. We cannot but therefore look to further time and place for the attainment of this ripeness. 'The soul must surely grow, as with the continuity of an asymptote, towards the throne of the supremely good, for ever and for ever approaching though never there.'[1] Our potentiality for endless origination, confined as it is here within the limits of the customary, constitutes the riddle of our present phase of being, and points and presses for its solution to a higher phase. It is because our nature is all too large for its surroundings, and our potentiality too vast for its realisation amidst these surroundings, that we are compelled to believe in a destiny which stretches beyond the present into the boundless future. You feel it an insult to call a child a cub. Why? Because the child has that in him which the cub has not—the potentiality for becoming a man. He is by nature rational, though only as he grows up will this rationality show itself. Even his destiny as a child he will fulfil only in proportion as he soars above this childhood and leaves it beneath him. And therefore it offends us to be termed simply animals, seeing there

[1] Pritchard on the Continuity of the Human with the Divine, 20.

is that within us which no mere animal possesses—the potentiality for indefinite progression by unlimited acts of originative thought and will. Man has a power of spontaneous emergence out of the swaddling clothes of animalism; he carries in himself as man a contradiction of himself as animal; he is at once a naturalised supernatural, an enslaved prince, a spirit made flesh. And the accomplishment of the destiny involved in such a nature requires a stage of being in which the supernatural shall break the limitations of the natural, the prince be set free from his slavery, the spirit be emancipated from the flesh. Our potentiality guarantees our permanence.[1] Nor is this argument wanting in the sacred books. The Psalmist assures himself, 'I shall behold thy face in righteousness; I shall be satisfied when I awake with thy likeness.'[2] That is, 'Then first shall my nature come to its perfection when it shall reach its stage of thorough conformity to Thee!' And with the same thought St. Paul encourages us to diligence in all things proper to our nature here: 'Be ye steadfast, unmovable, always abounding in the work of the Lord, forasmuch as ye know that your labour is not in vain in the Lord.'[3]

What full authority therefore have we for the glowing anticipations of the poet!

>    This is the bud of being; the dim dawn;
>    The twilight of our day; the vestibule!
>    Life's theatre as yet is shut, and death,
>    Strong death alone can heave the massy bar,

---

[1] See Erdmann, Psychologische Briefe, 55, 'Das menschliche Individuum ist natürliches Übernatürliches, unterworfenes Unabhängiges.'

[2] Psalm xvii. 15. This awakening is '*das Erwachen vom Tode,*' 2 Kings iv. 31; Jer. li. 39; Job. xiv. 12; Isaiah xxvi. 19; Dan. xii. 2. And the beholding is '*das Anschauen* Gottes in der ewigen Seligkeit.'—De Wette.

[3] 1 Cor. xv. 58.

This gross impediment of clay remove,
And make us, embryos of existence, free!
From real life but little more remote
Is he, not yet a candidate for light,
The future embryo, slumbering in his sire.
Embryos we must be till we burst the shell,
Yon ambient azure shell, and spring to life,
The life of gods, oh transport! and of men!'[1]

[1] Young's Night Thoughts, Bk. I.

OF GOD.

'I had rather believe all the fables in the Legend, and the Talmud, and the Alcoran, than that this universal frame is without a mind. It is true that a little philosophy inclineth man's mind to atheism, but depth in philosophy bringeth men's minds about to religion; for while the mind of man looketh upon second causes *scattered*, it may sometimes rest in them and go no further; but when it beholdeth *the chain of them confederate and linked together*, it must needs fly to providence and Deity.'—BACON, *Essay* xvii.

'The omnipresence of something which passes comprehension, is a belief which has nothing to fear from the most inexorable logic, but on the contrary is a belief which the most inexorable logic shows to be profoundly true.'—H. SPENCER, *First Principles*, 113.

'The reasoning on to God lies properly within the domain of science. For it belongs to science, starting from phenomena, to stop not till it raise us to the hidden ground of these phenomena.'—Sir I. NEWTON.

'Ce monde, œuvre de liberté, d'intelligence et d'amour, *c'est l'expression vivante de son principe*. Partout, dans l'immensité des espaces et des temps, domine une loi de convenance et d'harmonie, loi divine, loi souveraine qui régle les rapports de tous les êtres, triomphe de toute résistance, efface tout désaccord accidentel, et conduit chaque être, a travers des transformations appropriées, à toute la beauté, à toute la perfection, à toute la félicité que comportent sa nature particulière et l'ordre universel.'—SAISSET, *Phil. rel.* ii. 195.

## LETTER VI.

### THE BEING OF GOD.

My dear Friend,—

It has often been observed, that all knowledge depends on attention and retention. We must 'mark' what is put before us with our whole mind, and we must 'inwardly digest' it afterwards by continuous rumination. And hence the advantage of returning often on our steps, and taking up afresh the course of thought along which we have been travelling.

Now that course, hitherto, has been this. We began with seeking some fundamental decisions concerning *Man*. And to obtain these we addressed ourselves to *Facts* of observation and experience. And these facts brought before us man as a being self-subsisting, sensitive, causative, intellective, moral, religious, progressive; from all which qualities we found ourselves entitled, nay obliged, to ascribe to him the further attribute of permanency amidst the several changes of relation to which he is exposed.

But we found him further, though self-subsisting, yet subsisting in various relations with other entities different from himself. The very observation which tells me that 'I am,' tells me at the same time that I am in intimate conjunction with a world which is not I. The very self-investigation which assures me that I am a substantial

entity—a Subject in which my sensations inhere, and from which my acts emerge—assures me that these sensations are *conditioned* by somewhat not myself, and these acts *condition* this somewhat in return. For my *sensations*, though assuredly *mine*, and modifications of my proper self, yet are not in my own power; they spring not independently from me the subject of them, and are neither producible nor removable at my own pleasure. They imply, therefore, somewhat beside myself as the *occasion* of their production in me. And in like manner *my acts*, though truly *mine*, and exertions of the force within me, are yet acts of pressure against pressure. They involve the existence therefore of a somewhat not myself which exerts pressure on myself, and on which (again) I press. 'It is in the exercise of *force*,' says Mr. Bain, 'that we must look for the feeling of the externality of objects. The sum total of all the *occasions* for our putting forth active energy is our external world.'[1]

Nothing, indeed, is more certain than that all my thoughts, feelings, and volitions are simply changes which take place in the sphere of my own self. For we cannot pass beyond this sphere, we can only travel from conception to conception within it; all sensation is a modification of our inward self, all action an efflux from our inward self. Yet still the occasions for such modifications lie not within us but without us. Had we, for instance, the power of generating the phenomena of vision, we might regard these phenomena as merely a rapid succession of subjective mental products. But this is not the case. All we are conscious of as coming from our own volition is the movement of the eye;

[1] Bain, The Senses and the Intellect, pp. 371, 372.

yet every such movement is accompanied, without any further effort of our own, by a distinct and a varied perception. As the mind, therefore, is one and indivisible, and as all its states assume the form of a succession or series, it cannot possibly recognise a multiplicity of co-existing phenomena as mere modes of its own existence. It must of necessity regard them as standing apart from itself and forming an extended surface in space.

Now this external world which I am thus compelled to recognise as 'apart from myself,' is made up of numberless phenomena. But phenomena, as we have formerly seen, are simply outward shows of inward substances. And these phenomena change with the changes of relation between me and those substances. Hence my connection with this external world is one not merely of juxtaposition but of interaction. I affect the elements of it; and they affect me. Our independence is only partial. We are finite beings in a finite world; each limited by each, and all by all. 'Just as philosophers tell us that every word we utter, every breath we inhale, has, through a million of intermediate links in the chain of cause and effect, a definite influence on the dancing of the leaves in an American forest or on the course of a hurricane in the Indian seas, so we recognise the fact that the action of every unit of a nation or a party tells upon the total result of human achievement.'[1]

---

[1] Dallas, The Gay Science, ii. 274; and compare the *Cornhill Mag.*, March 1871: 'We are sons of yesterday, not of the morning. The past is our mortal mother, no dead thing. Our future constantly reflects her to the soul. Nor is it ever the new man of to-day which grasps his future good and ill: we are pushed to it by the hundreds of days we have buried— eager ghosts. And if you have not the habit of taking counsel with them, you are but an instrument in their hands.'

Still, many and various as are the ways in which the elementary substances limit one another, this fact is certain, that there is order, method, plan, in this limitation. The phenomena do not present themselves in utter confusion. They show themselves as parts of one great whole, organised to one great end. And therefore these phenomena, taken together, have long ago been termed, with reference to this order and adjustment, a 'Cosmos;'[1] and with reference to this organic unity, 'The Universe.' 'The aspect of external nature,' says Humboldt, 'is that of unity in diversity, and of connection, resemblance, and order among things most dissimilar in their form; one fair harmonious whole.'[2] And so I. H. Fichte: 'The endless multiplicity of things constitute a universe; i.e. being concatenated by an inward connection with each other, they exhibit a perfect unity. One single all-determining principle runs through them, and manifests itself by means of them; and however diverse they may seem, this very diversity results from their unity, the outward differences indicating not an inward contrariety but rather the reciprocal *integration* of all things each by each; their eternal conjunction by means of their mutual limitation.'[3]

Here, then, we have two undeniable facts in the world

---

[1] This term the Septuagint has applied to the new-formed world considered as 'a host' or orderly array. For it renders 'thus the heavens and the earth were finished and all *the host* of them,' by 'all the Cosmos of them.'—Gen. ii. 1.

'Quem κόσμον Græci nomine ornamenti appellavere, eum nos à perfecta absolutaque elegantia mundum.'—*Pliny*, xi. 4.

And hence Sir Thomas Browne speaks, with deep devotion, of 'the First Composer.' 'For there is in music a shadowed lesson of the whole world of God; such a melody to the ear as the world, well understood, would afford the understanding.'—Lord Lytton, *Miscell.* i. 179.

[2] Humboldt's Cosmos, i. 5.

[3] I. H. Fichte, Vorschule der Theol, p. 5.

of which we form a part. First, that the movements of all things are limited, conditional, subordinate, secondary. And next, that these movements are thus limited, not confusedly, not without meaning, but according to a *law* of organisation, an *idea* of unity which pervades and actuates all.

Now, what follows from these facts? To what is your mind carried onward by what Mr. Spencer calls 'the momentum of thought,' which urges us from things observed to the ground and manner of these things; from *what* things are to *why* and *how* they are? This follows: that movements limited and secondary must owe their origin to a Prime Mover; and that movements organised into one great whole show this Prime Mover to be intelligent and full of purpose.

1. Consider how all the movements you are acquainted with—your own and those of all the elements in conjunction with you—are manifestly limited, secondary, conditioned each by each; and see if this does not bring you of necessity to the recognition of a Prime Mover, transcending yourself and all things else.[1] It so brought Aristotle, when he ascended from all observable movements and principles of motion, up to what he calls 'the principle of principles,' 'the first immovable mover,' which 'being itself immovable, causes all things else to move.' For you are conscious that you do not move yourself absolutely from yourself. So far as you can trace your movements, you always find some cause not in yourself, concurrent with yourself. And the same is true of all

---

[1] 'The very nature of the phenomena demonstrates that they must have had a beginning, and that they must have an end.'—Huxley, *Lay Sermons*, p. 17.

other persons and things, so far as observation enables you to judge. Other elements of being do not move themselves, nor move each other absolutely from themselves alone. Your movements are conditioned by theirs, theirs by yours. There is universal interaction, reciprocal limitation. There is no prime movement in anything you know. Whence then do all these only secondary movements have their origin? Whence, but in a somewhat transcending them all—a life which is our life, and yet lies deeper than our life?

This is well put by Mr. Parker: 'We are not sufficient of ourselves, not self-originated, not self-sustained. A few years ago and we were not; a few years hence and our bodies shall not be. A mystery is gathered about our little life. We have but small control over things around us; are limited and hemmed in on all sides. Our schemes fail. Our plans miscarry. One after another our lights go out. Our realities prove dreams. Our hopes waste away. We are not where we would be, nor what we would be. We find that it is not in man that walketh to direct his steps. We find our circumference very near the centre, everywhere. And we feel an irresistible tendency to refer all things, and ourselves with them, to a power beyond us, sublime and mysterious, which we cannot measure nor even comprehend.' So, again, the author of 'Henry Holbeach:' 'Everything runs up into *the* mystery of *life*. I myself am. I have life. All nature around me is full of individual lives. And beneath, though pervading me and these, is the universal life of the world. And so my own self, other selfs, and *the force in my self and other selfs*, are equally *facts*, presented to my observation. They manifest themselves to me. I do not simply infer, imagine, invent either of the three. There they are; *given* in experience. I must deal with them as I find them. I must adjust my thoughts to them and construct my whole theory of being out of them as *data*. And what much-abused *meta*-physics is there in this? Here is simply being, and then unavoidably ontology or a theory of being; i.e. an adjustment of the *facts* presented to me concerning being.'[1]

And thus the *facts* of being lead unavoidably to the acknowledgment of a One invisible source of being of whom all visible existences are but the offspring, one life of whom all lives are but the manifestation.

And this argument is involved in the very modes of speaking of the sacred Scriptures. As when our Lord describes the Father as 'having life in himself,' and so able to 'give life' to whom he will.[2] And when the Prophets mark out the true God from all false deities by this emphatic title, 'The Lord is the true God, for he is *the living God* and the King of eternity. He is the living God and steadfast for ever.'[3] And when God himself says to Moses, 'I am what I am! This is my name for ever, and this my memorial throughout all generations.'[4]

2. But when you look at the phenomena in nature, you find them not only conditioned each by each, and amidst the partial independence of each centre of force exhibiting interdependence among all; but you find them thus interdependent, conditioning and conditioned, according to *laws* of organisation, particular, general, and universal,

---

[1] See Appendix, Note XIV.  [2] John v. 26.
[3] Daniel vi. 26.  [4] Exod. iii. 15.

which unite them as subordinate wholes into one all-comprehending whole, hence called 'The Universe.'

Now of all organisation, small or great, this principle is certain, that the whole presupposes an Idea of this whole, and such Idea working efficiently to produce and keep up this whole. 'An Idea,' says Coleridge, 'is, in order of thought always and of necessity, contemplated as antecedent. In the idea or principle of life, for instance, the vital functions are the result of the organisation; but this organisation supposes and presupposes the vital principle. The bearings of the planets on the sun are determined by the ponderable matter of which they consist; but the *principle* of gravity, the *law* in the material creation, the *Idea*, is presupposed in order to the existence, yea to the very conception of the existence, of matter itself.'[1] And so through the whole ascending series of organisms, from the simplest cell-force up to the universe of being. Concatenation, adjustment, interaction, adaptation of means to ends, suppose throughout a Thought predetermining the result, and this Thought active and efficient towards the accomplishment of this result.

And hence, from the presence of such thought, in each organism by itself, and in all together, we are obliged to recognise not only (as before) a Prime Mover, an all-pervading Life; but this Life, this Prime Mover as *intelligent*, as acting according to design and purpose, in short, as *mental* force, or (which is the same thing) rational will.[2]

This is the well-known argument of Socrates. Take it as stated by Zeller: 'A consideration of the world as a whole, and its reasonable arrangement, conducted Socrates

---

[1] Coleridge, Church and State, p. 14.
[2] See Appendix, Note XV.

to the notion of the One Supreme. God appeared to him as reason, ruling the world and holding the same relation to it as the soul does to the body. As the soul without being visible affects the body, so God affects the world. As the soul exercises dominion over the body, so God over the world. As the soul is present in all parts of the body, so God in the world. And as the soul, though limited, can perceive what is distant, and have thoughts of the most various kinds, so the knowledge and care of God must be able to embrace the whole universe at once.'[1] And thus the universal *providence* of God is included in the argument for his *existence* drawn from this relation in all things of means to ends.

In the same way Newton argues: 'All these movements according to rule and purpose cannot have their origin in merely mechanical forces. This most exquisite combination of sun, and planets, and comets can have sprung from nothing short of the counsel and dominion of a Being at once intelligent and mighty. For a blind metaphysical necessity is at all times and in all places the same; and from such can never spring *the variation of things*. That universal diversity which you see adjusted to *suit times* and *places* can have its origin solely in the ideas and volitions of an entity existing of and from itself. And this view of God is furnished us by the phenomena of nature itself, and is therefore a proper integral part of natural philosophy.'

And so again Herbart: 'The assumption that the order we observe in the world not only terminates in certain ends accomplished by it, but has its origin in the preconception and predetermination of these ends, and is

---

[1] Zeller's Socrates, by Reichel, 145.

worked out by an ever active spirit, may indeed, in a system rigidly scientific, be called an hypothesis only, as distinguished from demonstration. But still, how firm a foundation such an hypothesis supplies for faith is unanswerably proved by the corresponding force which it has in another case. Whence do we know that *men* exist? that not merely human forms but human beings are round about us? We have never seen these beings. We know nothing of them but by their doings. But these doings, being characterised by method, and adjustment of means to ends, we ascribe at once, from analogy with our own experience of our self as the unseen source of similar manifestations, to thinking, willing, and acting *persons*. No one can say, " I have *seen* this assumed person." No one can deny that our certainty of his existence is simply a belief added on to what we actually see.'[1] And (let me say) legitimately added on, by that process of thought which travels from things visible to things invisible; from a premiss to the conclusion contained in it.

This argument is well put by the Duke of Argyll: 'Ideal conformity and unity of conception is the one unquestionable fact in which we recognise directly the working of a Mind with which our own has very near relations. No possible theory in respect to the physical means employed to preserve the correspondence of parts which runs through all creation can affect the certainty of that mental plan and purpose which alone makes such correspondence intelligible to us. And yet scientific men sometimes tell us that ' we must be very cautious how we ascribe intention to nature. Things do indeed fit into

[1] Herbart, Lehrb. der Phil. 213.

each other as if they were designed, but all we know about them is that these correspondences exist!' Well, but still they *do exist*. The perception of them is as much a fact as the sight or touch of the things in which they appear. They may have been produced by growth; they may be the result of a process of development; but it is not the less the development of a *mental purpose*. Take the case of the poison of a deadly snake. This is a secretion not simply exuding by some law of growth from one animal, but *adjusted to the organisation* of other animals, so as to rush in upon the citadel of their life. And there is but one explanation of this: a *Mind*, having perfect knowledge of the structure of both, has *designed* the one to be capable of inflicting death upon the other. This mental purpose is the one thing which our intelligence perceives with intuitive recognition. Or take Mr. Darwin's book 'On the Fertilization of Orchids.' He points out an infinity of adjustments to secure a certain end. And in doing so, to this advanced disciple of pure naturalism 'caution in ascribing intentions to nature' does not seem to occur as possible. Intention is the one thing which he does see, and which, when he does not see, he seeks for diligently till he finds it. Mark his words: 'Contrivance,' 'curious contrivance,' 'beautiful contrivance;' 'The *labellum* is developed into a long nectary in *order* to attract *lepidoptera*;' 'The nectar is *purposely* so lodged in *order* to give time;' and so on. Nay more, the idea of special use as the controlling principle of construction is so impressed on Mr. Darwin's mind that in any detail of structure, however singular and obscure, he has absolute faith that in *this* lies the ultimate explanation. For instance: 'The strange position of the *labellum* perched on the summit of the column *ought to have shown me* that here was the place for experiment. I ought to have scorned the notion that the *labellum* was thus placed *for no good purpose*. I neglected this plain guide, and for a long time completely failed to understand the flower.'[1]

Hence, then, the perfect validity of the argument, from an organised world to an organising God. 'To rise,' says I. H. Fichte, ' from the world to God, we assume nothing but the manifest fact that this world is *a whole*; that its many and various substances constitute together a universe : which means, that being linked together and sustained by an intimate co-relation they exhibit an absolute unity. One single principle determining all things pervades them and manifests itself through them. And diverse as they seem from each other, yet this very diversity results from their hidden unity. The outward distinctions do not indicate an inward difference, but rather point to the reciprocal completion of each by each; to an eternal combination by means of their mutual limitation. And thus the manifold mounts up into the highest possible unity; the individual limitations into a somewhat which limits all; the particular causes into a first cause. You cannot recognise things as forming a universe without by the same act recognising this cause, as *given*, in and along with this universe.'[2]

And so Mr. Smith : ' Examine the individual phenomena, and you will find that the whole is as necessary to the parts as the parts are to the whole. And it is this unity, or this *organic* nature, of all things, which brings us to the great truth that a Divine Idea lies at the origin of all things. The whole must necessarily be conceived

[1] Argyll, Reign of Law, 33-43.   [2] I. H. Fichte, Vorschule, p. 5.

of as a manifested *Idea*; and the forces of nature are nothing else than the power by which such manifestation is accomplished. The Idea, and the Power of manifestation of it, form our conception of God. And by God I can understand no other than a *Person*, because I cannot conceive intelligence without personality.'[1]

And thus we arrive at the idea of God as not only a *some What*, transcending all things, but also as a *some One*, by whom all things are adjusted to each other, and are being continually developed towards the accomplishment of a preconceived end. That is to say, we learn not only that God *is*, but that He is as *Mind and Will*. But what mind and will are we know only from the consciousness of our own personality. Therefore, by analogy with this personality, we conclude concerning Him who is the Primary transcendent Mind and Will that He has personality like our own.

For with this analogy we have begun, and from this analogy we cannot depart. The existence of God I must accept as proved, by the same sort of process, from the same sort of facts, as those which prove the existence of my own self. In both cases we reason onward from things visible to their necessary complement in somewhat invisible; and our faith in this somewhat invisible is in both cases equally a logical deduction from acknowledged facts. From the facts of my consciousness I reason on to the conclusion of a hidden self, as the ground of these facts. And so equally from the facts of the universal world, I reason on to the conclusion of a hidden ground of these facts. And this hidden ground I call God. As sure, therefore, as *I* am, and as sure as *the world* is, so surely God is.

[1] Thorndale, 442–448.

And just this is the Scripture argument, drawn sometimes from the facts of the world, sometimes from the fact of our own existence. From the *facts of the world*, in Hebrews xi. 1–3, 'through faith,' as the rational conclusion from observed facts, 'we come to the conviction (νοοῦμεν) that the worlds were framed by the word (i.e. the fiat or will) of God; so that the visible whole (τὸ βλεπόμενον) derives its birth and development (γεγονέναι) not from itself (the phenomena which we see).' And again, in Rom. i. 19, 20, 'whatever is knowable concerning God (τὸ γνωστὸν τοῦ Θεοῦ) is manifest to men, for God himself hath made it so. For the invisible facts concerning him, namely, his eternal power and Godhead, are clearly discerned through reasoning onward (νοούμενα καθορᾶται) from the things that are made.' And the same conclusion is got from the *fact of our own existence*, in Acts xvii. 27, 28, where it is argued by St. Paul to the Athenians, 'We need not *search* after God, for he is not far from any one of us; for in him we live and move and have our being.' Our life proves his life as its necessary ground.

## LETTER VII.

### THE PERSONALITY OF GOD.

MY DEAR FRIEND,—

You must often have remarked how marvellously the ambiguities of language impose on the acutest minds. An instance of this occurs in connection with the subject to which I go on in this letter. And it affects the answer to the question, Is or is not *faith* of the nature of knowledge? Can we trust its testimony as fully as the testimony of what are called our senses? The Poet Laureate thinks not. He makes the sphere of knowledge conterminous with that of sense:

> We have but faith, we cannot know;
> For knowledge is of things we see.

And he puts *faith* in antithesis to *proof*:

> Whom we that have not seen thy face,
> By faith, and faith alone, embrace,
> *Believing* what we cannot *prove*!

And herein he only follows the lead of a certain school of thinkers, who limit knowledge to observation, and make seeing alone believing; who trust only what we see with our eyes, as distinguished from what we see with our mind. But here it is forgotten that what they call seeing with our eyes is, in fact, seeing with our mind; for all perception is a product of two factors, the one without us, the other within us. And further, they forget that what we see with our mind is really the most trustworthy knowledge we have. Observation may deceive us; continually does deceive us. We are obliged incessantly to correct its testimony by reason. Whereas ratiocination does not deceive us, cannot deceive us so long as we conduct it according to the fundamental logic of the human mind. You see the sun with your eyes; yet the notion of it which you thus gain you have to correct by the more trustworthy suggestions of your reason. Your knowledge of all things that you merely *see* is an imperfect knowledge, nay, a false knowledge. But the notions you obtain of them by means of *reason applied to sight* are true knowledge. These notions are suggested by rigid logic. They constitute for us not δόξα but ἐπιστήμη.

And so it is with faith, as compared with *fact*. For faith is no mere surmise, conjecture, baseless imagination. It is legitimate anticipation. It is the logical conclusion arrived at by reasoning onward from fact. Faith, according to the Pauline definition of it, is emphatically 'That conviction of things not seen which emerges by legitimate inference from things seen.' Observation supplies us with materials, data; the conclusions from which data are as certain as the premises whence they are drawn. Newton *observed* the falling of an apple. He drew conclusions from this fact. Was he less certain of his conclusions than he was of the fact whence he drew them? Did he not, on the contrary, trust his conclusions as valid for all space, when his fact was observed in only one infinitesimal portion of space?

Now, by just a similar process have we travelled from

the observed facts of the world up to the conclusion
flowing from these facts, of the existence of a some One
as the living ground of this world. As surely as we see
by the eye what we call existences, so surely do we see
by the mind the *base* of such existences. As suerly as I
know that I myself *am*, so surely do I know that, as the
necessary base of this myself, God *is*. And as surely as
I know that I myself am intelligent will, so surely do I
know that, as the absolute source whence this property in
myself must be derived, God is Intelligent Will.[1]

Yet this last certainty is questioned by many who admit
the preceding one. Granting that first certainty thus
arrived at, of the *existence* of God; granting, as Mr.
Spencer puts it, 'the omnipresence of something which
passes comprehension,' this 'unseen reality,' this 'ultimate
cause,' this 'ultimate religious truth of the highest possible
certainty, in which religions in general are at one with
each other, and with a philosophy antagonistic to their
special dogmas, and respecting which there is a latent
agreement among all mankind,' still this same writer,
together with Mr. Lewes, Dr. Tyndall and others, denies
the possibility of our *knowing* this transcendent Being,
and asserts that 'the Power which the universe manifests
is utterly inscrutable.'

To which I must reply, 'Just so much inscrutable as
the Power which your book manifests to me; but no
more. You, your *Self*, are "utterly inscrutable" to me;

---

[1] All being is only the veil before the face of God, the shadow of the idea. And this veil is not to be despised because merely phenomenal. It is lovely and holy; not merely the covering, but the only possible manifestation of the inner verity. As the theologians say, 'unless ye believe neither shall ye understand,' so we, 'unless ye will be content with the shadows ye shall not see light.'—G. Bruno, *Macmillan's Mag.*, Feb. 1871.

but yet I can and do *know you* by your utterances, i.e. by the outerance which you make of yourself, by what you do and say. And these utterances I can judge of, can admire, love, agree with, conform to, guide myself by, as they commend themselves to my judgment and conscience. And just so, and no more, is God utterly inscrutable in *Himself*, and his essence; and yet scrutable through his utterances; through the outerance of Himself which He is continuously making in the world around me, in my own mind within me. And by the same power of judgment and conscience these utterances I can *apprehend*, even though I may be unable, in their whole depth and compass, to *comprehend* them.' Yet Mr. Lewes says, 'The reason of man is incompetent to know God, because reason is finite, and the finite cannot embrace the infinite;'[1] where the juggle lies in the word 'know,' as if we could 'know' nothing unless we had *perfect* knowledge of it; as if *ap*prehension involved *com*prehension. I may 'know' something of Plato, though totally incompetent to sound the depths of his mind; I may 'know' Mr. Lewes, though unable to follow all his judgments and inferences. The finite truly cannot *comprehend* the infinite, cannot (literally) hold it within its grasp; but the finite can *apprehend* such manifestations of the infinite as come within this grasp. And it is just such manifestations which come to us by means of the world without us and within us. Therefore, though we cannot know God by intuition and direct beholding, we can and do know Him by those rays which are reflected on us by the facts of nature and mind. God, in Himself, is truly ' inscrutable;' but God in his relation to the world, to you, and

[1] Hist. Phil., 1st edit., ii. 198.

to me, is as much scrutable by the way in which He acts to us as you are scrutable to me, or other men are scrutable to me, by ways and acts. The first part of the proposition is laid down as absolutely in Scripture as by our modern philosophers; the second part nevertheless is equally laid down in Scripture as perfectly compatible with that first. What says St. John? 'No one' (οὐδείς, not simply no *man*, but no one whatever of the loftiest created intellect, angel or archangel) 'hath seen God at any time.' And yet he adds, 'The only begotten Son which is in the bosom of the Father' (the intimate associate of his mind) 'he has made him clear to us.'[1] And what says St. Paul? 'God is the blessed and only potentate, the king of kings and lord of lords, who only hath immortality, dwelling in the light that no man can approach unto' (dazzling all beholders, like the blazing sun), 'whom no man therefore hath seen nor can see.'[2] Yet what says the same Apostle in other places? 'Now ye have known God;'[3] 'God who commanded the light to shine out of darkness hath shined in our hearts to give the light of the knowledge of the glory of God reflected on us from the face of Jesus Christ;'[4] 'The invisible things of God *are clearly seen*, being arrived at by inference from observation of the things that are made.'[5] And this was just the meaning of the promise vouchsafed to Moses, when he cried so earnestly, 'Show me thy glory!' and the Lord said, 'Thou canst not see my *face*, for there shall no one see me and live; but I will make *my goodness* pass before thee' (my character of love in relation to you shall be manifested), 'and I will

---

[1] John i. 18.   [2] 1 Tim. vi. 15, 16.   [3] Gal. iv. 9.
[4] 2 Cor. iv. 6.   [5] Rom. i. 20.

proclaim the *name* of the LORD' (those *relative* attributes by which I may be known and named) 'before thee, and will be gracious to whom I will be gracious and will show mercy to whom I will show mercy.'[1] And thus, while Paul in his letter to the Romans claims the testimony of God's *works* as witnessing his *Power*, in his address to the people of Lystra he claims the testimony of God's *ways*, as witnessing his *goodness*: 'He left not himself without witness' (without any testimony to the *relative character* of the Absolute Unknown), 'in that he *did good*, and gave us rain from heaven and fruitful seasons, filling our hearts with food and gladness.'[2]

And so the more we learn of the works and ways of God, which the outer and inner world display to us, the more do we come to know, not indeed God in his essence, but God in his character in relation to ourselves. 'In proportion,' says I. H. Fichte, ' to the comprehensiveness and the sagacity with which we investigate the manifest harmony of the world, and its completeness as a whole, the more will there be unfolded to us of the depth and richness of that highest ground of the world; for it is precisely in these things seen that the great cause of them reveals Himself.' And Barrow asks, 'Is the ocean less visible because, standing upon the shore, we cannot discern its utmost bounds?' And Cudworth says, 'We may approach near to a mountain, and touch it with our hands, though we cannot encompass it all round and enclasp it with our arms.'[3]

As surely, therefore, as we can know ourselves and our fellow-men, so surely can we know God. From the

---

[1] Exod. xxxiii. 19, 20.   [2] Acts xiv. 17.
[3] Cudworth, Intel. System, iii. 221. See more in Appendix, Note XVI.

phenomena of your own consciousness, you infer not only *that* you are, but also *what* you are—a being distinguished by the qualities of thought, feeling, and will. You *know* yourself. Then, again, from similar phenomena observable in similar beings, you infer the possession of the same qualities by them. You *know* men. And from just the same sort of phenomena observable in the universe, you are both entitled and bound to infer, nay, to 'clearly see,' that the Being whose existence you have already admitted as the necessary ground of this universe, in whom it *is* and is *one*, possesses the same sort of qualities which from similar manifestations you have already inferred and 'clearly seen' to exist in yourself and in your fellow-men. That is, you *know* God. You know Him to this extent, and with this certainty, that He must be a being, like yourself, of thought, feeling, and will.

But then, it will be objected, 'This is anthropomorphism! This is clothing the great inscrutable Supreme with attributes borrowed from the petty experiences of petty men!' True, this is anthropomorphism. It obliges us to conceive God, however transcending us in *degree*, yet like us in *kind*. But such anthropomorphism is unavoidable. When two natures are similar, whatever be their inequality, we can conceive the higher, and describe the higher, only in terms of the lower. And still more, it is only in proportion to the exaltation by due culture of the lower that we can approximate to just conceptions of the higher. Erroneous views of the character of God have sprung, not from the absolute dissimilarity of human nature and divine, but from a low stage of development of human nature. And in proportion as this nature is unfolded, we arrive at just, if not adequate, conceptions of the character of God. The likeness of God in man resides in the moral sentiments; and the more refined these sentiments become in us the better do we know God, for God is the ideal of these ideas. 'No one hath seen God at any time; but if we love one another God dwelleth in us, and the love which is in him completes itself in us. So every one that loveth knoweth God.'[1]

Still, it is urged by some, 'In thus conceiving of God as the ideal of man, you are ascribing to him that *personality* which distinguishes man. And personality cannot be ascribed to the Absolute, for the very notion of personality includes that of relation to other beings, and so of limitation by them. "I" am "I" in relation to "you." And thus we are reciprocals, and condition each other.' But here the error lies in a wrong conception of what constitutes personality. Our personality, which we ascribe by analogy to God, lies not in the distinction of me from not me, not in the relation of my self to other selfs, but in the relation of my self to *my own mind*; the relation of that which constitutes the *ground* of my being to the various *states* of being which I observe in myself. The sense of personality arises not from comparison of our self with others, but from the cognizance and the control of all the thoughts, feelings, and volitions which emanate from us, and present themselves as internal phenomena to our contemplation. 'By this word personality,' says I. H. Fichte, 'all languages express the property by which the mind throws its glance

---

[1] 1 John iv. 12, 7. See the Scholiast in Matthæi: ὁ ἀόρατος θεὸς καὶ ἀνέφικτος διὰ τῆς εἰς ἀλλήλους ἀγάπης ἐν ἡμῖν μένει. On the truth, though inadequacy, of representative language, see Appendix, Note XVII.

over all that belongs to it, and occurs in it; collects this into a whole as its own, and exercises over it control, as being itself the centre, and at the same time the master, of its own emanations.'[1] Personality, therefore, consists not (as the objection supposes) in the recognition of our self as one amidst many other selfs, but as one amidst the multitude of our own thoughts, as having them within our ken and our grasp. And so, the Absolute Being stands not in a relation of *co-ordination* with other beings, but in a relation of *comprehension* to his own ideas, which are generative of all being. In other words, God is not a unit but a unity; not a mathematical point but an all-containing sphere. As Dr. Clarke expresses it when he says, 'God includes and surrounds everything with his boundless presence.'[2] And Bishop Jeremy Taylor, 'We may imagine God to be as the air and the sea, and we all inclosed in his circle, wrapt up in the lap of his infinite nature, or as infants in the womb of their pregnant mothers; so that we can no more be removed from the presence of God than from our own being.'[3] And this is what Scripture means when it asks, 'Am I a God at hand, saith the Lord, and not a God afar off? Can any hide himself in secret places that I shall not see him? saith the Lord. Do not I fill heaven and earth? saith the Lord;'[4] and when it says of the Son of God, the 'Word,' or utterance of the invisible ideas in visible forms, 'It pleased the Father that in him should all his fulness dwell;' and 'In him dwelleth all the fulness of the Godhead bodily;'[5] and when it declares of God,

---

[1] I. H. Fichte, Psychologie, p. 15; and see Appendix, Note XVIII.
[2] Being of God, 101.   [3] Holy Living, i. 3.
[4] Jer. xxiii. 23, 24.   [5] Col. i. 19; ii. 9.

'Of him, and through him, and to him are all things, to whom be glory for ever. Amen.'[1]

God, then, as the intelligent ground of all things, can be fitly conceived and spoken of by us only in terms derived from our consciousness of our own self, as the intelligent ground of our own thoughts, feelings, and acts. And we must ascribe to Him, by the same analogy, the like perfections in kind, though infinitely transcendent in degree, which mark and constitute our human personality. His *essence* we cannot know (nor can we know any essences[2]), but his *character* we learn from its manifestations in nature and in ourselves; and this character is that of a *Person*, wise in thought, righteous in sentiment, and mighty in will.

For if we conceive of God in the terms of our own consciousness, the first thing which presents itself to us in this region is the quality of *Intelligence*. We find in ourselves intelligence, and therefore we must ascribe a similar intelligence to Him whose offspring we are. As the streams, so must be the source. There can be no perfection in us, however limited, which exists not primarily with unlimited fulness in him who made us in his image. This argument is drawn out by Dr. Clarke: ' 'Tis impossible that any effect should have any perfection which was not in its cause;' 'If, then, intelligence be a distinct quality, then beings endued with intelligence can never have arisen out of that which had no such

---

[1] Rom. xi. 36.
[2] Little flower, if I could understand
   *What* you are, root and all, and all in all,
   I should know what God and man is!
                   Tennyson, *Poems*, 1871.

quality as intelligence; because nothing can ever give to another any perfection which it hath not actually in itself.'[1]

And this perfection which we thus deduce from analogy with our own mind, we find exhibited *in fact* in all the works and ways of God in the world. 'We must believe,' says the Duke of Argyll,[2] 'in a supreme intelligence, for this our own intelligence not only enables us to conceive of, but compels us to recognise in the whole economy of nature. Her whole aspect (as Dr. Tulloch says) answers intelligently to our intelligence, mind responding to mind as in a glass.' This same conviction is expressed by the well-known sayings, 'All minds are of the same family;' and 'The principia of Newton would be true upon the planet Saturn;' and by the maxim of Plato, 'God geometrises.' And the proof of the universal manifestation of such intelligence throughout all being is drawn out with great force by Mr. Murphy; from which his conclusion is, 'If the intelligence that adapts organic structures to their functions is fundamentally identical with the mental intelligence of man, it follows that the intelligence which forms the lenses of the eye is the same intelligence which, in the mind of man, understands the *theory* of the lens; the intelligence that hollows out the bones and the wing-feathers of the bird, in order to combine lightness with strength, and places the feathery fringes where they are needed (and which is probably the most wonderful adaptation in the motor system of any animal), is the same intelligence which, in the mind of the engineer, has devised the construction of iron pillars,

[1] Being of God, 48-50.  [2] Reign of Law, p. 22.

hollowed out like those bones and feathers; and the intelligence that guides the bee in his unconscious shaping of hexagonal cells is also that which, in our minds, understands the properties of the hexagon.' 'There is a *principle of intelligence* which guides all organic formation and all motor instincts, and finally becomes conscious in the brains of higher animals, and conscious of itself in man.'[1]

Well, therefore, may we join adoringly with the many utterances of Scripture which recognise and extol this universal wisdom of God. 'He that planted the ear shall not he hear? He that formed the eye shall he not see? He that teacheth man knowledge shall he not know?'[2] 'The Lord giveth wisdom, out of his mouth cometh knowledge and understanding;'[3] 'I wisdom dwell with prudence and find out knowledge of witty inventions. The Lord possessed me in the beginning of his way, before his works of old. I was set up from everlasting, from the beginning, or ever the earth was. When he prepared the heavens I was there; when he set a compass on the face of the depth; when he established the clouds above; when he strengthened the fountains of the deep; when he gave to the sea his decree that the waters should not pass his commandment; when he laid the foundations of the earth, then I was by him as one brought up with him, and I was daily his delight, rejoicing always before him!'[4] 'The Lord by wisdom hath founded the earth, by understanding hath he established the heavens;'[5] 'O Lord, how manifold are thy works! In wisdom hast thou made them all!'[6]

[1] Habit and Intelligence, ii. 5, 6.  [2] Ps. xciv. 9, 10.  [3] Prov. ii. 6.
[4] Prov. viii. 18-30.  [5] Prov. iii. 19.  [6] Ps. civ. 24.

But among the constituents of our human personality there stands prominently out a class of experiences which we term the feelings, and the highest division of which, the so-called *sentiments*, comprises those movements which are stirred in us by the presence of whatsoever is true, and beautiful, and good. Now similar sentiments, or sentiments which we can express in no more appropriate language, we must, from the evidence of facts, accept as resident in God.[1] For facts show to us in the realm of nature manifestations of truth, of beauty, of goodness. And such facts point us onward and upward to One who, as the ground of nature, must be the very truth, the very beauty, the very goodness whence the scattered rays of these qualities radiate through the world. That which we observe in nature, that which we find in ourselves, however partially and however faintly, this must exist in God in full completeness and splendour. For God actually manifests, in the world which He permeates, all that we mean by a taste and relish for the true, the beautiful, and the good. Whence He is called in Scripture 'the God of truth,' and is represented as dwelling on his works with an artistic complacency, as having come out *true* to his idea of them: 'God looked round on all his work that he had made, and behold it was very good.'[2] And God has (still more) for the very essence of his character that *moral* sense, that taste for 'whatsoever things are true, and noble, and just, and pure, and lovely,' which characterises our own human moral sense. 'The Lord is righteous in all his ways and holy in all his works.'[3] 'The righteous Lord loveth righteousness; his countenance doth behold with

---

[1] See Appendix, Note XIX.   [2] Gen. i. 31.   [3] Ps. cxlv. 17.

pleasure the upright.'[1] 'He is excellent in judgment and in plenty of justice.'[2] 'Far be it from God that he should do wickedness, and from the Almighty that he should commit iniquity. Yea surely God will not do wickedly, neither will the Almighty pervert judgment.'[3] And 'God is love!'[4] As truly therefore as Plato said of the divine *mind*, 'God geometrises'—He has the sense for geometrical truth even as ourselves; so truly may we say of the divine *spirit*, 'God poetises'—He has the sense for the sublime and beautiful as we see these qualities spread through the world, and find them recognised in our own minds. And above all, 'God loves!' He has a *heart* like ours, to feel for others' welfare; to pour itself out to them in acts of righteousness, justice, compassion, mercy, care. 'As the external universe,' says I. H. Fichte, 'reveals the infinity of his eternal *nature*, and the might of his organising *intellect*, so in the principles of beauty which pervade this universe there is revealed the highest æsthetic *taste*, while in his relation to the human spirit the proofs of his *moral* disposition come out in all their fulness; so that in this last characteristic, as it is the distinguishing element of human character, we behold the distinguishing element of the Divine character.'

And similarly, the Rev. E. H. Bickersteth: 'All beauty is a gleam from the fountain of beauty. No work of beauty can be more beautiful than the mind which designed it. I do not think a sculptor can possibly chisel a marble so as to make it more beautiful than his own ideal conception. I do not think a painter can produce a paint-

---

[1] Ps. xi. 7.    [2] Job xxxvii. 23.    [3] Job xxxiv. 10, 12.
[4] 1 John iv. 8.

ing more beautiful than the thought of his mind which led up to it; I do not think a musician can express in sound, or a poet on paper, anything beyond the thought within him. I know, indeed, that the conception of either may grow with the process by which it is presented to others, and that the man may, as he proceeds, have a fairer and nobler view of what he is trying to express; but, after all, the mind of the sculptor is more beautiful than the marble which he has sculptured; and the mind of the painter is a more beautiful thing than the work of art which he has painted; and the mind of the musician is better, and higher, and nobler than the most exquisite symphony which he has composed and reduced to writing; and the mind of the poet is better than his most beautiful piece of poetry. And so we must rise from all the fragments of beauty which God has scattered so widely over his world to say with Milton—

> Thine this universal frame
> Thus wondrous fair; Thyself how wondrous then!'

Yes, assuredly, whatever the dimness of our conceptions as to the other attributes of God, of this we are clear that He is a holy God; a righteous God; a good God; that is, that He possesses in perfection just those qualities of which *our* moral nature shows but faint and fitful gleams—the qualities of justice, equity, and love. And if anyone therefore even seem to suppose God's moral principles to be different from our own, God's justice, equity, and love to be something not merely more comprehensive, and therefore, in their action, often unfathomable to our limited understanding, but different in *kind* from what He has implanted in our own bosoms, I wonder not that such a seeming should have called forth the passionate protest of Mr. Mill: 'To maintain, not merely that an absolute being is unknowable in Himself, but that the *relative attributes* of an absolute being are unknowable also, is to say that we do not know what wisdom, justice, benevolence, mercy are as they exist in God.' 'It is to suppose that the infinite goodness ascribed to God is not the goodness which we know and love in our fellow-creatures, distinguished only as infinite in degree, but is *different in kind* and another quality altogether.' But 'if, instead of the glad tidings that there is a Being in whom all the excellencies which the highest human form can conceive exist in a degree inconceivable to us, I am informed that the world is ruled by a Being whose attributes are infinite, but what they are we cannot learn, except that the highest morality does not sanction them, and I am told that I must believe this, and at the same time call this Being by the names which express and affirm the highest human morality, I say, in plain terms, that I will not.'

But no such mistake is made by Cudworth, when he claims for God a *moral* as well as *mental* likeness to ourselves: 'Those ancients who affirmed that *Mind* was Lord over all and the Supreme King of heaven and earth, held at the same time that *Good* was the sovereign monarch of the universe; Good reigning in mind and together with it, because mind is that which makes all things for the sake of Good, and whatsoever doth otherwise was, according to them, not wisdom but unwisdom, not mind but madness, and consequently no God.' So Celsus in Origen: 'God is a prince and governor, not of discordant passions, neither of aimless disorder, but of a right and righteous nature.' And so Origen himself: 'We maintain that God can never do that which is wrong, since then you would have a God who could become no God; for a God who can do wrong is no God.' And again, 'God never wills anything unbecoming to Him, for this would be destructive of his very being as God. The Deity is not to be conceived as mere arbitrariness, but as an overflowing fountain of love and goodness, justly and wisely dispensing itself and omnipotently reaching all things. The will of God is goodness, justice, and wisdom; or decorousness, fitness, and ought itself, willing; so that the perfection of excellence, that which is absolutely the best, is an indispensable law to this will, seeing that it constitutes the very essence of it.'[1]

Thus, then, the character of God is revealed to us, and must be conceived by us, as including *wisdom of thought* and *righteousness of sentiment*. It is not less distinguished by *mightiness of will*. What *will* is we know from our own experience. It is initiative force. It is that which make us *causative*, self-moving, beings. Whence Aristotle's definition of the soul, that it is ἀειχίνητος, of incessant activity. And this same property of will we find displaying itself in God. The whole universe is an expression of his will, and is governed by his will. God is manifestly not a mere idea shining out upon the world, but a force working in the world. And a force not only originative of all other forces, but actuating and dominating all. This is what Sir Isaac Newton took pains to lay down as indispensable to our right notion of God, when he wrote: 'We must not conceive of God as some mere soul of the world dispersed through its various

---

[1] Cudworth, Intellectual System, iii. 402.

phenomena, nor as an abstraction without *life*. He is both distinct from the world and yet actuating the world. It is not enough for us to regard Him as a being, eternal, infinite, absolute; nay, it is not enough for us to admire Him as the wise and beneficent builder of the universe; we must fall down before Him as our *Lord and Sovereign*. And hence men do not say " *my* eternal" or " *my* infinite," but they do say, and this rightly, "*my* God," that is, my *Lord*. God, without dominion, superintendence, and the actuating everything as means subservient to his ends, would be no better than fate and necessity. The true God is a *living* God, who moves, controls, and governs the universe. This even natural philosophy declares to us. This conclusion lies within the sphere of science. For it belongs to science, starting from phenomena, to stop not till it raise us to the hidden ground of these phenomena.' And just this sovereignty of a divine *Will* is what Scripture insists on in such a variety of forms, when it tells us that God is ' the *living* God and an everlasting *King* ;'[1] that ' the heavens with all their host, the earth, the seas, and all that is therein, are all preserved by Him;'[2] that they all ' continue this day according to his ordinances, for all are his servants ;'[3] that He is ' the God in whose hand our breath is, and whose are all our ways ;'[4] that He ' worketh incessantly, without pause ;'[5] and that He ' doeth according to his will, in the army of heaven and among the inhabitants of the earth; and none can stay his hand or say to him, what doest thou ?'[6]

[1] Jeremiah x. 10.  [2] Nehemiah ix. 6.  [3] Ps. cxix. 91.
[4] Daniel v. 23.  [5] John v. 17.  [6] Daniel iv. 35.

OF THE CORRELATION

OF

GOD AND MEN.

'My Father worketh without pause, and I work.'—*John* v. 17.

'One God and Father of all, who is above all, and through all, and in you all.'—*Ephes.* iv. 6.

'God is so great and wonderful a being, as at once to see all things, to hear all things, to be present in all things, and to take care of all things.'— SOCRATES, *Xen. Mem.* i. 4, 4.

> That God which ever lives and loves,
>   One God, one law, one element,
>   And one far-off divine event,
> To which the whole creation moves.
>                               TENNYSON, *In Mem.* p. 211.

'Not merely here and there, and now and then, does God lay hold of men; but He enters into them to dwell with them; He unites Himself permanently to them; and thereby He frees them from the entanglements of imperfection and of sin, and raises them to that completeness for which He has given them a divine capacity.'—I. H. FICHTE, *Specul. Theol.* ii. 648.

## LETTER VIII.

### THE DEALINGS OF GOD WITH MEN.

My dear Friend,—

Some one has quaintly asked, 'Why was there revealed to Jacob, at Bethel, a *ladder* set up between earth and heaven, when the angels might have descended and ascended without this help?' And it has been as quaintly answered, 'In order to encourage Jacob with the thought that for him, too, though wingless, there might be an ascent towards God; slow indeed, and only step by step, but still by a ladder of ratiocination, which, though planted on earth, has its top reaching to heaven.'

Now, up the several rounds of such a ladder I have been endeavouring to help you. I have fixed your attention first on *facts*, planted firmly on earth. The fact of your own existence as an individual unit. The fact of your existence in intimate relation with other units, which, nevertheless, you modify, and which modify you with incessant reciprocity. The fact of these other units forming with yourself a whole, in such manifest correlation of parts and movements as to constitute a *system* of forces, co-ordinated and co-operative towards predetermined ends. And then up these visible rounds of observed facts we have climbed together to the not less certain, though invisible, summit, on which the most rigid logic lands us, that within this system of beings there must exist another Being, the ground of its life, order, concinnity, and adjustment, who must be conceived by us, from the testimony of his works and ways, as possessing a personality like our own.

And thus we have fixed the two great points which it most concerns us to know, *man* and *God*. *Man*, as we *find* him in ourselves and others; *God*, as we *find* Him, with equal evidence, in the phenomena of the world And these phenomena have proved to us (i.e. have *shown* us by unmistakable facts) not only his *existence*, but his *character* in relation to the world, of which He is the ground.

The particulars of this *relation*, more especially in reference to *men*, I now wish to unfold to you. God is correlated with men; men are correlated with God. What are the *dealings of God* with men? And what the corresponding *duties of men* towards God?

Now, that God is indeed *dealing with* men is sufficiently obvious from all the facts which we observe in ourselves and things around us. We are parts of one great whole. And we partake of the movements, we are subject to the *law* of movement, discoverable throughout this whole. What is this law? It is the law of evolution; of a graduated process of development from lower to higher forms of existence, and in each separate form from lower to higher stages of perfection. There is throughout the universe as a whole, and in each department of this universe, a continuous advance from primitive simplicity, through successive stages of differentiation and integration, onwards towards an ultimate equilibration.

Of this law the best exponent is Mr. Herbert Spencer, who shows at large its operation in the several departments of geology, of biology, of psychology, and of sociology. And his definition of it is: 'Evolution is a change from an indefinite, incoherent homogeneity, to a definite, coherent heterogeneity, through continuous differentiations and integrations, and the causes of this change can be expressed only in terms of matter, motion, and force.'[1] See also the work of Mr. Murphy on the same subject, in which he shows how this development is ever and in all things being carried on, not by blind, or so-called 'natural,' but by *intelligent* force, i.e. by the all-pervading will (for 'will' is 'intelligent force') of the great Supreme. For he maintains: 'There is something in organic progress which mere "natural selection" among spontaneous variations will not account for. And this something, I believe, is that *Organising Intelligence* which guides the action of the inorganic forces, and forms structures which neither natural selection nor any other unintelligent agency could form.'[2]

It is then to the application of this law of development by this 'Organising Intelligence' whom we term God, to his *dealings with men* specifically, that I now ask your attention. God is carrying on a process of development for humanity. As the first step of this process He has endowed us with a rational nature like his own. This nature He is raising to its highest power even amidst our many aberrations from it. And this rise He is working out by a continuous education, beginning in the individual and spreading through the race of man.

1. First we must remind ourselves how everything manifests a *process* of development, in the world of mind as well as in the world of nature. We recognise God as

[1] First Principles, 216, 223.   [2] Habit and Intelligence, i. 348.

not only the *ground* of all things, causing them to BE, but as the *formative force* in all things, prescribing and producing what they are to BECOME. All facts show this. All intelligent observers of these facts agree in holding this.

I doubt not through the ages one increasing purpose runs,
And the thoughts of men are widened by the process of the suns.

This was long ago affirmed by Bishop Butler: 'Our existence is not only successive, as it must be of necessity, but one state of our life and being is appointed by God to be a preparation for another; and that to be the means of attaining to another succeeding one; infancy to childhood, childhood to youth, youth to mature age. Men are impatient and for precipitating things; but the Author of nature appears deliberate throughout his operations, accomplishing his ends by slow successive steps; making one thing subservient to another, this to somewhat further, and so on through *a progressive series* of means which extend both backward and forward beyond our utmost view.' And such a view of the divine procedure involves in it the constant operation of a Providence particular as well as general in and over all things and all men. 'Every view of the world, as having its ground in God, involves in it the belief that this God exercises a divine *Providence*. And this, not in the sense of a mere upholding of those *universal* laws which are inwoven with nature and with human life as their essential warp, but, far more, in the sense of an *individual* just and gracious guidance of the destiny of each separate person.' 'And this view of a particular providence is so inseparable from the more general notion of an historical providence that they must stand or fall together. For in the province of history there is nothing small or great in itself. It is only our one-sided opinion which makes it so. Even the great, the universal, can bring out the unity of the plan of the world only so far as the individual in whose complications this unity is imbedded responds precisely thereto. If then there be a plan of the world (and for this the whole sum of its facts is sufficient guarantee), then the smallest particular must form part and parcel of this plan. So true is the saying of Hamann, "Only a Providence which extends to the smallest parts can make good the design for the whole." Looked at indeed superficially, history is no more than a sum of petty particulars. And yet it is by these particulars that what is great, the divinely human purport of these particulars, accomplishes itself. And, therefore, the minutest occurrences, which sometimes amount to no more than involuntary commissions or omissions on our part, must in reality be under the guidance of that universal regulating force, even though we may be unable to point out clearly its action in particular instances. Nor is such an indication needful, seeing this would establish only an *à posteriori* certainty.'[1]

And with the same distinctness and decision Parker says : 'The notion that God continually watches over the world and all its contents is very dear to mankind. It appears in all forms of conscious religion. Men distinguish, it is true, a general and a special providence, but

---

[1] I. H. Fichte, Seelenfrage, 207. And so Blasche: 'Divine providence is at once universal and particular; nay, because it is absolutely universal it must extend itself to the most particular and minutest points. For the particular can exist only in the bosom of the universal; and the universal can work and manifest itself only in the details of the particular.'—*Das Böse im Einklange mit der Weltordnung*, p. 206.

these distinctions lose themselves in the true idea of a *universal* Providence. A law that is perfectly special, providing for each, is also completely general, providing for all. In other words, it is universal. God's providence must be infinite, like his nature. And its action is not against, but in and with, the laws of each class of things. He takes care of material things without violating their constitution, but acting always according to the nature of the things that He has made. So also in the animal world. And so, therefore, in the human world, by means of man's consciousness and partial freedom, not against them. Atheism tells you of a world without a God, a great going, but a going with none to direct. But with absolute religion we have absolute trust in the motive of God; absolute trust in the means which He has provided in the nature and constitution of things. The human faculties become then the instruments of Providence. Every man is under the protection of God. And all fear of the final result, for you, for me, for all mankind, quite vanishes away. The details, indeed, we know not. Experience reveals them a dayfull at a time. But the result we are sure of. Ignorance is full of dread, and trembles at the earthquake and the storm. But science justifies the ways of God to matter, knowing all and loving all; and discloses everywhere the immanent and ever active force. Where science does not understand the mode of action, nor read the title of perfection clearly in the *work*, it points to the infinite perfection of the *Author*, and we fear no more.'[1] And so Mr. Adams: 'In a profoundly religious and philosophical sense, a particular providence is included in a general providence, and a general provi-

---

[1] Parker, Theism, pp. 170, 186.

dence includes a particular providence, just as all the parts are included in the whole, and the whole includes all its parts.' And again : 'Since the idea of a providence is derived from that of a cause of law, it follows that its characteristics must agree with the nature of its origin, and that we must conceive of a providence, not as exhibited in peculiar, extraordinary, and irregular interferences with the operation of law, either in the natural or in the moral world, but as consisting in a divine presence and power, not only active in the origination of all things, but permanent and all-pervading, sustaining all phenomena, energising all law, moving in all motion, thinking in all thought, living in all life, existing in all being, and presiding over all events.'[1]

The world then is, throughout, the offspring of *intention*, and through all space and time is being actuated by intention. It is under the perpetual governance of an Intelligent Will ; and this governance is being incessantly exercised towards its development, as a whole and in all its parts, according to preconceived and predetermined ends.

What, then, are these ends, with reference to *man* ? Here, as everywhere, we must begin with *facts*. And facts show us plainly, by their actual though gradual approximation towards a certain goal, what this goal is, and what, therefore, is the intention manifested in our being gradually guided towards it. The history of an *individual* man is the history of his development, from mere unconscious animalism up to the perception, not only of things around him but things within him ; and not only of things around him and within him, but of laws and princi-

[1] Adams, Theories of History, 37, 236.

ples inwoven in these things, to which laws and principles he finds an involuntary responsiveness in his own mind.

From one stage to another of mental growth the child is brought to recognise, to accept, to adjust himself to *laws*—material laws, vital laws, mental laws, moral laws. And he finds, too, that just in proportion as he does adjust himself to these laws, his consciousness that he is fulfilling the end of his being is increased, and the self-respect and happiness which result from such fulfilment are enjoyed.

And, as with the individual man, so is it with the race of men. We have here equally *facts*. And these facts show us that from the earliest dawn of humanity, as discovered in the pre-historic remains, there has been going on one continuous course of slow yet sure development, out of merely animal existence on to the exercise of thought, of purpose, of invention, of skill, of labour, prompted by the prevision of certain ends, and guided towards the means for their accomplishment, up to that magnificent maturity of manhood which marks the present age. Nor even here is there any sign of this development having reached its destined height. The progressive power of man seems inexhaustible. We have probably hitherto but imperfect intimations of what is yet to come for us. And therefore, from the facts of the past and present, and the anticipations which these facts not only justify, but require for the future, the race of men must be recognised as under a law of development, from the faintest possibility of rational life to its fullest approximation towards the character, and therewith the blessedness, of God. 'We may shake off any lingering feeling of humiliation at the recollection of our poor relations by remembering that there are no backward footprints on the sands of time. We cannot retrace our steps. What is, cannot be what it was. We may be something more, we cannot be something less, than man, in the future. Man is a fourth kingdom—a kingdom by himself—the human kingdom ("le règne humain"). And what is its peculiar distinction? That it is *historical*. "The character that distinguishes man from all other organised beings is precisely that which you forget in the definition and discussion of man. This characteristic is, to be *a historical world*; to metamorphose himself, in the course of time, not only as an individual, but as a race; to grow from generation to generation; to secrete around himself a social historical envelope, a world of successive traditions; to have, as man alone has, *a history*, of which he is himself the increment and the food; when for all other organic beings there is only a *description*. Behold man and his kingdom as opposed to all other realms of nature. Alius in alio tempore, linguam, genus vivendi, mores, artes mutat. Solus historiam occupat et implet. Behold the features that I sought. They are not in Linnæus. But they are written everywhere in human nature." [1]

And it is *in order* to such ultimate development, that our Heavenly Father has endowed us with a *nature like his own*. The nature which distinguishes us as men is, as we have formerly seen, that capacity for discerning differences which includes in it the perception, approval, and relish of truth, beauty, and goodness. And such a nature, as we have also seen, is that of God Himself. Therefore, our capacity for this discernment, even when only in its feeblest germ, constitutes us, in this sense and

[1] Quinet, La creation, in the *Times* review of it.

to this extent, like God; marks us as the offspring of God; and akin to God.

This capacity, observe, recognised under the name of *reason*, has been among all peoples regarded as constituting man, by its very existence, however feebly, *like God*. Because of this, Cicero calls the human mind 'celestial,' and 'of divine nature.'[1] Because of this he terms reason 'a derived resemblance to the eternal reason;'[2] and 'the bond of fellowship between God and men.'[3] Because of this, 'to follow reason' is, with other philosophers, synonymous with the 'following God;' and 'to obey right reason and to obey God are one and the same thing.'[4] And because of this, the sacred Scriptures represent man as possessing 'the image of God.' Thus, we read in Genesis i. 26, 27, 'God said, Let us make man in our image after our likeness. So God created man in his own image; in the image of God created he him.' And then, in Genesis v. 1, 3, to assure us that this image has never departed from man, but descends from father to son, it is added: 'In the day that God created man (or Adam), in the likeness of God made he him. And Adam begat a son in his likeness, after his image.' That is, plainly, 'In the same image, with the same likeness to God in which Adam himself was created, did he beget his son.' Whence the perpetual law against destroying man for food, as we may destroy animals, is based on this perpetually true distinction

---

[1] 'Est animus *cælestis*, ex altissimo domicilio depressus et quasi demersus in terram, locum *divinæ naturæ* æternitatique contrarium.'—*De Senect.* 21.

[2] Participata similitudo rationis æternæ.

[3] Vinculum Dei et hominis.

[4] See Jno. Smith, Discourses, 388.

between man and animals. 'Whoso sheddeth man's blood, by man shall his blood be shed, *for* in the image of God made he man.'[1] And this permanence of God's image in man, thus asserted in the Old Testament, is re-asserted as true for all men, and distinctive of the race, in the New. 'A man ought not to cover his head, forasmuch as he is' (not 'has been,' but 'is' in all time and place) 'the image and glory of God.'[2] 'With the tongue we bless God, and therewith curse we men which are made' (constituted) 'after the similitude of God.'[3] And this point is insisted on with equal earnestness by secular as by sacred writers. By Plato: 'What is there in the soul of a diviner nature than this capacity of knowing and considering? Therein, therefore, it is that we are similar to God.'[4] By Cicero: 'There is in man a similitude to God.'[5] And again, 'The mind is a kind of image of God.'[6] Whence Manilius says: 'Each man is a reduced copy of the Supreme.'[7] And by Sir Thomas Browne: 'There is surely a piece of divinity in us; something that was before the heavens, and owes no homage unto the sun. Nature tells me I am the image of God, as well as Scripture.'[8]

But as being thus *like God*, man is said to be as em-

---

[1] Gen. ix. 6. If, as geologists assert, all men were in pre-historic times anthropophagi, this prohibition, and the reason for it, as the godlike in humanity began to show itself, was the more necessary.

[2] 1 Cor. xi. 7.          [3] James iii. 9.

[4] Ἔχομεν οὖν εἰπεῖν ὅ,τι ἐστὶ τῆς ψυχῆς θειότερον ἢ τοῦτο περὶ ὃ τὸ εἰδέναι τε καὶ φρονεῖν ;—Alcib. i. (Bipont, v. 65).

[5] 'Est homini cum Deo similitudo.'—*De Legg*. i. 8. Compare Stobæus, *Anthol.* iii. 387: 'Homo solus omnium in terra degentium Dei est imitamentum, et similes Ei virtutes habet.'

[6] Dei imago quædam animus est.

[7] Exemplumque Dei quisque est in imagine parva.

[8] See Lord Lytton's Miscell. i. 180.

phatically *the offspring of God*. Because he possesses the divine capacity of reason, he must be specially, as lower beings are not, of divine origin, or birth. Thus Socrates declares : 'The soul of man, if any portion of him, must be that which partakes of the divinity, for it is manifest that this it is that ruleth within us;'[1] where you have not only the conviction uttered, but the reason for this conviction: 'The soul must be divine, for it is *imperial*, dominant over sense.' And so Plato, 'Now, concerning the ruling part in our soul, we should well consider this : that God has vouchsafed this to each one, as a sort of divine guardian, dwelling in the very summit of the body, drawing us up from earth to our kinsfolk in heaven, as plants not of earthly but heavenly origin. For thither whence our soul had first its birth, a divine power, raising aloft our head, directs our whole frame.'[2] And Cicero tells us that 'Pythagoras had no sort of doubt that the souls of men are derived from the soul of the universe;'[3] and his own belief was that, 'A being so prescient, sagacious, many-sided, acute, with such a memory, and so replete with reason and wisdom, as man is, must be in a peculiar way the offspring of the high God. For man alone, amidst so many varieties of being, is participant of reason and reflection. And what can be, not only in man but throughout heaven and earth, more divine than reason? Consequently, since nothing, whether in man or God, can be better than reason, there must be a certain primitive affinity through reason be-

---

[1] Ἀνθρώπου γε ψυχή εἴπερ τι καὶ ἄλλο τῶν ἀνθρωπίνων, τοῦ θείου μετέχει, ὅτι μὲν γὰρ βασιλεύει ἐν ἡμῖν φανερόν.—Xenoph. Mem. iv. 3, 6.

[2] Plato, Timæus (Bipont, ix. 431).

[3] Cicero, *De Senectute*, 21 : 'ex universa mente divina delibatos animos.'

between man and animals. 'Whoso sheddeth man's blood, by man shall his blood be shed, *for* in the image of God made he man.'[1] And this permanence of God's image in man, thus asserted in the Old Testament, is reasserted as true for all men, and distinctive of the race, in the New. 'A man ought not to cover his head, forasmuch as he is' (not 'has been,' but 'is' in all time and place) 'the image and glory of God.'[2] 'With the tongue we bless God, and therewith curse we men which are made' (constituted) 'after the similitude of God.'[3] And this point is insisted on with equal earnestness by secular as by sacred writers. By Plato: 'What is there in the soul of a diviner nature than this capacity of knowing and considering? Therein, therefore, it is that we are similar to God.'[4] By Cicero: 'There is in man a similitude to God.'[5] And again, 'The mind is a kind of image of God.'[6] Whence Manilius says: 'Each man is a reduced copy of the Supreme.'[7] And by Sir Thomas Browne: 'There is surely a piece of divinity in us; something that was before the heavens, and owes no homage unto the sun. Nature tells me I am the image of God, as well as Scripture.'[8]

But as being thus *like God*, man is said to be as em-

---

[1] Gen. ix. 6. If, as geologists assert, all men were in pre-historic times anthropophagi, this prohibition, and the reason for it, as the godlike in humanity began to show itself, was the more necessary.

[2] 1 Cor. xi. 7.     [3] James iii. 9.

[4] Ἔχομεν οὖν εἰπεῖν ὅ,τι ἐστὶ τῆς ψυχῆς θειότερον ἢ τοῦτο περὶ ὃ τὸ εἰδέναι τε καὶ φρονεῖν;—Alcib. i. (Bipont, v. 65).

[5] 'Est homini cum Deo similitudo.'—*De Legg.* i. 8. Compare Stobæus, *Anthol.* iii. 387: 'Homo solus omnium in terra degentium Dei est imitamentum, et similes Ei virtutes habet.'

[6] Dei imago quædam animus est.

[7] Exemplumque Dei quisque est in imagine parva.

[8] See Lord Lytton's Miscell. i. 180.

heathen faith without their counterpart and confirmation in the sacred Scriptures. For St. Paul himself adopts the words of Aratus as the text of his argument with the Athenians; pressing on them a spiritual worship, because they, as men, partake the spiritual nature of God: 'He is not far from any one of us, for in him we live and move and have our being; nay, we are also *his offspring*, as one of your own poets has said. *Therefore* if we' (manifestly we all) 'are thus the *offspring* of God' (are akin to God, and God akin to us), 'then we ought never to think of the Godhead as like to gold, or silver, or stone;'[1]—He from whom man springs must be like man. And because of this affinity of nature with the Supreme the Scriptures call the first human father of the race '*the son* of God:' 'Enos was the son of Seth, which was the son of Adam, which (Adam) was the son of God.'[2] And they exhort us, 'Bear up patiently under chastisement, for God in this dealeth with you *as with sons*; for what son is he whom his father chasteneth not.'[3] And if we should suppose that here there is indicated a relation of *character*, and not of *race*, we shall find our mistake corrected by the antithesis which immediately follows: 'We have had *fathers of our flesh* which corrected us, and we gave them reverence; shall we not much rather be in subjection to the *Father of our spirits* and live?'[4] And this same sort of contrast between an earthly and a heavenly parent our Lord makes in as comprehensive terms when he says, 'If a son ask bread of *any of you that is a father*, will he give him a stone? If ye then, though evil, know how to give good gifts to your children, how much

---

[1] Acts xvii. 27-29.
[2] Luke iii. 38.
[3] Heb. xii. 7.
[4] Ibid. xii. 9.

more shall *your Heavenly Father* give the Holy Spirit to them that ask him?'[1] Whence also, with the same breadth of comparison, he points out as the pattern for our imitation, not our human brethren, but our divine parent: 'Be ye perfect as *your Father which is in heaven is perfect;*'[2] and he teaches us to pray, with a similar contrast between the parents of our bodies and the parent of our souls, '*Our Father which art in heaven!*'[3] And if it should be urged on you, 'That exhortation, and this prayer, are given to Christ's *disciples*, and therefore you must confine the idea of fatherhood to those who have a *moral* affinity with God;' then you may answer the objector unanswerably, from the touching parable which pictures the return of *heathen* and of *outcasts*, far away from God in character. For here you have God imaged as *from the first* the Father of the prodigal— the representative of *heathen* and of *outcasts*—('A certain man had two *sons*'). And *from* this Father the sin of heathen and of outcasts is a departure; *to* this Father repentance is a coming back; and *by* this Father these heathen and these outcasts are received home again; not as *now first* through repentance *becoming* sons, but simply *recognised* as sons; reinstated in the birthright they had forfeited; clothed with the garments and invested with the ring of their original dignity in the household; and welcomed with the acclamation: 'This *my son* was dead and is alive again; he was lost and is found!'[4]

Well, therefore, may I close this letter with the elevating words with which John Smith, of Cambridge, has extolled the dignity of the human soul: 'God hath

---

[1] Luke xi. 11-13.　　[2] Matt. v. 48.
[3] Ibid. vi. 9.　　[4] Luke xv. 11-24.

stamped a copy of his own archetypal loveliness upon the soul, that man, by reflecting into himself, might behold there the glory of God ; see within his soul all those ideas of truth which concern the nature and essence of God, *by reason of its own resemblance to God*, and so beget within himself the most free and generous motions of love to God! For reason in man is " light of light," the derived resemblance of the law of God.'[1]

[1] Discourses, 382.

## LETTER IX.

*OF EVIL IN RELATION TO GOD'S DEALINGS WITH MEN.*

IN my last letter we gained a point of view, whence there began to spread out before us a glorious prospect of the destiny of man. Our relation to God being that of children to a wise and loving parent, the dealings of God with us take the form of successive steps in a process of development, by which He is raising us from affinity with Himself in capacity, to similarity with Himself in character. We have been endowed with Godlike prerogatives, that we may use these for the building up within us a Godlike personality.

But here, I think I see you draw back with surprise and incredulity from a view so inspiriting. I think I hear you murmuring, 'All very fine! It dazzles for a moment! The bursting sunlight sheds a momentary splendour over dull reality. But are there no clouds remaining? Do I not see stealing upward, at the very moment that I gaze delighted on the fairy scene, a thick cold mist of earthly exhalations which efface it from my view? Have we not left the solid ground of fact for the delusive atmosphere of fancy? You speak of God having endowed us with a rational nature like his own, in order to raise this nature ultimately to its highest power. But what see we in actual humanity

—in all existing men? A glimmering reason only, amidst a prevalent unreason. Some feeble sentiments of goodness amidst strong universal badness. If endowed with divine gifts, we have abused them to our ruin. If made partakers of our Father's goods, we are wasting them in riotous living. If planted a noble vine, wholly a right seed, how are we turned into a degenerate plant, as of a strange vine! The gold has become dim! —the most fine gold changed! The crown is fallen from our head! Woe, woe unto us, for we have sinned!'

True, my friend; too true! And therefore I must pause upon these facts for a moment, to endeavour to show you how, notwithstanding their existence, we may be assured that God is carrying on his process of development for humanity. This process He still keeps in view. In order to this process he has endowed us with a nature similar to his own. And toward this development he is using the very aberrations which seem to you so antagonistic to it.

That such aberrations do exist every one concedes. Bias says, 'The majority are wicked.'[1] Seneca, 'Hardly any one is free from vice.'[2] Sophocles, 'It is common to all men to miss the mark.'[3] Seneca again, 'We all of us have sinned, some with heavy offences, some with lighter; some with determination, others through impulse or example; some from want of strength to stand firm to our good intentions, and slipping away from innocence with reluctance and resistance.'[4] And hence the compas-

---

[1] Οἱ πλεῖστοι κακοί.—Bias in Diog. Laërt. i. 5.
[2] 'Nemo pæne sine vitio est.'—Seneca, Controv. iv. 25.
[3] Ἀνθρώποισι γὰρ τοῖς πᾶσι κοινόν ἐστι τοὐξαμαρτάνειν.—Antig. 1023.
[4] 'Peccavimus omnes, alii gravia, alii leviora, alii ex destinato, alii forte

sionate sympathy of Plutarch, when he says, 'We commiserate the infirmity of human nature, seeing that even minds the most worthy and the most distinguished for virtue have no power to work out what is right unmixed with blame.'[1] Well, therefore, may we exclaim, with Petronius, 'Not one of our race is free from sin, for we are men, not gods;'[2] and with Simonides, 'For man to be righteous is impossible. It surpasses human nature. Such honour belongs to God alone;'[3] and with Job, 'What is man that he should be clean, and he that is born of a woman that he should be righteous?'[4] and with Solomon, 'There is not a just man upon earth that sinneth not;'[5] and with Paul, 'There is none righteous, no, not one.'[6] But then, in these very bewailings there is included an inextinguishable feeling that sin is literally '*aberration*;' not the true path of man, but a *wandering from it*; not what is proper to our nature and lineage, but what is *depravation* of this nature, *degeneration* from this lineage. The very fact that all men see, and notice, and bewail the darkness, testifies to a light within them by which they see it, alien from this darkness—antagonistic to this darkness. In the very act, therefore, of observing such aberrations, we observe them as not primary but secondary, not in the line of our proper

---

impulsi, aut aliena nequitia ablati, alii in bonis consiliis parum fortiter stetimus et innocentiam inviti ac renitentes perdidimus.'—Seneca, *De Clem*.

[1] Οἰκτείροντες τῆς ἀνθρωπίνης φύσεως τὴν ἀσθένειαν, εἰ μηδ' ἐν ἤθεσιν οὕτως ἀξιολόγοις καὶ διαφόροις πρὸς ἀρετὴν ἱκανοῖς εὑρεῖν δύναται τὸ καλὸν ἀνεπίμικτον.— Plutarch, Cleom. 16.

[2] 'Nemo non nostrum peccat. Homines sumus non dei.'—Petron. *Sat*. 75, 1.

[3] Εἶναι ἄνδρα ἀγαθὸν ἀδύνατον καὶ οὐκ ἀνθρώπειον, ἀλλὰ θεὸς μόνος τοῦτο ἔχει τὸ γέρας.—Simonides, in Plato.

[4] Job xv. 14.    [5] Eccl. vii. 20.    [6] Rom. iii. 10.

tendency, but departures from this tendency. Evil is a state of things *superinduced* on good, made *subservient* to the bringing out of higher good, and when its transitional work has been accomplished, to be *superseded* by the highest good.[1]

1. That evil is a state of things *superinduced* on good, is universally felt. All the traditions among all nations of a golden age of purity and happiness, a primitive Eden in which sin and sorrow were unknown and God had his delights with men, are symbols and exponents of this feeling. Look only at the touching contrast set before you in the Sacred Books. You open the first and second chapters of Genesis, and you find it written : ' God created man in his own image, male and female created he them. And they were both naked and were not ashamed.' You turn to the third chapter of Genesis, and you find this man and woman having their eyes opened to know that they were naked, and hiding from the presence of the Lord amidst the trees of the garden, because they had eaten of the tree of which he had commanded them saying, Thou shalt not eat of it ! You find, again, the whole of nature brilliant in beauty before the eyes of its Creator, so that ' God saw everything that he had made, and behold it was very good.' And then you find a change and a corruption ; ' Cursed is the ground for thy sake ; thorns and thistles shall it bring forth to thee !' Always, good is contemplated as preceding evil, evil as a departure from primeval good. The idea of things perfect. Facts, a deflexion from this idea. ' As no one,' says Epictetus, ' sets up a mark in order to miss it, so can there be no

---

[1] For the *ground* of such evil, see my Fatherhood of God, 83-168. The thoughts suggested here are supplementary.

essential evil in the nature of the world.'[1] On which Simplicius remarks, 'Evil is the *depravation* of its subject, by which it *swerves* from nature. It is not *in* nature, as good is; but is an additional thing superinduced on good. Just as we may conceive sickness in relation to health; or stumbling, which is an accident beside the purpose of our primary action. For whatsoever is contrary to nature is an accidental addition to that which is agreeable to nature. Good was first, then evil; not evil first and afterwards good.' And you know the striking way in which Paley puts this fact, 'Evil no doubt exists, but it is never the object of contrivance. Teeth are contrived to eat not to ache; their aching now and then is incidental to the contrivance, perhaps inseparable from it; but it is not the *object* of it. No anatomist ever discovered a system of organisation calculated to produce pain or disease; or, in explaining the parts of the human body, ever said, This is to irritate; this is to inflame; this duct is to convey the gravel to the kidneys; this gland to secrete the humour which forms the gout.'[2]

And it is the assurance of this fact which has led to so many and decided protests against the attributing evil in any way to the Supreme Himself. What says Euripides? 'If the gods do anything evil, they are no longer gods.'[3] What, Plato? 'God is good; and of all things good He is the only cause. But of things evil, if we must seek

---

[1] "Ὥσπερ σκοπὸς πρὸς τὸ ἀποτυχεῖν οὐ τίθεται· οὕτως οὐδὲ κακοῦ φύσις ἐν κόσμῳ γίνεται.—Epict. Enchir. 34 (Edit. Simpson).

[2] Paley, Moral Phil. ch v. Evil, according to Herbart, lies *in the making* of things; it is a transition state. 'It is with good and evil as with the metals, whether precious or vile. These you do not find in the primitive rocks, nor in the upper clay, but only in *the transition strata*.'—*Ueber das Böse*, 161.

[3] Euripides, apud Plutarch.

their cause, it must not be in God.'[1] What, M. Antoninus? 'The reason which governs the universe has in itself no ground for doing evil; for it has no malice. Nor does it in fact do evil to anything, nor is anything ever injured by it.'[2] What, Seneca? 'Whence comes the good which the gods bestow? From their own essential goodness. It is an utter mistake to suppose that they have ever ill-will towards anything. This were impossible. They can neither suffer nor inflict wrong. They cannot cause evil any more than they can be evil. They chastise us indeed; they coerce; they punish; but these things have no more than the show of evil, not its reality.'[3] What, again, says Coleridge? 'The origin of evil is a question interesting only to the metaphysician. We are content to be certain, first that evil must have had a beginning, since otherwise it must either be God or a co-eternal and co-equal rival of God. Secondly, that it could not originate in God; for if so it would be at once evil and not evil; or God would be at once God (i.e. infinite goodness) and not God.'[4] And to the same effect Naville: 'If it were maintained that evil is the principle of all things, the objection must be answered, Why has good appeared in the world? Our libraries are full of treatises on the origin of evil, but I have never met with one on the origin of good. It appears, then, that reason has always admitted by a sort of instinct the identity of good

---

[1] Plato, Rep. ii. 251 (Bipont): τῶν μὲν ἀγαθῶν οὐδένα ἄλλον αἰτιατέον· τῶν δὲ κακῶν ἄλλ' ἄττα δεῖ ζητεῖν τὰ αἴτια, ἀλλ' οὐ τὸν θεόν.

[2] Anton. vi. 1.

[3] Seneca, *Epistol.* 95: 'Quæ causa est Diis bene faciendi? Natura. Errat si quis putat eos nocere velle; non possunt. Nec accipere injuriam queunt nec facere. Nec dant malum nec habent; ceterum castigant et coercent, et pœnas irrogant, et aliquando *specie mali* puniunt.' See Theile on James i. 13.

[4] Coleridge, Aids, 249.

with the principle of being.'[1] And the writer of 'Henry Holbeach:' 'No human being ever denied the existence of the mountains with their awful shadows. The mountains *are*; and their shadow has lain, lies, must lie on every human soul at times. But the question is, *What are the mountains? What are the mountains for? Or again, Which shall we live by?* The shadows, or *the light that falling on the mountains makes these shadows?*'

And this, which is true of all evil, has its special application to *moral* evil, or sin. Moral evil, too, is secondary, not primary. Our very sense of moral evil testifies to pre-existing moral good as the criterion and the condemnation of moral evil. 'Moral order,' says Mr. Adams, ' is a *positive* idea. Moral disorder is a *negative* idea. Moral order may exist and may be conceived to exist, without moral disorder. Moral disorder cannot be conceived to exist, and cannot exist in fact, except as *an antagonism, or rebellion, against moral order*. To whatever extent moral order exists it proves itself. To whatever extent moral disorder exists *it proves its opposite*. It bears testimony to the existence and reality of the moral order whose authority and laws it contradicts.'[2] And, therefore, all moral disorder we must always ascribe to ourselves and not to God. True, indeed, that the transgressor, in the midst of his transgressions, teased and goaded by the unrest they bring upon him, will strive to shake off the burden of self-blame, and throw it on his making, or his Maker, or his fate. 'It is not I,' cries one, 'who should be blamed for my wrong-doing ! It is Zeus, and Fate, and the avenger that walks in darkness!'[3] 'It was

---

[1] Naville, The Heavenly Father, 338.
[2] Adams, Theories of History, 71.     [3] Iliad, xix. 86.

God,' declares another, 'who drove me to this deed!'[1]
'I blame Apollo,' says Orestes, 'who stirred me up to
such most unholy work!'[2] But everyone who, in the
calm composure of his mind, contemplates sin, at once
throws back from himself all whispers of this kind. 'The
source of evil,' says Plato, 'is in the man who chooses
evil; not in God.'[3] And Seneca, 'No one is made mis-
chievous by fate.' 'You mistake if you suppose that vices
are born with us. They are superinduced. They are
an intrusion into us.'[4] 'Let no man,' says the Apostle
James, 'complain when he is tempted, I am tempted of
God; for even as God can never himself be tempted
with evil, so neither tempteth he anyone to evil. But
every man is tempted when he is drawn away and seduced
(as by the blandishments of a harlot),[5] by *his own lust*;
and this lust, when it has conceived, brings forth sin,
and sin when it comes to maturity brings forth death.
For nothing but *good* gifts, nothing but *perfect* gifts come
down from the Father of lights' (the pure bright Sun of
the world), 'with whom' (unlike the lights in the firmament) 'there is no variableness, neither shadow of turning.'
He never deflects a hairsbreadth from the perfect rectitude
of his essential nature!'[6]

2. But we must now go a step further on this subject,
and observe that evil is not merely only *superinduced* on
good, but is made *subservient* to the bringing out a higher
good. 'The divine art and skill,' says Cudworth, 'most
of all appeareth in bonifying evils, and making them, like

---

[1] Plautus, Aulul.      [2] Euripides, Orest. 285.
[3] Plato, Rep. x.: αἰτία ἑλομένου, θεὸς ἀναίτιος.
[4] Seneca, Œdip. 1019; Epist. 94. 51: 'supervenerunt, ingesta sunt.'
[5] Ἐξελκόμενος καὶ δελεαζόμενος.
[6] James i. 13-17. Add. Appendix, Note XX.

discords in music, to contribute to the harmony of the whole.'¹ Evil is used in the hands of an all-bonifying God as a stage of transition, a moment of development of the very purpose which it seems to hinder and retard; the discipline, education, and perfectionment of humanity. It is overruled to bring men onward from moral infancy to a conscious, well-weighed, and determined moral manhood. It breathes them. It stimulates them. It drills them. It strengthens them. It makes them cautious, humble, dependent, prayerful. It impels them towards a power greater than their own, and so makes them more than conquerors over itself. They become no longer (as Mr. Parker says) 'moral fossils, nor moral animals, but moral *men*. They become conscious co-workers with the Infinite.' For, as Clement of Alexandria argues, 'Though we are formed by nature with an aptitude for virtue, yet we do not *possess* this virtue from our birth, but *attain* it by our own exertions. The salvation which God intends for us must be wrought in us by our own selves. And, therefore, He has made it the essential nature of our soul to set its own self in action. And the aptitude He has implanted in it is, indeed, a bias towards virtue, but is not virtue itself.'² And in like manner Pfleiderer: 'God wills his creature's spontaneous self-development. And He permits evil as a means of this development. It is the condition throughout nature of any being rising in the scale of worth. And this spontaneous self-development becomes stronger and more active in proportion as the creature is destined for a higher and more perfect end. Our destiny is to grow into harmony with God. But harmony can

---

¹ Cudworth, Intel. System, iii. 468.
² Clemens Alex. Stromata, vi. 662.

exist only between distinct and separate wills. God, therefore, has endowed us with a will distinct from his own, that by the spontaneous energising of this will, against antagonisms, and even through many aberrations, we may raise ourselves at last into that *voluntary harmony* with his will, which alone constitutes *free love*, and which alone, therefore, is fitting for sons of God.'[1]

And this which is just in theory we find to be true in fact. We do get good out of evil. Our gracious Educator does evolve for us out of corruption, temptation, and sin, new purpose, new skill, new triumphs. If evil is present only as a thing to be *removed*, permitted only to be cast out, then what is called the development of humanity assumes the freer, nobler form of *deliverance*, redemption, restoration. Our process is not simply that of *advance* towards God, but of *recovery* to God. In every sphere of good we make progress by antagonisms. Our life is polar. From a point of indifference it becomes differentiated into antitheses, and then, in the reconciliation of these antitheses, it finds its synthesis of perfectionment. Truth, for instance, is reached only through successive *deliverances* from error. We become adepts in good *taste* only by successive eliminations of bad taste. And we rise into *virtue* by successive battles with vice. The necessities of life stir us up out of sloth. Its perplexities sharpen in us invention and resource ('curis acuens mortalia corda'). And its sufferings are the medicines which heal the soul ($\pi\alpha\theta\dot{\eta}\mu\alpha\tau\alpha$ $\mu\alpha\theta\dot{\eta}\mu\alpha\tau\alpha$).

> Zeus, who leadeth men in wisdom's way
> Hath fixed fast the law,
> Wisdom by pain to gain;

[1] Pfleiderer, Die Religion, i. 320.

And, slowly dropping on the heart in sleep,
  Sends crime-recording care,
And makes the unworthy yield to wiser thoughts.[1]

3. But then, beyond this overruling of intermediate evil into subserviency to a higher good, we are entitled to assure ourselves that what has been superinduced as a transition state of things is therefore, necessarily, only for a time. It will pass away with the functions which it is made to fulfil. It will at last *be superseded* by the highest good, for the world, and for God's offspring, man. This has been ever the dream and hope of every lover of truth, and beauty, and goodness. It has formed the theme of poets and of sages, and of righteous men in every age. It was held out by Socrates as the stay of his disciples, that ' all who have been purified and perfected shall, when they reach the higher world, take up their abode with the gods.'[2] It gave the sage himself consolation in the presence of his judges : ' To me the way of living above will be admirable, for all there are far more blessed than anyone here below, and through the rest of time shall die no more.'[3] This hope was enshrined in the Sibyline books ; this fired the glowing lines of Virgil ;[4] this has made for itself utterance in noble words in our own time. ' It is a part of the very definition of evil,' says the author of "Henry Holbeach," ' that it is *a thing*

---

[1] Æschyl. Agamemnon, 170.  See Appendix, Note XXI.
[2] Plato, Phædo (Bipont, i. 157): ὁ δὲ κεκαθαρμένος τε καὶ τετελεσμένος, ἐκεῖσε ἀφικόμενος, μετὰ θεῶν οἰκήσει.
[3] Apol. Socrat. (Bipont, i. 94): εὐδαιμονέστεροί εἰσιν οἱ ἐκεῖ τῶν ἐνθάδε, καὶ ἤδη τὸν λοιπὸν χρόνον ἀθάνατοί εἰσιν.
[4] Pollio, 4–6 :
  ' Ultima Cumæi venit jam carminis ætas;
  Magnus ab integro sæclorum nascitur ordo.
  Jam redit et Virgo, redeunt Saturnia regna.'

*to be removed.* There is no other meaning in the word. Unless wrong be evanescent, there is no right to be worshipped. Evil is a thing that is subject, not superior. The case is this. I look around the world and I see certain forms of evil which displease me. If I find suffering in another I wish to remove it. If I find wrong-doing I disapprove, my disapproval sometimes rising to the height of passionate indignation. Now of two things one. The maker of the world and *of my heart* sympathises with me in this desire to remove all evil, or He does not. If the maker of the world does not sympathise with my hatred of evil, and my will to make it cease, I know my part; it is contained in a word—resistance, not religion.' (This is the grand thought which pervades the fable of Prometheus.) 'If the maker of the world hates evil as I do, and has (in kind) the same will to remove it, then I pass at one bound from out of the shadows of doubt. For, bethink you, my will to remove evil is boundless, i.e. there is no evil that I would choose to let stand. I cannot accomplish this will, except in part, simply because I have only an imperfect control of the tendency of things. But the maker of all that is must have a perfect control of that tendency. In other words, it is his will that there should be no evil. This is the absolute to which all schemes must be relative.' And so says Carlyle : ' In the huge mass of evil, as it rolls and swells, there is ever some good working imprisoned, working towards deliverance and triumph.' And so writes Spencer: ' Can things increase in heterogeneity through all future time ? Or do they work towards some ultimate state, admitting no further modification of like kind? In all cases there is *a progress* towards equilibrium. That universal existence of antagonist forces which necessitates the universality of rhythm, and which necessitates the decomposition of every force into divergent forces, at the same time necessitates *the ultimate establishment of a balance.'*—First Princ. 440. And so sings Tennyson :

> All we thought, and loved, and did,
> And hoped, and suffered, is but seed
> Of what in them is flower and fruit.

And again :

> I can but trust that good shall fall
> At last, far-off, at last, to all,
> And every winter change to spring.

And once more :

> That God which ever lives and moves,
>   One God, one law, one element,
>   And one far-off divine intent
> To which the whole creation moves.

Nor is this other than the faith and hope which glowed in the Scripture sages, prophets, and apostles. You find it in Isaiah : 'The former troubles are forgotten; they are hid from mine eyes; for behold I create new heavens and a new earth. Men shall not labour in vain, nor bring forth for trouble. The wolf and the lamb shall feed together; and they shall not hurt nor destroy in all my holy mountain, saith the Lord!' 'In this mountain shall the Lord of Hosts make to all people a feast of fat things; and He will destroy the face of the covering cast over all people and the vail that is spread over all nations. He will swallow up death in victory and the Lord God will wipe away tears from off all faces.'[1] You find it in Hosea : 'I will ransom them from the power of the grave; I will redeem them from death; O death I will be

---

[1] Isaiah xxv. 6; lxv. 17-25.

thy plagues! O grave I will be thy destruction!'[1] You find it in St. Paul: 'The creature shall be delivered from the bondage of corruption into the glorious liberty of the children of God.'[2] 'For he must reign till he hath put all enemies under his feet. The last enemy that shall be destroyed is death. . . . that God may be all in all.' . . . 'For this corruptible must put on incorruption: and this mortal must put on immortality! So, when this corruptible shall have put on incorruption, and this mortal shall have put on immortality, then shall be brought to pass the saying that is written, Death is swallowed up in victory!'[3] 'In the dispensation of the fulness of times he will reduce back into one whole' (ἀνακεφαλαιώσασθαι) 'all things in Christ.'[4] 'It pleased the Father, having made peace by the blood of his cross, to bring back all things into harmony with himself (ἀποκαταλλάξαι τὰ πάντα εἰς αὐτὸν), whether they be things in heaven or things in earth.'[5] That is, all things are perfect in their type. They are exposed to aberration during the process of becoming actualised. But they shall be carried on at last into perfect harmony with their original Idea. The evil therefore which now marks them is subordinate to their ultimate perfectionments.[6] And hence the final triumphant visions of the Apocalyptic Seer: 'I saw a new heaven and a new earth: for the first heaven and the first earth were passed away: and there was no more sea. And I saw the holy city, New

---

[1] Hosea xiii. 14.    [2] Rom. viii. 21.    [3] 1 Cor. xv. 25, 53.
[4] Eph. i. 9.    [5] Col. i. 20.
[6] And thus you have an anticipation of the Coleridgean formula. Prothesis, evolving itself into opposites, thesis, and antithesis, and brought round again in the final synthesis. Nay, and that of Hegel, The process of the universe begins with affirmation, proceeds to denial, and issues in denial of this denial, which is equivalent to re-affirmation.

Jerusalem, coming down from God, out of heaven, prepared as a bride adorned for her husband. And I heard a voice out of heaven saying, Behold the tabernacle of God is with men, and he will dwell with them, and they shall be his people, and God himself shall be with them and be their God. And God shall wipe away all tears from their eyes, and there shall be no more death, neither sorrow nor crying, neither shall there be any more pain; for the former things are passed away; and he that sat upon the throne said, Behold, I make all things new!'[1]

[1] Rev. xxi. 1–5.

## LETTER X.

### *OF GOD'S WORK IN MEN.*

It is curious to observe how different is the aspect that the same thought wears to different minds. The doctrine of evolution, or development—or (as I would prefer to term it) of continuous transformation, by means of concurring agencies, from one stage into another of existence—excites in some alarm and reprobation. They are startled, perhaps, by the adjective usually prefixed to it, '*natural* development,' and '*natural* selection ;' forgetting that whatever is natural is at the same time perforce divine ; that 'nature' is only a term for whatever 'comes out into existence ;' and therefore that as surely as there emerge before our eyes the forms of a progressive nature, so surely must there emerge before our mind the idea of a ground for these forms, in whom *sub*sists the essence of this *ex*istence, and from whom this existence unfolds itself into form, not by any momentary act, but by a continuous activity. Translating therefore that suspicious term 'natural' into its real equivalent, we get the idea of a divine activity begetting, at every stage of existence, from the simplest elements up to the most complex organisms, a new and fuller manifestation of the eternal types which reside in the mind of God. And what is there so sublime, what so consonant with the metaphysic of the Bible as this? To conceive the world as not first *made*, then *marred*, then *mended* by successive efforts springing from successive after-thoughts, but as contained already in idea within the ken of the Eternal Mind; destined by this Mind to an ultimate perfectionment to which we can imagine no bounds; and actuated by this Mind without intermission, through an ascending series of transformations which emerge and expand in spiral evolution, towards this Perfectionment—fills me with adoration, trust, hope. For I see in it what St. James meant when he said, 'Known unto God are all his works from the beginning of the world!' I see in it, extended to all occurrences, what the Lord, by his prophet Isaiah, declares concerning political events: 'I am God, and there is none else! I am God, and there is none like me! Declaring the end from the beginning, and from ancient times the things that are not yet done; saying, My counsel shall stand, and I will do all my pleasure.' And so I end with the rapturous exclamation of St. Paul, 'O the depth of the riches' (the inexhaustible fulness of resource) 'both of the wisdom and knowledge of God! For of him, and through him, and to him, are all things; to whom be glory for ever! Amen!'[1]

But this doctrine of divine development, transferred from the universe at large to the dealings of God with *men* in particular, brings before us the Father of our spirits, designing the ultimate assimilation of his children into perfect harmony with the idea of humanity in which He formed us; ordering towards this assimilation every stage of our intermediate history, both as individuals and as a race of beings; overruling for this end whatever seem to our bewildered vision, hindrances, antagonisms, aber-

---

[1] See Appendix, Note XXI.

rations; and organising as factors to work out its ultimate accomplishment all the forces of individual, family, tribal, national, and world-wide life. God made us to become like Himself. God is bringing us step by step towards actual likeness with Himself. God is ordering for this end all intermediate circumstances and events. God is furthering this end even by those things which seem most to thwart it. And God communicates Himself directly to human minds to enlighten and enable them as co-operant towards this end.

For God's perpetual relation to the world is threefold. Not its producer only is He, but also its preserver, and its perfecter. He works, as Augustin says, 'Creans, et nutriens, et perficiens.'[1] He is incessantly efficient in the creation, the conservation, and the consummation of all things. And while in relation to the first result He is transcendent, and to the second immanent,[2] He is, in relation to the last, *concurrent*; concurrent with the wills which he Himself has called into activity and partial independence, in order to *rule* them in accordance with his law, to *recover* them from their departures from this law, and to *raise* them into ultimate harmony with this law. To this end it is that He has made us capable of direct communication from Himself. To this end, that He has endowed us with the power of responding to such communication, co-operating with such communication, reflecting and diffusing such communication over congenial minds. And to this end, that He does in fact, through the course of ages, awake men to their need of Himself, raise up gifted spirits filled with his own light and life to respond to this need, and through the instru-

---

[1] August. Conf. i. 4.     [2] See Appendix, Note XXII.

mentality of these his human agents (or intermediators) call into being an ascending series of communities in which the divine idea becomes realised, both intensively and extensively, with ever-increasing fulness.

1. The first step which the Father of spirits takes to bring his children towards ultimate likeness with Himself (that is, towards the realisation of the idea in which He created us), is the *awaking men to their need of Himself.*

'In the image of God made he man.' God is the ideal after which humanity is modelled. We are made like Him in capacity that we may become like Him in character. And as we are thus formed for God, to become conformed to God, no one can ever feel at rest till he finds himself thus conformed, or in the way of becoming conformed, to God.[1] But of this, all are at first ignorant. Of this, the mass of men have neither notion nor desire. And therefore the very first step to raise us towards our proper stature as men, is the awakening in us this notion, the stirring in us this desire. Without conformity to God we have no rest, because we have not found our proper centre. And only in proportion as the idea of such conformity dawns upon us can we begin to gravitate towards this our proper centre. The wandering soul searches through the universe for the object on which its inborn desire is fixed, and never can be satisfied till this object is revealed to it. 'God,' says the Apostle Paul, 'hath made of one blood all nations of

---

[1] Milton's two epic poems are Paradise Lost and Paradise Regained. But the true epic of humanity, the epic which is in a constant course of evolution from the beginning until the end of time, the epic which is daily poured forth from the heart of the whole human race, sometimes in rejoicing pæans, but oftener amid woeful lamentations, tears, and disappointed hopes —what is it but Paradise Sought for?—Ferrier, *Lect.* i. 273.

men, that they should seek the Lord, if haply they might *feel after him*;'—grope for Him, as a blind man touches one thing after another in his search for what he wants. For 'Thou hast made us,' says Augustin, 'for Thyself, and never, therefore, is our heart at rest till it has found repose in Thee.'[1] 'God,' says Archbishop Leighton, 'hath suited every creature He hath made with a convenient' (appropriate) 'good to which it tends, and in the obtainment of which it rests and is satisfied. Natural bodies have all their own natural place, whither, if not hindered, they move incessantly till they be in it; and they declare by resting in it that they are where they would be. Sensitive creatures are carried to seek a sensitive good, as agreeable to their rank in being, and attaining that, aim no further. But in this is the excellency of man, that he is made capable of communion with his Maker, and because capable of it, unsatisfied without it. The soul, being cut out (so to speak) to that largeness, cannot be filled with less; though we are fallen from our right to that good, yet not from a capacity of it, no, nor from a necessity of it for the answering and filling of this capacity. For the heart, even in its wandering, retains that natural relation to God as its centre, that it hath no rest elsewhere, nor can by any means find it. It is made for Him, and is therefore still restless till it meet with Him. The soul, the immortal soul, descended from heaven, must either be more happy or remain miserable. The highest, the uncreated Spirit, is the proper good; the Father of spirits is that pure and full good which raises the soul above itself; whereas all

---

[1] 'Fecisti nos ad te, et inquietum est cor nostrum donec requiescat in te.'—Aug. *Conf.* i. 1.

other things draw it down below itself. So, then, it is never well with the soul but when it is near to God, yea, in union with Him, married to Him. Mismatching itself elsewhere it hath never anything but shame and sorrow.'[1] And the same thought is embalmed in poetry by Isaac Williams:—

> O beautiful and strange epitome
> Of this our life, while through the vale we trace
> Homeless Ulysses on the land and sea!
> From childhood to old age it is the face
> Of heaven-lost yearning man; from place to place
> Whether he wander forth abroad, or knows
> No change but of home-nature and of grace,
> Still is he as one seeking for repose—
> A man of many thoughts, a man of many woes![2]

2. But not only does God, in his education of the world, awake men to feel their need of Himself; He provides, moreover, for the supply of this need by *raising up gifted spirits* to respond to it.

For it is by such, endowed with light and life beyond their contemporaries, that the onward movement of the world—all that constitutes its real *history*—takes place. 'Great men,' says Carlyle, 'are the inspired (speaking and acting) texts of that divine book of Revelations whereof a chapter is completed from epoch to epoch, and by some named *History*.'[3] And so I. H. Fichte: 'Every step in advance in history, every mental act which introduces into its chain of occurrences something absolutely *new*, results entirely from the inflowing of God into man. God alone makes *history*, by sending down

---

[1] Leighton; as quoted by Coleridge, Aids, 121.
[2] Williams, Christian Scholar.   [3] Sartor Res, 108.

from Himself each new element that carries it on. But then He does this only by the agency of men. All truly historical events are brought about by God's raising up gifted men, or "geniuses,"[1] and breathing into them his own light and life. Seized by this divine influence, and submitting themselves to it, such men are conscious that the works they do, though truly their own, have their source above themselves, and spring not from their own origination, but are literally infused into them.'[2] And similarly Mr. Martineau: 'In societies as in individuals the order of reformation will be found to be from the centre to the circumference; from a solitary point, deep-buried and unnoticed, first to the circumjacent region and then over the whole surface; from the native force and inspired insight of some individual mind that kindles first itself and then, by its irresistible intensity, a wider and wider sphere of souls; spirit being born of spirit, life of life, thought of thought. Of all the more remarkable social revolutions, the seminal principle, the primitive type, may be traced to some one man whose spiritual greatness had force enough to convert generations, and constitute an era in the world's life; who preached with power some mighty repentance or transition of sentiment within the hearts of men, and thus rendered more and more near at hand that "kingdom of heaven" for which all men sigh and good men toil.'[3]

And thus such men contribute to fill the generations after them with more of light and life than even they

---

[1] Comp. Milner, *Ch. Hist.* 500: 'Wiclif might have stood among the foremost of those *geniuses*, who have been raised up by Providence to instruct and reform the human race.'
[2] I. H. Fichte, Spec. Theol. 651.
[3] Endeavours after the Christian Life, i. 140.

themselves possessed. As Roger Bacon foretold: 'The wise men of the present day are ignorant of many things which hereafter shall be known to the very mob of students.' And yet in their place and for their time they are the divinely-kindled lights of the world. Whence in China such sages are regarded as sent 'by heaven,' and Confucius is declared to have been used 'by heaven' as 'the alarum of the world.' And your classical recollections will tell you how universally in all ages and among all nations this conviction of all wisdom, and skill, and virtue being infused into their possessors from above has prevailed. Artists and artificers, orators, poets, philosophers, statesmen, prophets, are all regarded as distinguished from the herd of men by *divine* endowments. As one says of Scopas the sculptor: 'Impelled by a certain inspiration, he threw himself with divine fervour on the making of his statues.'[1] And Plato declares of philosophers: 'They would not venture to teach others were they not excited to this by God Himself.'[2] And Arrian says of Alexander: 'I hold that such a man, who was like no ordinary mortal, was not born into this world without some special providence.' And Sir Walter Raleigh writes of all great men: 'Such spirits have been stirred in sundry ages of the world and in divers parts thereof, to erect and cast down again, to establish and to destroy; and to bring all things, persons and states to the same certain ends, which the infinite *spirit of the* **Universal**, moving and governing all things, hath ordained.' And Cicero, of poets: 'They manifest themselves as inspired by a certain divine influence;' and of all distinguished men in every sphere: 'Never was there a man of mark

---

[1] See Sonntag, De Inspirat. 6.   [2] Apol. i. 69.

without some kind of divine inbreathing in his soul.'[1] For what Mr. Ferrier says of poetry is true of all invention and all genius : 'Poetry represents the *derivative and unconscious*, just as Philosophy represents the free and conscious elements of humanity ; and is itself, according to every notion of it from the earliest times down to the present, an *inspired* or fatalistic development. This is evident from the fact that all great powers have ever referred away their power from themselves to " the God," " the Goddess," " the Muse," or some similar source of inspiration, always foreign to themselves. Whence the saying, " Poeta nascitur, non fit." And Virgil says, " Est Deus in nobis, agitante calescimus illo." '[2]

Nor less do we find the Sacred writings ascribing all human knowledge to God. Even of ordinary skill in *husbandry* they say: 'Doth the plowman plow all day to sow? doth he open and break the clods of his ground ? doth he cast abroad the fitches, and scatter the cummin and cast in the principal wheat, and the appointed barley and the rye in their place ? It is his God that doth instruct him to discretion and doth teach him. This also cometh forth from the Lord of Hosts, which is wonderful in counsel and excellent in working.'[3] And therefore, still more, whatever of excellence in *art or science or character* attracts the eyes of men, this especially is ascribed to the inworking of the Spirit of God. Thus, of Bezaleel the *artificer*, God says, 'I have filled him with the spirit of God, in wisdom and in understanding, and in knowledge to devise cunning works, to work in gold and in silver and in brass, and in cutting of stones and in carving of timber, and in all

---

[1] De Nat. Deor. ii. 66.  [2] Ferrier's Lectures, ii. 151.
[3] Isai. xxviii. 24-29.

manner of workmanship. And in the hearts of all that are wise-hearted I have put wisdom that they may make all that I have commanded thee.'[1] Of Gideon and Jephthah and Samson, and other *heroes* of Jewish history, it is said, 'The Spirit of the Lord came upon them.' Of Othniel and David, as *rulers* of men, 'The Spirit of the Lord came upon them for the governing of Israel.' Of *wise men* we are told, ' Blessed be the name of God for ever and ever, for wisdom and might are his; he giveth *wisdom unto the wise* and knowledge to them that know understanding; he revealeth the deep and secret things.'[2] And more emphatically still, of that wisdom which is conversant about *divine* things, we read of Balaam, 'The Spirit of God came upon him;'[3] of Saul, 'The Spirit of the Lord shall come upon thee, and thou shalt prophecy' (or, speak as divinely moved) 'and shalt be turned into another man.'[4] And of *all* the prophets or teachers of God's truth, 'Prophecy came not in old time by the will of man, but holy men of God spake as they were moved by the Holy Ghost.'[5] And as to those who, in their *whole character*, were beyond others, epoch-makers in history, their piety and their power are always ascribed to the indwelling in them of God. Such was Enoch, and such Noah, ' who walked with God.'[6] Such Abraham, who is called 'The friend of God.'[7] Such Moses, to whom the Lord said, 'Go, and I will be with thy mouth and teach thee what thou shalt say,'[8] and who was with the Lord in the holy mount.[9] Such was David, 'the man after God's own heart,' as

[1] Exod. xxxi. 3–6.   [2] Daniel ii. 22.   [3] Numb. xxiv. 2.
[4] 1 Sam. x. 6.   [5] 2 Pet. i. 21.   [6] Gen. v. 22; vi. 9.
[7] James ii. 23; 2 Chron. xx. 7.   [8] Exod. iv. 12.
[9] Ibid. xxiv. 15.

ruler of his people.'¹  Such John the Baptist, to whom 'the word of God came.'²  Such the Apostles, and Paul, and the Christian prophets, who were 'filled with the Holy Ghost.'³

Yet beyond all these, of old times and of new, you see One towering in supereminent Majesty, the special representative and agent of God, JESUS; *the* Prophet, the Lawgiver, the King; in whom God incessantly dwelt and worked. Of Him it is declared that 'God gave not the Spirit by measure to him'⁴ (in limited degree, and temporary illapses, as He did to other gifted men); for 'the WORD of God himself in him became flesh and dwelt among us;'⁵ and the words therefore which He spoke, and the works which He wrought, these He spoke and wrought, not of Himself, but by the Father which was in Him.⁶ And hence, to see this Son of God was to see the Father. JESUS, accordingly, was the One Great Epoch-maker in the history of mankind. In Him converged all the previous lines of human development. From Him have radiated all its subsequent progressions. 'God who at sundry times and in divers manners had spoken to the fathers by the prophets, in the last days spoke to us by his *Son*.'⁷ Of this *Son* He proclaimed, 'The heavens shall perish, but thou remainest; and they all shall wax old as doth a garment; and as a vesture shalt thou fold them up, and they shall be changed; but thou art the same and thy years shall not fail.'⁸ And by this *Son* He changed, and is continuously changing, the whole face of the world; moulding it as a new creation, till it become

[1] 1 Sam., xiii. 14.  [2] Luke iii. 2.  [3] Acts iv. 31.
[4] John iii. 34.  [5] Ibid. i. 14.  [6] Ibid. xiv. 10.
[7] Heb. i. 1, 2.  [8] Ibid. i. 11, 12.

at last 'a new heaven and a new earth, wherein dwelleth righteousness.'

But now, from this view, which all Scripture gives us, of the way in which God teaches man, you will see how mistaken is the ordinary distinction (or disruption, rather) between reason and revelation. Reason is (in kind, though not in degree) as much the gift of God as revelation. Revelation is no more essentially from God's inspiration than reason. 'The Spirit of man, which searcheth all the inward parts, is the *candle of the Lord.*'[1] It is the light by which we are enabled to discern, compare, co-ordinate, all our thoughts. And revelation is but the breathing on this light a diviner air, to brighten up in us perceptions, previsions, presages, presentiments, beyond our ordinary ken. At all times, those in whom this light burns brightly, see more and further than their fellow-men. The poet is also a *prophet* (vates). Compare Acts xvii. 28, 'As certain also of your own *poets* have said,' with Titus i. 12, 'One of themselves, a *prophet* of their own, hath said.' And even of a prophet not of the favoured race, it is declared '*God came* unto Balaam.'[2] Whence he says, himself, 'I cannot go beyond the *word of the Lord.*'[3] In like manner also the *philosopher*, as a lover of truth, feels that he is inspired by the God of truth, and is bound to be to Him who enlightens him a faithful spokesman and servant. 'I am moved,' said Socrates, 'by a certain divine and spiritual influence.' And again: 'Be well assured that this *the Deity* commands.' Whence his bold

---

[1] Prov. xx. 27, where the Hebrew word means, to search for, to search out ( = inter-lego), to select, discriminate. See Ps. lxxvii. 6.
[2] Numb. xxii. 9.   [3] Ibid. 18.

determination, so similar to that of Christ's Apostles, [1] 'I shall obey God rather than you.' [2]

There is, therefore, no distinction of *kind* between reason and revelation. It is only of degree ; degree of purity, extent, conviction ; degree of the lesser or greater inflowing of God into the mind. Whence St. Paul calls faith, 'a *rational conviction* of things not seen.' [3] And the conclusions of reason have always been felt to accord with the mind of God Himself ('God geometrises,' said Plato) ; and the intuitions awakened by revelation are but more *immediate and rapid* convictions, of greater clearness, reach, and certainty. Reason *divines* what revelation *declares*. You find a noble assertion of this view in Lactantius : ' If you will constantly fix your gaze towards heaven, and keep before you the sun as the guide of your course, your feet will of themselves step onward in the right path ; and that celestial light, which to the healthy mind is brighter far than the sun, will so direct you as to bring you with no mistake to the highest wisdom and virtue. For this end, therefore, we must take the *law of God* for our guide ; that sacred heavenly law concerning which Marcus Tullius, in words almost divine, declares : "The true law for us is right reason in harmony with nature, diffused through all things, never changing, ever living, which summons us to duty by its prescriptions, and warns us off from wrong by its prohibitions ; which is not one code at Rome, another at Athens, one system to-day another to-morrow, but which to all nations in all ages remains the same, eternal and immutable ; the common lord and emperor and god of all men. For God it is who is the author of this law,

---

[1] Acts iv. 19.   [2] Plato, Apol. (i. 69, Bipont).
[3] Heb. xi. 1, ἐλεγχος.

who enacts it, who maintains it; and whosoever refuses to obey it flies from his own self, spurns from him the very nature of man, and for this reason, by this very act, must bring upon himself the highest penalties, even if he escape what are usually styled punishments."' 'And, now then,' continues Lactantius, 'who is there acquainted with the mystery of God, who can more clearly set forth the law of God than this man, who was far removed from revealed truth? I, for my part, must look on men who thus unwittingly utter truth as diviners moved by the Spirit. And if, in addition to this perception of the force and authority of sacred law, he had known how to tell us in what precepts this law consists, he would have been not merely a philosopher but a prophet of God.'[1] And a similar conviction of this presence of the Spirit of truth among all people, in essence though not in degree and detail, is avowed by St. Augustin when he says: 'What is now called the Christian religion has existed among the ancients, and was not altogether absent even from the beginning of the human race up to the coming of Christ in the flesh; though from this last epoch, that true religion which existed already began to be termed specifically the Christian religion.'[2]

What then are the *marks* of this divine inbreathing, among all persons and in all times? This question may be answered in the words of I. H. Fichte: 'The form in which the Divine Spirit accomplishes every important change in the world is that of gifted men, by means of whom he diffuses his own ideas, and works them out. And thus the gifted man becomes the mediator of the Divine Spirit, in behalf of those who are not seized at

---

[1] Lactantius, Instit. vi. 8.   [2] As quoted by Max Müller, Chips, i. xi.

first hand by these ideas. He knows himself to be this by two signs: the one, his consciousness of self-sacrificing enthusiasm; the other, his consciousness of originative power. The last is no proof of divine inspiration separate from the first; and the first is equally insufficient without the last. The test lies in the co-presence of these two factors. The real man of God is conscious of being seized on by a might superior to his own, to whose behests he consecrates himself; and thenceforward he speaks and acts, not in his own name for his own interests, but in the name of this higher power of which he has become the instrument.'[1] And this view may be illustrated by the Brahminical saying: 'The Veda is "sruti" (hearing), but the other books are only "souriti" (recollection);' and by the devout exclamation of Haydn, who hearing, in his old age, his 'Let there be light!' raised his hands to heaven, weeping, and cried, 'Not from me, but from above it all has come!'

And this view is authorised by the Sacred Writings. As when the Prophet Jeremiah exclaims, 'O Lord thou hast deceived me, and I was deceived' (hast persuaded me, overcome my reluctance to speak). 'Thou art stronger than I, and hast prevailed; thy word was in my heart as a burning fire shut up in my bones, and I was weary with forbearing' (with endeavouring to hold it in), 'and I could not stay.'[2] And when our Lord says,

[1] Spec. Theol. 655.
[2] Jer. xx. 7–9. And it is such a *seizure* of the interpreter of divine oracles overbearing the individual will, which is illustrated by those strong lines of Virgil, Æn. vi. 77, 'At Phœbi nondum patiens:'—

    Struggling in vain, impatient of her load,
    And labouring underneath the ponderous god;
    The more she strove to shake him from her breast,
    With more and far superior force he prest;
    Commands his entrance, and without control,
    Usurps her organs, and inspires her soul.—*Dryden*, 120–4.

'The Son can do nothing of himself' (on his own individual impulse), 'but only what he seeth the Father do' (what is set before his mind by God).[1] 'The words that I speak to you I speak not of myself' (of my own motion merely),[2] 'but the Father that dwelleth in me, he doeth the works' (whether of word or deed) 'which I work.'[3] And again, 'My doctrine is not mine' (the product of my own mind, 'quod ex meo ingenio cogitavi'), 'but his that sent me.'[5]

And if now you proceed to enquire after the *means* by which God thus constitutes gifted spirits his interpreters and agents, to transmit to less favoured minds his word and will, you will find that He qualifies them for their sacred work, by the breathing into them divine *light* and *life*.

And first, divine *light*. Very slight observation will show you that our mental illumination takes place in a twofold way : (1) the ordinary one, in which new light is *acquired* by gradual increments, through the suggestions of men and things, and our own patient thought—hence the knowledge we thus obtain is called 'learning ;' and (2) an extraordinary one, in which new light is *received*, in happy moments, without any effort on our part, through the sudden opening of the mind's eye to a brightness from above. And this is therefore called 'intuition,' 'insight ;' and announces itself by such phrases as, 'I have found it!' 'I see!' 'It strikes me!' 'It flashed upon me!' 'It was borne in upon my mind!'

Now this last sort of illumination is ascribed in Scripture to the Divine Spirit. As in Job, where Elihu pleads in

---

[1] John v. 19.  
[2] 'Non ex meo ingenio.'—*Tittmann*.  
[3] John xiv. 10.  
[4] Ibid. vii. 16.

excuse for his presumption in venturing to teach his
'learned' friends: 'I felt at first that days should speak
and multitude of years should teach wisdom, but I am
conscious that there is a Spirit in man, and that the inspiration of the Almighty giveth understanding; that
great men are not always wise, neither do the aged necessarily understand judgment' (it is not learning, experience, nor reflection alone which brings truth before us);
'but I am full of matter; the spirit within me constraineth
me; behold, my belly is as wine which hath no vent; it
is ready to burst, like new wineskins; I must speak, that
I may get breath, I will open my mouth and answer.'[1]
And in the same sense our Lord congratulates Peter as
enlightened to discern important truth by a *direct ray
from above*: 'Blessed art thou Simon Barjona, for flesh
and blood hath not revealed this to you' (mere human
insight has not conveyed to you this conviction), 'but my
Father which is in heaven!'[2] And so St. Paul says of his
recognition of Jesus as the Christ, 'I neither *received* it'
(by tradition), 'nor was I *taught* it' (by apostolic instruction), 'but it came to me by the revelation of Jesus
Christ'—by a light flashed from the Lord himself.[3] And
similarly the same Apostle declares concerning what constituted peculiarly 'his gospel' (the proclamation, namely,
of unlimited salvation): 'This mystery' (or hitherto un-
suspected truth) 'was not in other ages made known to
the sons of men as it is now revealed' (unveiled) 'to the
holy apostles and prophets' (of the Christian faith) 'by
the Spirit;'[4] and again, 'Eye hath not seen, nor ear heard,
neither have entered into the heart of man' (no one hath

---

[1] Job xxxii. 8–20.  [2] Matt. xvi. 17.
[3] Gal. i. 12.  [4] Eph. iii. 5.

gathered by ordinary thought), 'the things which God destined for the sight of them that love him, and hath now unveiled to us by his Spirit. For the Spirit pryeth into all things, even the deepest thoughts of God; and by the illumination of this Spirit we know the things that are so freely bestowed on us by God.'[1]

And of such illumination, by rays direct from heaven, the Lord Jesus Christ was in full possession, both through his essential union with the Father, and his habitual communion with his Spirit. For as to his essential union with the fountain of all light St. John declares, 'No one else hath seen God' (beheld the mind of God) 'at any time, but the only begotten Son' (because thus peculiarly his Son), 'being in the bosom of his father' (the intimate of his secrets),[2] 'he hath made clear to us his mind.'[3] And so again, 'No one hath seen the Father save he which is of God, he hath seen the Father' (has intimately known his mind and will).[4] Whence Jesus says again, 'I speak that which' (not simply I learn from others, or think out for myself, but) 'I have seen with my Father.'[5] And as the illumination of Jesus is ascribed to his essential *union* with the Father, so also is it to his habitual *communion* with the Spirit of this Father, while on earth. Thus John the Baptist says of him, 'He who receives the testimony of this man come from above, sets to his seal that *God*, from whom he comes, is true' (reposes his confidence in God Himself), 'for the man whom God hath sent speaketh the words of *God*' (it is the same as God

---

[1] 1 Cor. ii. 9–12.   [2] Comp. John xiii. 23, 24.   [3] John i. 18.
[4] John vi. 46, where 'he which is of God' is παρὰ τοῦ Θεοῦ, and παρὰ means 'necessarius et familiaris' (Fritzsche on Mark iii. 21), and is equivalent to πρὸς τὸν Θεόν, John i. 1, and εἰς τὸν κόλπον τοῦ πατρός, John i. 18.
[5] John viii. 38.

Himself speaking by Him), 'because God giveth not his spirit by measure to him'—does not infuse it partially and only for a time, as He does to other interpreters of his mind and will.[1] And hence Jesus affirms of Himself that He, in contradistinction from all other 'lights' or reflectors of the divine mind (such as John the Baptist, for instance, who was a burning and a shining light [2]), is '*the* light,' the one perfect reflector of God's light. 'I,' He says, ' am The Light of the world; he that followeth me shall not walk in darkness, but shall have the light which guides to life;'[3] by which He means what He declares in other words, 'He that seeth me hath seen the Father, for the words that I speak to you I speak not of myself' (as the conclusions of my own sagacity), 'but the Father that dwelleth in me, he doeth' (originateth) ' all my works.'[4] Whence further, Jesus represents Himself as 'The way, the truth, and the life;' through whom alone anyone can be guided to the Father;[5] the only complete revealer of the Father's mind and will; for 'as no one knoweth the Son but the Father, so knoweth no one the Father but the Son, and he to whom the Son unveils him.'[6] From which it follows that life eternal depends upon our knowing this Father in the light in which the Son reveals Him to us. 'This is life eternal, to know thee, the only true God, through the teaching of him whom thou hast sent.'[7]

Here, then, we reach the doctrine of *revelation*, as distinguished from reason in its ordinary processes of inference, surmise, conjecture. *Revelation*, which is the

---

[1] John iii. 33-35.    [2] Ibid. v. 5.    [3] Ibid. viii. 12.
[4] Ibid. xiv. 9.    [5] Ibid. xiv. 6.    [6] Matt. xi. 27.
[7] John xvii. 3.

flashing on the eyes of specially gifted men a light from heaven, above the brightness of the sun at mid-day; the unveiling of the thoughts of God to those who are called emphatically his 'elect,' his 'beloved,' his 'servants the prophets;' and this unveiling made, in its purest splendour, to that Servant whom he specially upheld, that Elect in whom his soul delighted,—his only beloved Son.

And such revelation I deem to be a *fact*. That men of God, in every age, have been raised up by divine providence; filled with divine light; actuated by the Divine Spirit; and thus made manifestors, in a special manner, of the divine mind and will; and that He whom Christians reverence as the highest term in this godlike series of inspired teachers, is, in a still *more* special manner, 'The WORD,' or utterance (i.e. outerance) of this mind and will; seem to me *facts*, as well attested as the facts of mind, and the facts of nature on which we have hitherto dwelt. They are facts of *history*, in its broadest sense, the history of the gradual development, under divine guidance, of the race of men.

And therefore, from the Ideas thus revealed, I think we are entitled to form for ourselves a connected view of God's dealings with men, through all the successive moments of that process of development by which He is educating them up to their proper stature. Such facts of history, with the conclusions from them, may indeed be called in question; even as some call in question the facts of mind, as psychological delusions, and the facts of design in nature, as projected into it from our own imagination. But anyone who may be perplexed by the difficulties which beset some of these facts, I would respectfully remind that, in whatever way to be interpreted, they still form part and parcel of the whole series of events which constitute the general history of mankind, and are constituent elements in that ' purpose widening by the process of the suns,' which we find to be still at work. Even, therefore, if you should fail to follow me in all the beliefs which I base on these historical events, you will see that I am pursuing the same *method* which we have hitherto adopted. I use these documents of history only as I have used the documents in mind and in nature; as points of departure and bases of belief; according to the light which is given me. And I offer the conclusions which I draw from them simply as *aids* to your own investigation and your own judgment. Here also, as before, we can only be ' helpers of each other's faith.' Here also, as before, I can only wait on the divine Teacher who is educating us all, assured that ' if in anything you be otherwise minded, He will reveal even this to you;' will ' make your faith grow exceedingly;' and will shed on both of us that ' shining light which shineth more and more unto the perfect day.'

But when I hold, as matter of *historical fact*, that God has in all ages raised up revealers of his mind and will, ' seers' of the divine ideas, and interpreters of these ideas to their less favoured brethren, I do not forget that such men can be no more than *interpreters*—translators, i.e. into the language of ordinary thought, as it exists at each successive stage of development, of the eternal truths which have been flashed upon themselves. And therefore, these truths, so coming to us, through the medium of human interpreters, must come reduced into the form and clothed with the imagery, and conditioned by the prevalent conceptions of the age and people to which they are sent.

The prophet must express the *notions*, as much as he must speak the language of those to whom he prophesies. Nay, he must himself conceive the truths revealed to him, in forms and images suited to that stage of development to which his own mind is limited by his time and country. And as he conceives them, so he must give them utterance. For of prophecy it is equally true as of poetry,

> The Poet's eye in a fine frenzy rolling,
> Doth glance from heaven to earth, from earth to heaven;
> And as imagination bodies forth
> The forms of things unknown, the poet's pen
> Turns them to shapes, and gives to airy nothing
> A local habitation and a name!

And hence it follows that while the divine *ideas*, or 'forms of things,' are flashed on the prophet's eye direct from God, the 'shapes' in which he presents these ideas to others must always be affected by the limitation belonging to all conceptions; by their inadequacy to the full expression of the ideas to which they give shape; and by their inseparable relation to the stage of progress of the age, the nation, the individual seer. Directly the recipients of divine light begin to reflect its rays on those around them, these rays *must* be coloured and refracted by the atmosphere of the prophet's mind through which they pass, and of the people's mind into which they enter. The pure ideas, translated into conceptions for the seer's own mind, and into images for the minds of his hearers, *must* assume the imperfect shapes of all merely human (ordinary, concrete) thought and speech.[1]

---

[1] See 2 Cor. xii. 4: 'In paradise I heard unspeakable words, which it is not possible to convey to others' ('quibus enarrandis homo non par est' (Emmerling). (For οὐκ ἐξὸν=οὐ δυνατόν ἐστι.—Phavorinus.)

These 'shapes,' therefore, are not of the *essence* of the revelation, but are only its *accidents*. They give not absolute truth but only approximations to it, symbols of it; and such approximations and symbols as are suited to (and conditioned by) the age, the country, the way of thinking of the speaker or writer. Whence such approximations and symbols require to be estimated with relation to these factors, and to be converted into (equally conventional) equivalents for other ages, countries, stages of mental progress. It is the old story, with the old constantly-recurring difficulty, of an original seer (vates, poet) shaping with conscious insufficiency his ideas; and of these shapings becoming necessarily shaped afresh, in translations for other peoples in other ages of the world. You never have the pure essence. You have only embodiments of it in accessible *media*. All this has been already maintained by John Smith: 'In this state we are not able to behold truth in its own native beauty and lustre; but while we are vailed with mortality truth must vail itself too, that it may the more freely converse with us. God, to accommodate his truth to our weak capacities does, as it were, *embody* it in earthly expressions—according to that ancient maxim of the Cabbalists: "The divine light never descends to our level but in a suitable vail." Agreeable to which is that of Dionysius the Areopagite, often quoted by the schoolmen: "It is impossible for the divine light to shed itself on human minds but through the medium of various sacred vails."'[1] This again is laid down by Archbishop Leighton: 'We, comparing great things with small, can do

---

[1] Select Discourses, 378.

no more than faintly shadow forth those high invisible ideas in conceptions earthly and familiar to us ; nay, the sacred Scriptures themselves come down in these matters to our level ; even as the Hebrew writers say, "the law of God speaks the dialect of the sons of men."[1] And this is just the truth so strikingly symbolised in Holy Writ when it tells us that the pure light of the divine glory was unbearable by the people, and that Moses was obliged to vail his face when he spoke to them, because 'they were afraid to come nigh unto him.'[2]

But God's way of responding to the spiritual needs which He awakens in mankind, in order to their being brought to Himself, is not merely by flashing light into the minds of gifted men that they may reflect this light on their less endowed brethren ; but also by the stirring in these favoured persons a divine *life*, which shall similarly diffuse itself through them into other hearts. God works in man not only by *illumination* but by *inspiration* : not simply by an unveiling to us of new thoughts—the thoughts of God ; but by an infusion into us of new life—the life of God in the soul.

That such an infusion of divine life from God into men is possible follows from the inseparable relation of the spirit of man to the Spirit of God. God is a Spirit from whom have sprung, and by whom are sustained in existence, all the spirits of the universe. He is emphatically the 'Father of spirits.'[3] And 'in Him

---

[1] Leighton, *Prælectiones*, i. 6: 'Nos, parvis magna componentes res illas altas et invisibiles, terrenis et notis adumbramus tantum; imò et sacræ scripturæ in hoc nobis συγκαταβαίνουσι, quemadmodum Hebræi dicunt, *Lex Dei loquitur linguam filiorum hominum*. Cœlestem illam vitam sub hereditatis et divitiarum sub regni et coronæ nominibus repræsentant.'

[2] Exod. xxxiv. 29-35. Add Appendix, Note XXIII.   [3] Heb. xii. 9.

we live, and move, and have our being,' so that He is 'not far from any one of us.'[1] And with such intimate correlation there may, and must, be corresponding communication. And by this communication the Divine Spirit quickens the spirit of men, and fills them with his life. This is a doctrine maintained by the highest philosophers and divines, and confirmed by the testimony of Holy Writ.

You will find this thoroughly established, for instance, by I. H. Fichte: 'The universal law of being is, that the lower in the scale becomes possessed and mastered by the higher, so as to be thereby raised above itself, and made partaker of this higher.' 'And seeing that the spirit of a man can and does transfuse itself into the spirits of his brethren, we must grant the same inworking, and that more fully and effectually, to occur between the Divine Spirit and the souls which partake his likeness. For just as the so-called "natural laws" are nothing in themselves, cannot work *of* themselves, but are only the resultant of a divine *will* operant on the sphere of unconscious existence (a will, and not an impulse merely, for the force which is operant in this sphere is manifestly an *intelligent* force), just so is it with the "psychological laws" of the human mind. They have a providential character. It is through the working in us of a will for right, breathed into us by God, that we reach, through all the windings of delusion and self-deception, gradually but certainly, in this life or the next, to that full perfectionment of our nature, the sense of which constitutes our blessedness. And in this law of human development, just as much as in that of natural evolution, the divine

[1] Acts xvii. 28.

will is ever present and operative. The Father is incessantly operant in his creation (John v. 17). The very phrases in constant use among us imply all this. When we hear of reason as "the divine in man," of the conscience as "the voice of God," of goodness as attainable only through "a higher power than our own;" all this can possess no truth or meaning unless we admit a real, living correlation of the Divine Spirit with the human, an inworking of this Divine Spirit in this human, an "inspiration" or breathing into us a divine life. And to be made the organ of such inspiration, to experience with constantly increasing intimacy such life, this constitutes the highest perfectionment of the human soul.'[1] And again, 'As all the old poets, speaking from the testimony of their own experience, confess, the spirit of man is akin to God, and so and therefore open to the influences of the Spirit of God. Our spirit manifests itself as something supersensuous and eternal in the very midst of the sensuous and the transient in which it is plunged. It does so negatively, by its dissatisfaction with everything of mere time and sense, and positively by its ever soaring upwards beyond all its actual attainments, into a higher region. But just because of this affinity of our spirit with a Spirit higher than our own, we are capacitated for direct communications from this Spirit, and for the being filled and actuated by Him as instruments of his communication to other minds. Every development of the human consciousness, every step gained in human culture, both for the individual and the species, is explicable only on the supposition of this affinity of the spirit of man with the Spirit of God, and of real intercourse between the two.

[1] I. H. Fichte, Psychologie, 646-649.

The true author of all *new* thoughts in us is God. God Himself cannot be conceived by us without God. As we obtain the mass of our thoughts by the impression on us of outward things, so there is a higher class of thoughts which are awakened only by the impression on us of God within us. In the first case the relation into which we are brought is that of subject to external objects. In the second, we become objects to a higher subject. A higher than ourself glides into us, becomes one with us, manifests Himself by means of us. We cannot indeed *know* this higher as an object, but we *experience* Him as a *force*.'[1]

To the same effect Coleridge : 'This doctrine flows naturally from the admission of an omnipresent mind as the ground of the universe. If you have resolved that all belief of a divine Comforter' (i.e. strengthener, intensifier of the life within us) 'present to our inmost being, and aiding our infirmities, is fond and fanatical, in what better light can you regard prayer than as the groaning of a wounded lion in his solitary den ? The utter rejection of all present and living communion with the universal Spirit impoverishes Deism itself, and renders it as cheerless as Atheism, from which, indeed, it would then differ only by an obscure impersonation of what the Atheist conceives unpersonified under the name of fate or nature.'[2]

Nor less clear is the testimony of divines to this great doctrine of the life of God in the soul of man. 'The Spirit dwells in believers,' says Luther, ' not only by the gifts that He confers on them, but by the communication of his very life to them (quoad substantiam suam). For He does not so confer his gifts as if He were himself at a

---

[1] I. H. Fichte. Psychologie, Preface.     [2] Coleridge, Aids, 80.

distance or were asleep, but He is present along with his gifts, present in his creature to preserve, to actuate, to strengthen him with new force (addendo robur).'[1]

And so Mr. Martineau: 'To deny the purest and deepest movements of our nature to be from God, while it indicates a faint piety, is no sign of strong reason. For what emboldens you to contradict the universal testimony of souls aloft in worship: the natural language of poet, saint, and prophet? You say, perhaps, these movements are experienced by the worshipper's own mind, and must be parts of the nature that feels them. But it does not follow that because they are included in the consciousness of men they indicate no presence and living touch of God. Or, you say, there is no miracle in them, and they come and go by laws not quite untraceable. But this only shows that the divine agency is free from disorder and caprice, and loves to be constant in behalf of those who are faithful to its conditions. . . . And as there is no ground in *experience* for rejecting the old language of devotion, neither is there any in the claim of consistent *philosophy*. For we find men ready enough to allow that there is no place where God is not, perhaps no time when his *external* power is not active in some realm or other. Why, then, withhold from Him that *internal* sphere, of which all else is but the theatre and the temple? Shall we diffuse God as an atmosphere, and forget that He is a mind? plead for his mechanical action on matter, and doubt the contact of spirit with spirit? admit the agency of the artist on his work, and deny the embrace of the Father and the child? What possible ground is there for affirming God to be elsewhere, and *not* within our

[1] See Tittmann, Opuscula, 399.

souls? Far more plausible would the limitation be if we were to declare Him manifestly existent *here alone.* The decisions of the will are doubtless our own, and constitute the proper sphere of our personal agency. But in a region higher than the will (the region of spontaneous thought and emotion) there is scope enough for God's " abode with us." Whatever is most deep within us is the reflection of Himself. All our better love and higher aspirations are the answering movement of our nature in harmonious obedience to his Spirit. Whatever dawn of blessed sanctity and wakening of purer perfections opens on our consciousness are the sweet touch of his morning light within us. His inspiration is perennial. And He never ceases to work within us if we consent to will and to do his good pleasure. He befriends our moral efforts; encourages us to maintain our resolute fidelity and truth; accepts our co-operation with his designs against all evil; and reveals to us many things far too fair and deep for language to express. Christ felt how within the deeps of our spiritual nature the personalities of heaven and earth might become entwined together and indissolubly blended : " Thou, Father, art in me and I in thee, and they also one in us."'[1] And how completely this principle pervades our Articles, our Homilies, and our Liturgy, I need not remind you. Throughout, they assume the possibility and intreat the actuality of this ' entwining and blending' of the divine and human, for every Christian mind. 'It is the Holy Ghost and no other thing that doth quicken the minds of men, stirring up good and godly motions in their hearts, such as of their own crooked and perverse nature they should never

---

[1] Martineau, Endeavours, ii. 80.

have.'[1] 'We must needs agree that whatsoever good thing is in us, of grace, of nature, or of fortune, is of God only, as the only author and worker.'[2] 'Stir up the wills of thy faithful people!' 'Grant that by thy holy *inspiration* we may think those things that be good.' 'Cleanse the thoughts of our hearts by the *inspiration* of thy Holy Spirit.'[3]

And what metaphysicians allow, and divines contend for, Holy Scripture confirms. Its whole doctrine of 'grace' is a doctrine of the infusion of the divine into the human. Though Scripture has not the verb 'to inspire' at all, and uses the noun 'inspiration' only twice: first for the inspiration which enlightens the understanding of all men,[4] and next for that vouchsafed to the prophets of God in particular;[5] yet it continually ascribes, as does our Prayer-book, 'all holy desires, all good counsels, and all just works' to the operation of God on the soul. 'God,' says St. Paul, 'called me by his *grace*.'[6] And again, 'The grace of our Lord wrought in me abundance of faith.'[7] And again, 'By the grace of God I am whatever I am, and his grace which was bestowed upon me was not in vain, but I laboured more abundantly than they all, yet not I, but the grace of God which was with me.'[8]

---

[1] Homily for Whitsun Day.  [2] Homily for Rogation Week.
[3] Add Appendix, Note XXIV.  [4] Job xxxii. 8.
[5] 2 Tim. iii. 16.  [6] Gal. i. 15.
[7] 1 Tim. i. 14.  [8] 1 Cor. xv. 10.

## LETTER XI.

### OF GOD'S WORK IN COMMUNITIES.

You will go along with me, in the course of thought which I am now suggesting to you, only in proportion as you recognise the perpetual immanence and inworking of God throughout the whole of being. We can have no real belief in the relations of God with men, but as we regard Him as emphatically 'the Living God,' 'filling heaven and earth.' Without this, even the recognition of a ground of all things, a first cause, is no better practically than a denial of it. For without this, such recognition has no vitality, no force, no bearing on the needs and the aspirations of the human spirit. And, consequently, it is this which forms the distinguishing mark of all real Theism, and which is set forth from first to last, in the sacred writings, as marking off the true God from all the gods of the heathen. 'They have mouths but they speak not; eyes have they but they see not; they have ears but they hear not; but, O Israel, trust thou in the *Living One*' (Jehovah), 'for he is your help and your shield; he is mindful of us, he will bless us!' 'For *our* God is in the heavens, and he doeth whatsoever he pleaseth.'[1] 'The gods that have not made the heavens and the earth shall perish, but the Lord' (He who is significantly named Jehovah, the I AM, the Eternal) 'is the true God; he is

[1] Ps. cxv. 5-12.

the *living God* and an everlasting King; he causeth the vapours to ascend from the ends of the earth; he maketh lightnings with rain, and bringeth the wind out of his treasures.'[1]

And such a faith concerning God is justified and demanded by all that science discloses to us of his inworking through the whole extent of nature. Everywhere are found forces incessantly in action; and these forces acting with intelligence as means to ends. Everywhere the universe teems with life, and this life an intelligent life. Everywhere the continuous reign of law implies the continuous presence of a Law-enforcer. 'No one considers the so-called "acts" of the material world as anything else but acts of the present power and direct present attention of the Deity. The apple falls by laws of gravitation established ages ago, but no modern writer seems to think (not even the author of the "Vestiges") that it would do so, if that which originally founded the law was not there to enforce the law, or that divine interposition is unnecessary to preserve divine law. All admit that a law cannot enforce itself.'[2]

Shall, then, this presence and influence, recognised through all material existence, and actuating all unconscious organisms, be supposed to cease, as organisms rise in dignity and importance? Shall the unconscious workings of a divine vitality be thus acknowledged and not its conscious workings? Does God

> Live through all life, extend through all extent,
> Spread undivided, operate unspent,

[1] Jerem. x. 10–13.
[2] Mr. Simon, in Veitch's Life of Sir W. Hamilton, 348.

in lesser things, and must He not equally, nay supremely

> Breathe in our *soul*, inform our nobler part,
> As in a hair, so, perfect in a heart?

Assuredly, ' the hearts of men are in the hand of the Lord, as the rivers of water; and he turneth them whithersoever he will.'[1] 'The preparations of the heart in man and the answer of the tongue, are from the Lord.' 'A man's heart deviseth his way, but the Lord directeth his steps.'[2] 'Man's goings are of the Lord. How, then, can a man understand his own way?'[3] 'The way of man is not in himself: it is not in man that walketh to direct his steps.'[4] 'It is God which worketh in us both to will and to do of his good pleasure.'[5]

And truly is it for the ends of the divine '*good* pleasure' that God energises in men. It is because He has ' predestinated us to the adoption of children to himself, according to the *good* pleasure of his will,' that He awakes us to our need of Himself; raises up gifted spirits, filled with his own light and life, to respond to this need; and through their instrumentality carries on an ascending series of divine operations towards the ultimate accomplishment of his grand design, the bringing out in men the image of God.

These operations we have now to trace. I have shown you already how the light and life of God have been at all times diffused, however faintly, through the earth; how some flashes of true wisdom in poets, sages, moralists, of India, Persia, Greece, and Rome, not only illuminated the contracted circle of their immediate followers, but spread from age to age, and from country to country,

---

[1] Prov. xxi. 1.    [2] Ibid. xvi. 1, 9.    [3] Ibid. xx. 24.
[4] Jer. x. 23.    [5] Phil. ii. 13.

those preparatory thoughts which made the brighter illumination from Judea more intelligible and more welcome to innumerable waiting minds. In this way the conjectures of reason prepared admission for the certainties of revelation. Anticipation heralded assurance. Sages divined what prophets declared. But still, it was among a peculiar people, and through the stages of their history, that this divine light and life were specially manifested. With Abraham and his descendants did the Divine Educator of mankind commence and carry on in an ascending series a succession of religious influences and of resulting religious institutions, which spread onwards and outwards, from a sacred family to a sacred nation, till they culminated in a sacred brotherhood whose destiny it is to embrace at last the whole race of men.

Let us observe the commencement of this all-embracing scheme in the constitution of a *sacred family*. It was for this that God called Abram out of the darkness of heathenism, and illuminated him with the knowledge of Himself. Not for the mere personal benefit of the individual, but that this individual might become the founder of a *family* in which this knowledge might be preserved, increased, and extended from age to age. 'The Lord said to Abram, Get thee out of thy country, and from thy kindred, and *I will make of thee a great nation*; and in thee' (through the instrumentality of this nation) 'shall all families of the earth be blessed.'[1] And this, by the diffusion of that knowledge and worship of the true God to which Abram himself was called. 'Abraham shall surely become a great nation, and all the nations of the earth shall be blessed through him; *for* I know him

[1] Gen. xii. 1-3.

that he will command his children and his household after him, and they shall keep the way of the Lord, to do justice and judgment, that the Lord may bring upon Abraham that which he hath spoken of him.'[1] Where, observe well, it was by this friend of God, this gifted depositary of divine light and life, teaching others the *moral foundations* of all true religion, 'justice and equity;' the law of right and the law of recompense; that the original promise of God to make all men blessed through Abraham was to be accomplished. The light and life *in*fused into the individual were to be *dif*fused by him over his family and descendants, and *so* to become the blessing of all nations.

By this means, then, and for this end, you find the next stage of God's operations to be the constitution, in the descendants of Abraham, of a *sacred nation*, which, in its turn, becomes the depositary and the diffuser of the divine light and life. For this, when Abraham's family had swollen into tribes, and the tribes into an Abrahamic race, God raised up another and still more gifted spirit in the person of Moses, whose work was to consecrate these inheritors of the primary blessing to the sacred office of preserving, enlarging, and communicating the fundamental principles of true religion, as 'a *nation* of priests' or representatives of the true God. 'I bare you on eagles' wings and brought you to myself. Now therefore, if ye will obey my voice and keep my covenant, ye shall be a peculiar treasure unto me above all people, and ye shall be to me a kingdom of priests and a holy nation.'[2] And so 'Moses called all Israel and said to them, Hear, O Israel, the statutes and the judgments which I speak in

---

[1] Gen. xviii. 18.  [2] Exod. xix. 4–6.

your ears this day, that ye may *learn them and do them.*[1] Whence St. Paul places all the glory of his people in this their special function, that they were made depositaries of divine truth. 'What advantage hath the Jew?' (what superiority over other nations?) 'Chiefly that to them were committed' (entrusted as a sacred deposit) 'the oracles of God,' the divine communications of old time.[2] Nor were they to be only the depositaries, they were to be also the *diffusers* of the divine light and life entrusted to them. They were not only to ' teach them to their sons and their sons' sons,'[3] in lineal succession through the historic life of the sacred nation, but they were to fulfil the promise made to Abraham by spreading them beyond the confines of this sacred nation, for the gathering in of others from all lands, to partake of its privileges as the people of God. ' It shall come to pass in the last days,' says the Prophet Isaiah, ' that the mountain of the Lord's house shall be established in the top of the mountains and shall be exalted among the hills, and all nations shall flow to it. And many peoples shall say, Come and let us go up to the mountain of the Lord, to the house of the God of Jacob; and *he will teach us of his ways* and we will walk in his paths; for out of Zion shall *go forth* ' (for all peoples) ' the law, and the word of the Lord from Jerusalem.'[4]

And thus, the divine light and life infused into a gifted *individual*, and spreading, by means of a *sacred family* through a *sacred nation*, was brought by God along ascending stages of development to be enshrined in a *sacred Brotherhood*, composed of many individuals, families, and nations, and destined to embrace, at last, by

---

[1] Deut. v. 1.  [2] Rom. iii. 1.
[3] Deut. iv. 8, 9.  [4] Isaiah ii. 2, 3.

similar diffusion of the deposit entrusted to it, the whole race of men.¹

For, in this sacred nation, after a long but ever-ascending series of preparations, God raised up One, superior to all previous representatives of his truth and will, to be the Founder and Ruler of a new community, which should gather into itself all that had been previously revealed through preceding patriarchs, lawgivers, and prophets; and complete their imperfect fragmentary utterances by means of the fuller inspiration and indwelling of the Son of God. The same God who 'at sundry times and in divers manners had spoken in times past to the fathers by the prophets, in the last days spoke by his Son.'² The same God who had hitherto infused his Spirit into various 'elect ones' as 'vessels unto honour,' in various *measures* of inspiration, now breathed this Spirit into One who was emphatically *the Word*, or utterance of the divine mind, 'without measure;' so that whoever received his testimony was receiving the testimony of God Himself in all its fullness, because 'He whom God sent spake the words of God.'³

And thus this *Word* accomplished all that had been only darkly hinted and imperfectly effected by the previous gifted ones through whom God dealt with men. While serving God in their generation they were still only forerunners of a greater One to come. Abraham, the *friend* of God, was but a shadow of Him who was before Abraham, dwelling in the bosom of the Father. And therefore the promise made to 'the seed' of Abraham found its fulfilment in this one seed, Christ. Moses, the *prophet* of God, was but a palmary instance of the long

¹ See Appendix, Note XXV.   ² Heb. i. 1.   ³ Jno. iii. 32–34.

succession of inspired teachers which was closed and crowned by Him who could affirm, 'The words that I speak to you I speak not of myself but from the Father who dwelleth in me.'[1] And so the law of God, first proclaimed through Moses, and enforced by his successors, was sublimated and completed by this 'Prophet like to Moses,' raised up from the midst of his people, concerning whom it was prescribed, 'Him shall ye hear in all things whatsoever he shall command you.'[2] Aaron again, the *priest* of God, and all his race, with all their sacrifices, were but symbols of that 'great High Priest, higher than the heavens,' who superseded, by accomplishing, the whole hierarchical system, and by his one offering once offered threw open for all the world the portals of the heavenly temple, the way of access into the holiest.[3] And David, finally, with the whole line of theocratic *kings*, was but a type of that greater Prince, concerning whom God said, 'I have set my King upon my holy hill of Zion! Thou art my Son; this day have I begotten thee! Ask of me and I will give thee the heathen for thine inheritance, and the uttermost parts of the earth for thy possession!'[4] And so 'there is given him dominion and glory and a kingdom, that all people, nations, and languages should serve him; his dominion is an everlasting dominion which shall not pass away, and his kingdom that which shall not be destroyed.'[5]

And this dominion is the dominion of *the truth*; of that perfect religion which is designed and suited for all ages of the world. 'I am indeed a king,' said Jesus to his judge, but not a king whom his subjects are to

---

[1] John xiv. 10.  [2] Acts iii. 22–26.  [3] Heb. vii. 26; x. 10.
[4] Psalm ii. 6–8.  [5] Daniel vii. 14.

sustain upon his throne by force of arms. No! My office is to make *divine truth* paramount! And my subjects are all 'lovers of this truth.'[1] And therefore what the Sovereign of this new community is, that is the community itself—a brotherhood of those who *love the truth*. The Church, or universal Brotherhood under Christ, gathers into itself all the essential elements of religious feeling which have been scattered through different peoples in the ages gone by. It brings out into full relief those *principles of piety* which have ever formed the base of even the most grotesque forms of religious thought. It grasps the substance of which these forms were anticipative shadows. It supersedes these forms by unfolding the realities which underlie them. And from the many-coloured wrappings of ephemeral *opinion*, it brings out full and clear those *pure ideas* of religious belief which lie involved in them. The belief, I mean, that God communicates Himself to men, in order that men may be consecrated to his service, brought into communion with his Spirit, assimilated to his image, and perfected in his final kingdom.

The primary belief which underlies all forms of religion is, that God *communicates Himself to men;* consorts with men. I will not detain you with the Ethnic forms of this belief—the condescending visits of the gods to the favoured Ethiopians—the descent of guardian deities to direct, uphold, reprove, and comfort their human clients. I remind you only that in the sacred Scriptures we are told how the Lord became the guest of Abraham, in the plain of Mamre; how he came down to Moses and the prophets, speaking with them 'face to face, as a man speaketh with his friend;'[2] how Abraham 'built an altar

---

[1] John xviii. 37.  [2] Exod. xxxiii. 11.

to the Lord, who appeared to him,'[1] and Jacob called the name of a place 'Peniel,' for he said 'I have seen God face to face;'[2] how God called to Samuel, and revealed Himself in vision to Isaiah, and set before the eyes of Ezekiel 'the appearance of the likeness of the glory of the Lord.'[3] All these accounts bear witness to the primitive idea of a just and genuine faith that the Most High is never 'far from any one of us;' is habitually teaching, helping, cheering the spirits whom He has made. This idea lies at the base of all religion. Till we believe that God reveals Himself to us, there can be no responsiveness of heart towards God. And this idea it is which finds its noblest and truest form of utterance in the doctrine of 'The Word made flesh and dwelling among us,' so that 'whosoever seeth him seeth the Father.'[4]

But for what does God thus communicate Himself to man? To what end this descent of the divine into the human? It is in order to draw up the human into the divine, to reconcile men to Him from whom they have estranged themselves, and to *consecrate them* to his service. For this, God called out Abram from his idolatrous kindred, and said, 'I will make *a covenant between me and thee*, and thy seed after thee in their generations, to be a God to thee and to thy seed after thee!'[5] For this, He rescued Moses and his people from the land of Egypt, the house of bondage, and said, 'If ye will obey my voice and keep my covenant, then ye shall be a peculiar treasure unto me above all people, and a kingdom of priests, and a holy nation.'[6] And for this, He has accomplished through his Son a mightier deliver-

---

[1] Gen. xii. 7.   [2] Ibid. xxxii. 30.   [3] Ezek. i. 28.
[4] John i. 14; xiv. 9.   [5] Gen. xvii. 2, 7.   [6] Exod. xix. 5.

ance, a deeper reconciliation, a universal covenant of peace for 'all who are afar off, as many as the Lord our God shall call.'[1] 'God,' says St. Paul, 'was in Christ reconciling *the world* unto himself.'[2] And again, 'Jesus came and preached peace to them that were afar off as to them that were nigh, and through him both the grand divisions of mankind have access by one Spirit to the Father.'[3] And our Lord himself declared with reference to his becoming thus the uniting link between men and God, to consecrate them to his service: 'This is my blood of *the new covenant*, which is *shed for the many*, for the remission of sins.'[4] As there can be no religion without the belief that God communicates with man, so there can be no heart to welcome such communication, to respond to it, to embrace it, without this further belief that there is mercy with God, reconciliation with Him for them that have been afar off, return into his favour, access to his presence, permission to serve Him without fear, in righteousness and holiness before Him!

Access to his presence. For this is a third idea, the belief of which lies deep in the heart of all religious men, that God communicates Himself to us in order that we *may rise into communion* with Him. Such communion has been in all religions sought by those to whom God has spoken, whom He has called home into friendship with Himself. Enoch and Noah 'walked with God.'[5] Abraham 'took upon him to speak unto the Lord, though he was but dust and ashes.'[6] From the intensity of his communion with the divine countenance 'the skin of

---

[1] Acts ii. 39.    [2] 2 Cor. v. 19.
[3] Eph. ii. 17, 18.    [4] Matt. xxvi. 28.
[5] Gen. v. 24; vi. 9.    [6] Gen. xviii. 27.

Moses' face shone.'[1] The poets and prophets of the Lord 'poured out their hearts before him.' And He, above all, who is to us the Manifester of the Father, and our Reconciler with the Father, He, though coming down from heaven, dwelt still, in spirit, in heaven. He could affirm, 'The Father himself is with me; he hath not left me alone.'[2] And for our sharing with Him this communion, He sheds into every earnest mind the spirit of adoption, whereby we cry Abba, Father. So that his beloved Apostle testifies, for himself and for his brethren, 'Our fellowship is with the Father and with his Son Jesus Christ.'[3]

Nor is this all. These three fundamental ideas which find for themselves expression by facts and symbols in all religions—these indispensable beliefs that God speaks to us, accepts us, listens to us as to his children—are all preliminary only to a further end of God's dealing with mankind, the *assimilation of us* to his image. This fourth idea—of assimilation to God—lies equally at the base of all religious faith. You discover it in even the most imperfect theologies. Only, the notions under which it is veiled vary with the variations of human culture and character. The Greek conceived it under the form of elevation to divine wisdom. The Roman, of assumption to divine power. The Buddhist, of absorption into the divine essence. But in Christianity you find it disclosed in its true aspect—that of consimilarity with *the divine goodness*. For Christianity alone is essentially and thoroughly a *moral* religion, in harmony with the moral sentiments which constitute humanity; appealing to these, quickening these, unfolding these, refining these, satisfying these, and so

---

[1] Exod. xxxiv. 29.   [2] John viii. 29.   [3] 1 John i. 3.

effectually bringing out these in their full-orbed loveliness into the disposition and the life, that men become the shining temples of the Holy One, the habitation of God through the Spirit. Thus shone morality in our great Exemplar. 'No one convinced him of sin.' 'He did always such things as pleased God.' And thus it ought to shine in all his followers. 'As he who hath called you is holy, so be ye holy in all manner of behaviour; because it is written, Be ye holy for I am holy.'[1] 'The grace of God which bringeth salvation hath appeared to all men,' with this one lesson, for this one end, that, 'denying ungodliness and worldly lusts, we should live soberly, righteously, and godly, marked out and known as God's peculiar people by this one feature, *zeal for good works.*'[2]

And what is the prospect opened out for all who are thus called by God, reconciled to God, raised into communion with God, and renewed in the moral likeness of God? It opens out into eternity. The trail produces itself onward till it be lost in far-off glory. The shining light shineth more and more unto the perfect day. No religion ever stopped short with the first four ideas. No religion can consent to dwarf itself into the poor dimensions of this mere bud of being. No faith, the very essence of which is to soar beyond the visible, can restrain itself from soaring equally beyond the present. As surely as it is a conviction of things not seen, is it also and therewith a confidence in things hoped for.[3] In the most immature forms of religion this idea has, however dimly, been involved. The ancient heathen had their underworld, their Tartarus and their Elysian fields, their hopes of Astræa redux, of a descent again of right-

[1] 1 Peter i. 15, 16.  [2] Titus ii. 11-14.  [3] Heb. xi. 1.

eousness even to this distracted earth. For the Virgin is not altogether lost. She hovers over us in the sky, and she may once again drop down to us. Nor were the Jews without their hope of good to come. Of the patriarchs and of Moses it is affirmed, however vaguely, 'They were gathered to their people;' 'They slept with their fathers.'[1] The prophets trusted that those who walked in uprightness entered into peace and rested from their labours.[2] And as the sun rose higher in the heavens all clouds of doubt became dispersed, life and immortality had full light thrown upon them, till the last and brightest of the religious ideas beamed forth in meridian splendour— the idea, namely, of the *consummation of humanity* in the final kingdom of God. The Son of God became the firstfruits of this consummation. His soul was not left in Hades. God showed Him the path of life; He made Him full of joy with the light of his countenance. And with Him is involved the glory of his people.

> He dying rose, and rising with Him raised
> His brethren, ransomed with his own dear life!

Nay, this last fundamental element of all religious belief ministers not simply to the hope of saints, confines itself not to merely human interests; it embraces in its ample range the consummation of the world. The Stoics believed in a purifying fire by which the elements of nature should become renewed into their pristine perfectness.[3] And all religions, as they look backward to an age of primeval purity, so look forward to a final restoration of this age. Whence the magnificent expectations

---

[1] Gen. xxv. 8; 1 Kings ii. 10.   [2] Isaiah lvii. 2.
[3] 'Relinqui nihil præter ignem; a quo rursum, *animante deo*, renovatio mundi fieret atque idem ornatus oriretur.'—Cicero, *De Nat. Deor.* ii. 46.

of the sacred writings, the glorious visions of the Apocalyptic seer. 'New heavens and a new earth wherein dwelleth righteousness;' 'A new Jerusalem descending from God out of heaven; The tabernacle of God with men, and God himself with them as their God;' 'The whole creation delivered from the bondage of corruption into the glorious liberty of the children of God;' these are the brilliant images by means of which anticipative faith paints to the imagination what passes comprehension by the mind! And then cometh the end; when the Son shall have subdued all things to the Father; when He shall have put down all opposing rule and authority and power; when He shall have negatived the negatives, and reconciled the antagonisms, through which things travel onward to their ultimate affirmation and harmony; and when the whole scheme of the Father for all his creatures shall reach its consummation, and God Himself be all in all!

## LETTER XII.

### OUR DUTIES TO GOD AND MEN.

THE great problem which has occupied all thinkers, and yet still remains to be solved, is the problem of the one and the many: the question how unity can become self-severed into multiplicity.

This problem seems insoluble. Yet there it stands. We cannot get rid of it. All the facts of existence bring it before us. All the theories of existence demand its solution. The oneness of the universe (whence its very name) is as plain as its manifoldness. And so is the essential involution of this manifoldness in that oneness; its springing from the One, inhering in the One, and being actuated by the One.

And this problem presents itself, as with respect to all existences, so specially with reference to men. Men are multiplied before our eyes. And yet these multiplied men have their ground in a One not visible to us. We have no absolute standing in ourselves. We stand only in the root of our humanity. We have no absolute self-movement, self-direction, self-realisation. We are not simply in relation with the One; we are in a relation of subordinacy to the One. 'He has made us, and not we ourselves. We are his people and the sheep of his pasture.' 'The way of man is not in himself. It is not in man that walketh to direct his steps.' God is to us as a father to his family; as a sovereign to his subjects.[1] He is incessantly providing for our wants, responding to our yearnings, educating and training us, individually and collectively, in order to bring us onward from infancy to maturity, from the first germ of humanity in each to its full perfectionment in all. For this He made us in his image; for this, He awakens our desires towards Himself; for this, He sends gifted spirits to respond to these desires; for this, He has formed through them an ascending series of communities, from a single family to a universal brotherhood, within which He reveals Himself, through which He diffuses Himself, and which He will continue to develope till all the kingdoms of this world become the kingdoms of God and of his Christ, and He shall reign for ever and ever.

And hence the analogy which represents the Divine One as a KING; and all things as included in his kingdom. Hence the conviction that our privilege as rational creatures lies in being able to recognise this kingdom; and our duty, in becoming loyal subjects of this kingdom. What a favourite thought this is, for instance, with M. Antoninus. And how it elevates, comforts, delights him! 'The world' (he says) 'is a kind of political community. And the end for which all rational beings exist is to follow the reason and the law of this most ancient community. And if the poet exclaims "Dear city of Cecrops!" shall

---

[1] Where by 'sovereign' beware of imagining an arbitrary will, whose might is right; on the contrary, it is its right which is might. Even Homer addresses the Supreme as '*Father* Zeus,' although most glorious and powerful: Ζεῦ πάτερ, Ἴδηθεν μεδέων, κύδιστε, μέγιστε.—*Iliad.* iii. 276. The Divine Sovereign is in reality what the Roman emperors only arrogated to themselves, 'Pater patriæ,' 'The Father of the whole family in heaven and earth.'—Eph. iii. 15.

not I exclaim " Dear city of Zeus ! " ' [1] The same conviction you find in Philo : 'This world is one vast community, under one polity and one law !' And Cicero enlarges on it when he writes : 'Where there exists a law common to all, there must there be also a right common to all. And those to whom law and right are thus common must be looked on as members of the same commonwealth. Still more so, if they enjoy this law and right under one and the same authority. But this is what pertains to us as men. We do lie under this celestial authority. We are subject to this divine mind, which we call Almighty God. And we are therefore to regard the universe as constituting one vast commonwealth of gods and men. And, as in states certain classes are distinguished by their family relationships, so in the universe of nature how much more magnificent, how much more illustrious the privilege, that *men* take rank among the kindred and family of God!' [2]

Nor does this grand idea less manifest itself in the Sacred Scriptures. There, too, God is set forth as the universal King. 'The Lord hath prepared his throne in the heavens, and his kingdom ruleth over all!' [3] 'The state to which we belong,' says St. Paul, ' is a heavenly one.' And the principles on which God exercises this universal sovereignty are precisely those which He has constituted men to harmonise with, to respond to, to appreciate and adore. As He proclaims by Jeremiah : ' Let him that glorieth glory in this, that he *understandeth and knoweth me*, that I am the Lord which exercise loving-kindness, judgment, and righteousness in the earth ;

---

[1] Anton. iv. 23.   [2] Cicero, De Legg. i. 7.   [3] Psalm ciii. 19.

for in these things I delight, saith the Lord.'[1] Where note the distinct exposition of those three main functions of all right sovereignty to which the truest ethics also lead us; the administration of *order* ('righteousness'), which regulates the *rights* of the subject; of *justice* ('judgment'), which requites their *deserts*; and of *benevolence* ('loving-kindness'), which regards their wants.

Such, then, is the relation of God to men. And the duties (or dues) which we owe as subjects of this Divine King are correlatively, reverence for this order, recollection of this justice, and reliance on this benevolence.

1. The divine *order* is supreme over all. It regulates the rights of all. It assigns to each of us our place in God's commonwealth, and binds us to dutiful allegiance to Him in this place. And reverence for this order will beget, before all things, *fear* of Him who has appointed it. This, therefore, our Church Catechism sets at the base of all right disposition towards God: 'My duty to God is to *fear* Him.' This the Prophet gives utterance to: 'Forasmuch as there is none like unto thee, O Lord; thou art great, and thy name is great in might; who would not *fear* thee, O *King* of nations!'[2] And this forms the theme of the angelic chant of adoration: 'Great and marvellous are thy works, Lord God Almighty; just and true are thy ways, thou *King* of saints; who shall not *fear* thee, O Lord, and glorify thy name!'[3]

Nor will such inward fear of the Great Supreme be wanting in outward manifestations. It ever presses outwards into *worship*; the open, public ascription of *worth* to God as the object of our veneration. This is what lies at the foundation of all true worship; worship is the

[1] Jer. ix. 24.     [2] Ibid. x. 6.     [3] Rev. xv. 3, 4.

paying homage to the great King. It is the coming up to court to do Him suit and service. It is the 'serving the Lord with gladness and coming before his presence with singing,' because 'he hath made us and not we ourselves, we are his people and the sheep of his pasture.' It is the 'entering into his gates with thanksgiving and into his courts with praise.'[1] And hence it comprises all the duties that our Catechism details as following on the 'fear' of God; 'to worship Him; to give Him thanks; to call upon Him; to honour his holy name and his word.' Wherever there is 'fear' of false gods it displays itself in some act of worship. The true fear of the true God will do the same. Whence that contrast urged by the Lord upon the Israelites: 'Ye shall not fear other gods nor bow yourselves before them' (as subjects before their sovereign), 'nor serve them,' (i.e. worship them), 'nor sacrifice to them' (bringing loyal gifts); 'but *the Lord*, who brought you out of the land of Egypt, him shall ye fear, and him shall ye worship, and to him shall ye do sacrifice.'[2]

But reverence for the divine order includes, further, *zeal for God's honour*. Every loyal subject is what Elijah declared himself, 'jealous for the Lord God of hosts.'[3] And he therefore labours that his Sovereign be reverenced by others as by himself. 'Zeal for thine house,' cried the Psalmist, 'hath eaten me up.' And such zeal burned with pure white heat in the Son of God:[4] 'My meat is to do the will of him that sent me, and to finish his work.'[5]

2. God, however, as our Sovereign, not only assigns

---

[1] Ps. c.  [2] 2 Kings xvii. 35–37.  [3] 1 Kings xix. 10.
[4] John ii. 17.  [5] Ibid. iv. 34.

to each of us our place and work in the divine order, but watches over our behaviour in this place and work, and requites it with divine *justice*. The offices of sovereign and of judge are inseparable. They were at first exercised by one and the same person; and up to this age, in which their separation seems most complete, our judges are still but representatives of the monarch, who is supposed to sit, by means of them, in his courts, and deal out justice to his people. Whence the titles 'ruler' and 'judge' became synonymous; as Paul says to the Roman governor, 'Thou hast been many years a *judge* unto this nation.' And one great qualification of Moses for being a leader of Israel was the union in his temper of distributive and retributive justice. *Distributive*, passionate for *order*; whence he interposed between those who strove with each other: 'Wherefore smitest thou thy fellow?' And *retributive*, passionate for *requital*; whence he slew the Egyptian who had smitten one of his brethren.[1] And so, we are told, 'Moses sat to *judge* the people;' 'to *judge* between one and another, to make them know the statutes of God and his laws.' And it was not till his father-in-law had urged, 'Thou wilt surely wear away, for this thing is too heavy for thee: thou art not able to perform it thyself alone;' that Moses 'chose able men out of all Israel, and these judged the people.'[2]

And as with human rulers, so, by analogy, is it with our Divine King. He administers throughout all his dominions *justice and judgment*. He 'renders to every one according to his deeds.'[3] 'He brings every work into judgment, with every secret thing, whether it be good or

---

[1] Exod. ii. 11–14.  [2] Ibid. xviii. 13–26.  [3] Rom. ii. 5.

whether it be evil.'¹ He ordains that 'whatsoever a
man soweth that shall he also reap.'² And therefore our
correlative duty is to have this constantly in our recollection; to be awed by it, to be encouraged by it; to be
deterred by it from evil, animated by it to good! 'Re-
joice, O young man in thy youth, but bear in recollection all the while that for all thy ways God will bring
thee into judgment.'³ 'Be ye steadfast, unmovable, always
abounding in the work of the Lord; forasmuch as ye
know that your labour cannot be in vain in the Lord.'⁴

3. But now there remains one other essential element
of the regal relation towards all subjects of the realm—
*benevolence*, regard for their welfare; care for all their
interests, material, mental, and moral; the lifting up on
them the light of royal favour and complacency. It is
men's high esteem of this which comes out in the
favourite epithets given to princes, 'Your *grace*,' 'His
*serene* highness,' 'Our most *gracious* sovereign,' '*gentle*
prince,' 'hear me of thy *clemency*;' all recognising that
the main end of government is the good of the people
governed; that the reason for the administration over us
of order and justice is our welfare. The 'grace' of
monarchs is the brightest jewel in their crown. Whence in
our idea of princes there is included not only the general
feature that they are to act as fathers of their people, but
the particular prerogative of pardoning the penitent, pro-
tecting the helpless, and honouring the righteous. 'They
that exercise authority,' says Jesus, 'are called bene-
factors;' and the poet tells us how

> No ceremony that to great ones 'longs,
> Not the king's crown, nor the deputed sword,

¹ Eccles. xii. 14.   ² Gal. vi. 7.   ³ Eccles. xi. 9.   ⁴ 1 Cor. xv. 58.

The marshal's truncheon, nor the judge's robe,
Become them with one half so good a grace
As mercy does.

What, then, is the correlative of this? What the *return* due from the subject to the sovereign who displays this grace? What but corresponding *reliance* thereon, in all the forms in which it displays itself?

Just so, therefore, our duty to the *Great Supreme* as the Father of his people comprises first a general confidence in his *goodness*, such as the Psalmist delights to commemorate: 'The Lord is good to all, and his tender mercies are over all his works.' 'O taste and see that the Lord is good; blessed is the man that *trusteth in him*!'[1]

It comprises, next, a particular confidence in the *mercy* which monarchs reserve in their hands, wherewith to mitigate the terrors of law, and commute, or even remit altogether, the penalties of justice. This attribute was proclaimed to Moses as constituting an essential element in the 'name,' or character of the Lord. 'The Lord, the Lord God, merciful and gracious, long suffering and abundant in goodness and truth, keeping mercy for thousands' (reserving this prerogative of mercy to be exercised towards innumerable penitents), 'forgiving iniquity, and transgression, and sin.'[2] And hence the Psalmist *puts his trust* in this grace of his Divine Sovereign, crying, 'If thou, Lord, shouldst mark iniquities, who shall stand? But there is *forgiveness* with thee that thou mayest be feared' (that our allegiance, supported by hope, may not fail). 'Let Israel therefore hope in the

---

[1] Ps. cxlv. 9; xxxiv. 8.   [2] Exod. xxxiv. 6, 7.

Lord; for with the Lord there is mercy, and with him there is plenteous redemption.'[1]

It comprises, further, a universal confidence in the *care of the great King* over us in all our necessities. Such care for the helpless, the desolate, the destitute, has always been claimed for the Father of the people in the last resort. Hence the prerogative of kings to be the guardians of minors, orphans, widows, throughout their realms; a prerogative still exercised, even in these modern times, by means of their Courts of Chancery. And hence the trust which the sacred writers repose in the *Great King* in all such cases of human helplessness. 'The poor' (or destitute) 'committeth himself to thee, for thou art the helper of the fatherless.'[2] 'Happy is everyone who hath the God of Jacob for his help, whose hope is in the Lord his God; which executeth judgment for the oppressed; which giveth food to the hungry! The Lord looseth the prisoners; the Lord openeth the eyes of the blind; the Lord raiseth them that are bowed down; the Lord preserveth the strangers; he relieveth the fatherless and widows! The Lord shall reign for ever and ever.'[3]

Such are the duties of men to *God*, as viewed in the light which flows from the idea of his Divine Sovereignty. From the same idea we get a right view of the duties of men to *men*. They come before us as fellow-subjects with ourselves of the Great King. And we learn at once that we must yield to them as such all those dues on which the unity, harmony, and welfare of every state depends: respect for their rights; responsiveness to their claims; and regard for their wants.

[1] Ps. cxxx. 3–7.   [2] Ibid. x. 14.   [3] Ibid. cxlvi. 5–10.

Respect for the rights of our fellow-citizens is the first law of all social duty. And hence, when God established the sacred community of Israel, as an instance of that universal kingdom towards which it formed so important a stage in the march of his providence, you find Him basing all the duties of the citizens of this community towards each other on this one principle of reverence for *right*, as the only preservative of unity and peace. In the ten commandments which He proclaimed by Moses as the statutes of the new commonwealth, after having settled, in the first four statutes, his own rights as the Sovereign, and the correlative duties of his subjects towards Him; He settles, in the last six statutes, the rights of the people among themselves, and the correlative duty which these rights demand—the duty, namely, of *respect* for the position of our fellow-citizens; for their person; for their wedded peace; for their property; for their reputation; and for all their possessions. These six statutes comprise whatever the widest principles of social ethics require as needful for the *keeping the peace* between man and man. Their principle is, 'work no ill to thy neighbour.'

But our social duties are regulated not only by respect for the rights of all, but also by *responsiveness to their claims*. For the fundamental principle of justice on which these duties are based includes, not only that *distributive* justice which, assigning to each his place and prerogative, requires us to keep the peace by abstinence from all trespass on this place and prerogative, but it includes also that *retributive* justice which looks beyond mere peace to propriety; and balances the demeanour of others towards us by proportionate returns. And hence the upspringing in all states of courts of *equity* as well as law. Hence the claims we all feel that we have on others for a fair *requital* of our disposition and conduct towards them. Claims for *truth*, from those to whom we give credit; of *fidelity*, from those to whom we give confidence; of *gratitude*, from those to whom we do service; of acknowledgment and return in various forms, from those to whom we have *given* anything that deserves such acknowledgment and return. And this part of our duty is distinguished from the first, inasmuch as it is not mere abstinence from evil, but communication of good. It is not passive unwrongfulness, but active responsiveness. Its principle is, not merely 'work no ill to thy neighbour,' but 'whatsoever you would think it equitable he should do to you that do you even so to him.' 'Render unto all their dues.'

But very much further in the path of positive welldoing towards our fellow-subjects of the Great Supreme, advances the third leading principle of our duties to them; that which prescribes *regard for the wants* of all men. For communities are formed not only for mutual peace, and mutual confidence, but for mutual *benefit*. And no one has fulfilled his duty to others in such communities unless he not merely abstains from injuring them, and from disappointing their expectations, but also is spontaneously active to *help* them, in the development of their nature, the exaltation of their character, the perfectionment of their happiness; by contributing, in short, whatever he possesses of sympathy, and influence, and power to the supply of their material, mental, moral, and spiritual wants. For 'the body is not one member but many, and God hath tempered the body together that the members should have an equal care one for another; that no man should seek his own, but also every one another's welfare.'

And now we must go on to consider what is needful *in ourselves*, in order to the accomplishment of these duties towards God and towards men. What must the subject be, in order to be pure and strong in loyalty? What the citizen, in order to an efficient citizenship? And how are we to be this? to become increasingly this?

Here is the right place for the question of personal morality. This is no selfish self-perfectionment, for the end of self-enjoyment here, or self-exaltation hereafter. It is a *means* for the fulfilment of our duties as citizens of the divine commonwealth. The grand defect of the Stoic morality is its introverted reference to self alone; its worship of personal equanimity and dignity as the one ultimate aim. It has exalted a means into an end. It lifts itself contemptuously above the range of our relations to God and men, and confines itself to that self-culture which shall render us gods to ourselves and independent of men. 'Why be anxious about bettering your slave?' says Epictetus; 'Why make yourself sad because he is bad? Look only to your own equanimity!'[1] But here it is forgotten that all the virtues, like the Graces, are sisters. They must ever intertwine their arms and support each other. We must cultivate the realm of our own will *in order that* we may rightly fill our places in the realm of God. We must learn to rule the machinery within us, *in order to* its bearing on objects without us. And we must be con-

---

[1] Göethe's Self-Culture, 'The desire to raise the pyramid of my existence as high as possible' is just a similar selfishness. 'He attached value to *immoral* self-mastery as *an end*, and as in itself higher than any duty *for the sake of* which he might master himself.'—Hutton's *Essays*, ii. 69.

tinually improving this machinery, *in order* that we may become efficient towards those objects in the fullest extent.

1. And hence the first element of personal morality is *self-control*. The grand ideas of moral excellence present themselves as lights in the firmament of heaven. They are not *of* us, though they shine down upon us. And they are set in this firmament, not only to give light to us, but to *rule over* us. And yet the mind on which they shine is a chaotic, turbid sea of volitions, tossed by a thousand baleful influences rushing hither and thither in mighty currents. These currents must be checked. These volitions must be subdued into a calm, reflective of the heavenly lights. The tides of emotion must be regulated by these lights, must flow or ebb according to the influence of these lights. And for all this we require self-control; the calling up of those volitions which harmonise with the moral ideas, the checking those which work in antagonism with them. For while the ideas of goodness hover over us, our will is ever pressing onwards in its own currents, whether sluggish or strong. And thus we find it either harmonising with these ideas or not. If, by happy chance, it harmonise, then the duties to which these ideas point are fulfilled. Our conduct is in accordance with our conceptions. We have that self-consistency which distils such peace! But if this harmony of will with conscience be wanting, if our conduct do not correspond with our conceptions, then we have the painful sense of self-contradiction: we find ourselves the sport of jarring impulses; the machinery of our will is out of gear. And so we fail in a twofold way; the one of defect, the other of excess; the one in *coming short* of what our conscience points to, the other, in

*coming across* what it points to. The first failure is that of moral *weakness*, the second of moral *wickedness*. And with respect to both, the experience of self-contradiction brings with it the feeling of self-blame. And not till we have determined to reduce our will into subjection to our moral judgment, not till we have wrought out this determination into act, can we have peace.

2. But there is a second element of personal morality which must be vigorous within us, or we shall never be worthy citizens of the commonwealth of God. There must be *greatness* of character as well as goodness. Its circle must be not only complete, but expansive. We must not only respond to present duty, but we must educate ourselves into efficiency for constantly enlarging duty.[1] There must be not only self-consistency, but *self-completion*; and for this we require not merely self-control, but *self-culture*. Even where there remains little 'wickedness,' or antagonism to the divine laws, there may be much 'weakness,' or inefficient accomplishment of these laws. Where the spirit is willing the flesh may be weak. And to overcome this weakness, to make ourselves not only loyal but vigorous soldiers of Christ, we need the constant drilling of ourselves.[2] Weakness of character results from the volitions being few, feeble, fragmentary; strength of character must be sought by the multiplication of our volitions, their intensification, their combination.

3. But these personal duties of self-control and self-culture require an ever wakeful and persevering energy; and we have to carry them on amidst the strongest oppo-

---

[1] 'In virtute sunt multi adscensus.'—Cicero, *Pro Planc.*
[2] 'Non est ad astra mollis e terris via.'—*Seneca.* 'Ardua per præceps gloria vadit iter.'—*Ovid.*

sition, both from the world without us and the world within us. We can never accomplish them, therefore, without continuous *self-elevation to God*, as the Father who helps us in every effort at virtue, who can infuse into us a power above our own, who can assure to us ultimate success. All our *virtue* as citizens of the sacred commonwealth, whether it be social or personal, must be based on, sustained animated strengthened by, a *religious confidence* in the Sovereign of this commonwealth. Without this, all morality will ever be found wanting in depth, in breadth, in strength. It will not have over us the authority of a divine voice ; it will not extend itself to all cases and all persons without us, nor all thoughts and feelings within us ; it will not have hope enough, and therefore vigour enough, to fight manfully against the world, the flesh, and the devil. Our strength for goodness depends on our faith in the Good One.[1] The Goliath of immorality can never be conquered by merely human courage and human skill. There were brave men in the army of Saul against the giant of old ; there were skilful men, who could wield many a deadly weapon ; there were, no doubt, slingers as expert as the stripling David : but they all, ' when they saw the man, fled from him and were sore afraid.' And why? Because they calculated only their own strength and their own skill, and had no *faith in God*. David, on the contrary, fled not, was not afraid. And

---

[1] This is no mere theological dogma. It is recognised by the highest minds of all ages. There is no virtue without God. Ἀρετὴ ἂν εἴη οὔτε φύσει οὔτε διδακτὸν ἀλλὰ θείᾳ μοίρᾳ.—*Plato*. Σωφροσύνα δώρημα κάλλιστον θιῶν.— Eurip. *Med.* 635. Ζεῦ, μεγάλαι ἀρεταὶ θνητοῖς ἕπονται ἐκ σέθεν.—*Pindar*. ' Nemo vir magnus sine aliquo afflatu divino unquam fuit.'—*Cicero*. ' Pietas fundamentum est omnium virtutum.'—*Ibid*. And therefore, to become virtuous, we must pray to God. Ἀρετὴν γε μὲν ἐκ Διὸς αἰτεῖν.—*Theocritus*. Πάντα μὲν τ᾽ ἀγαθὰ τοὺς νοῦν ἔχοντας αἰτεῖσθαι δεῖ παρὰ τῶν θεῶν.—*Plutarch*.

why? Because he vainly fancied himself more courageous, more strong, more skilful than all the host of Israel and all its greatest captains? No! but for this one reason, that he *had*, what they were wanting in, *faith in God*; that he could say to the giant, what they failed to say, 'Thou comest to me with a sword, and a spear, and a shield, but I come to thee *in the name of the Lord of hosts*, the God of the armies of Israel, whom thou hast defied.' And such faith it is by which alone we can become strong for duty and victorious over sin; from faith must issue our morality, like the buds of spring-time from the sap in the tree. As Longfellow sings—

Believe and love: for works will follow spontaneous,
Even as day does the sun; the Right from the Good is an offspring.
And love is animate faith, as flowers are the animate spring-tide.

But faith must be nourished by *self-elevation to God*. And self-elevation to God is prayer. Prayer is the ascent of the mind to God. It is so described by the Psalmist: 'I lift up my soul unto thee!' It is so described by the Church: 'Lift up your hearts! We lift them up unto the Lord!' And prayer is the utterance of faith, and by such utterance the strengthener of faith. The two things are reciprocal. Faith lifts itself up in prayer, and prayer draws up with it faith.

> Enoch, as a brave God-fearing man,
> Bow'd himself down, and in that mystery
> When God in man is one with man in God,
> Prayed.

Thus then, as in order to fulfil our social duties to others, we need the personal duties of self-control and self-culture, so equally in order to fulfil these personal duties, which are *moral*, we need that additional personal duty which is *spiritual*, self-elevation to God. 'Enoch *walked with God*,' and so he was 'perfect' in the generation round him. Abram was called to 'walk before God,' and so to become 'perfect' in himself.

Take that duty of self-control. It comes from the contemplation of God's will in juxtaposition with our failure in doing this will. And its voice is, Reduce your will into accordance with God's will, or you can never be at peace! But this voice sounds in vain, when there is lacking in us faith in God. We may feel shame. We may be tortured by remorse. But we shall never have that which Paul calls, in distinction from these feelings, 'godly sorrow,' 'sorrow after a godly manner.' It is only as we recognise the guiding stars of duty as set in the firmament *by God*; only as we feel ourselves, in neglecting to steer by them, drifting away from God; only as we therefore determine by new will and effort to set our course and hold hard our helm, in strict accordance with them as the lights of God; that we rise from sorrow, shame, remorse, to the 'repentance which is not to be repented of.'

Paul had long counted the law of God 'holy and just and good;' he had long 'delighted' in the law of God in his inward man (his better spirit); morality he knew, he reverenced, he loved, he longed for, he struggled after; but yet, 'how to perform that which was good he knew not,' till there came to him through faith 'the law of the spirit of life, in Christ Jesus, to free him from the law of sin and death.' And then he 'walked in this Spirit,' he was 'led by this Spirit,' and 'by this Spirit he mortified the deeds of his body and lived!'

And just so with the duty of *self-culture*. As we cannot release ourselves from evil, so neither can we train ourselves in good, without habitual *self-elevation to God*. All multiplication, all intension, all unification of purpose, must come from filling the mind with thoughts of God, strengthening it by the Spirit of God, uniting it in its one centre, God. 'Unite my heart,' cries the Psalmist, 'to fear thy name.' We must be 'strengthened with all might,' says the Apostle, 'by God's Spirit in the inner man.' And to grow in grace, we must 'grow up into Christ in all things, as our Head, from whom alone the whole spiritual body, being fitly compacted by that which supplies each joint, according to his effectual working in the measure of every part, can make increase of the body, to the building itself up in love!'

'Speak to Him then, for He hears, and spirit with spirit can meet;
Closer is He than breathing, nearer than hands and feet!'

# APPENDIX.

'If he will not hear thee, then take with thee one or two more, that in the mouth of two or three witnesses every word may be established.'—MATT. xviii. 16.

'That our elder writers quoted to excess it would be the blindness of partiality to deny. On the other hand, it seems to me that we now avoid quotations with an anxiety that offends in the contrary extreme. It is the beauty and independent worth of the citations which have made 'Johnson's Dictionary' popular even as a reading-book.'—COLERIDGE, *Friend*, i. 80.

# NOTES.

## NOTE I.

### Page 7.

ON this necessity, that thought must transcend facts, and add something from itself to them, see Dallas, 'The Gay Science,' i. 296: 'Generalisation is a process of reasoning; but we never generalise without *adding something* which is not in the facts, and which is a creation of the mind. "All men are mortal." Nobody doubts this; but when logicians proceed to analyse it they find themselves unable to explain how we reach from particular examples to the general conclusion. All we know of a surety is, that a certain limited number of men have died; what has become of the rest we know not. But suppose we know for certain that all men hitherto *have died*, how do we arrive at the conclusion that in future, all men *must die?* Old Asgill seriously disputed the necessity of death passing upon all men. The leap to a generalisation is a creature of the mind. From the earliest dawn of reason the mind is in the habit of taking these leaps. It may generalise well or it may generalise ill, but generalise it must. The child burns its fingers with the flame of a candle; straightway it flies to the conclusion that all fire burns. There is a correct generalisation. Once is enough. It flies from the one to the all. But it also makes mistakes of generalisation: it calls every man it sees, Papa; it calls every bird Polly; it calls the dog, Puss; it runs to eat the snow for sugar. But, right or wrong, it generalises so continually that philosophers have raised a question whether knowledge in man begins with generals or with particulars.' We may well, therefore, take on this matter the warning of the Duke of Argyll: 'In no subject of inquiry should we be jealous of research; in all we must be jealous of presumption. Men who denounce any particular field of thought are always to be suspected. The presumption is, that valuable things which these men do not like are to be found there. There are many forms of priestcraft. "Whatever," says Mr. Lewes, "is inaccessible to reason should be strictly interdicted to research." Here we have the true ring of the old sacerdotal instincts. Who is to define beforehand what is and what is not "accessible to reason?" Are we to take such a definition on trust from the priests of this new philosophy? They tell us that all the proofs of mind in the universe, all wisdom of purpose, all conceptions of plan or design are the mere product of special "infirmities" of the human intellect. But we can never know what is "inaccessible to reason" till the way of access has been tried. In the highest interests of truth, we must resist any and every interdict against research. The philosophy which assumes to issue such an interdict must have reason to fear inquiry.'— Duke of Argyll in *Good Words* for March, 1868.

## NOTE II.

### Page 8.

This argument is insisted on by H. Ritter, 'Unsterblichkeit,' p. 24: 'No phenomena could present themselves before us, unless there existed something as their ground, something of which we can predicate these to be the phenomena. The very notion, therefore, of "appearances" requires for its completion the correlative notion of "grounds" for these appearances, of which grounds these appearances are the predicates. And these grounds for appearances we term "subjects," because they serve as subjects for the predicates in our propositions. But such subjects Metaphysics denominates "substances." Substances are the bases of phenomena—their grounds, without which we could not speak or think of "phenomena" at all;

for every phenomenon must be thought of as the phenomenon (or appearance) of a some*thing* as its ground or substance. This the laws of thought imperatively demand.' And yet Strauss affirms, 'The assumption of anything on the other side of sense (das Jenseits) is the one adversary which speculative criticism has to fight against and (if possible) overcome.'—*Glaubenslehre*, ii. 739.

But Strauss's 'if possible,' will be found very difficult of accomplishment under the vigorous counter-argument of a tract which I have just met with, on 'Matter, Force, and Atheism,' by the Rev. T. Kirkman, M.A., Rector of Croft.

He begins, where all solid reasoning must begin, with the *Ego*: 'No clear question can be asked or answered concerning being, which does not involve the datum *ego*. *I am* is a truth beyond the reach of scepticism.' But *I am* in two states of being, a passive and an active; a passive, receiving impressions on myself, an active, originating expressions of myself. I think, and I act. But *in acting* I experience *re-action* upon me; and from my experience of voluntary action under re-action I am certain that I am in space of three dimensions, which is divided into portions or *loci* wherein *forces are verily acting* which are demonstrable and measurable by my own will-force. To this certainty I have arrived with the same conviction that I have of my own existence. And do not object that the resistances whose reality I affirm are purely ideal after all; for, my acting Will I know to be in a relation of equilibrium or of inequality to another term of the relation. And of the reality of this *relation* I am as certain as that I live and act. Now there can be no true relation between a real and an imaginary; both terms must be real or both unreal. But I have firm hold of one term, my own conscious will-force; my very life in conflict with another force. This first-known term of the relation is real, therefore the second term is real; that is, the resistance which I encounter is a really acting force, and not ideal and imaginary.'

## NOTE III.

*Page 8.*

The whole passage of Xenophon should be well pondered: 'You will see the truth of what I say if, instead of waiting till you behold the forms of the gods, you would be satisfied with recognising and adoring *in their works* the gods themselves (τὰ ἔργα αὐτῶν ὁρῶντι σέβεσθαι καὶ τιμᾶν τοὺς θεούς). For he who has organised and kept together the whole world, and at every moment governs its affairs, is nevertheless invisible to us; just as the sun, which *seems* so visible, does not permit us to pry into his essence, but blinds us with excess of light. And thus it is equally with man. Our soul, above all other parts of our constitution, partakes most certainly of the divine nature. For it is plain enough that the soul rules in us, and yet it is not visible to us. Which facts well considering, we ought never to think contemptuously of the things invisible, but recognise, from their manifestations, the power they possess, and reverence the divine that is in them.'—Xenophon, 'Mem.' iv. 3–6. Add to this the words of Dean Mansel: 'The cardinal point of Sir W. Hamilton's system is the absolute necessity, under any system of philosophy whatever, of acknowledging the existence of a sphere of belief beyond the limits of the sphere of thought. "The main scope of my speculation," he says, in his letter to Calderwood, " is to show articulately that we must believe as actual much that we are unable (positively) to conceive as even possible."'[1] 'Faith in the inconceivable must become the ultimate refuge even of the pantheist and the atheist, no less than of the Christian.' Take the case of time : 'We may endeavour, with the Eleatics, to conceive pure existence, apart and distinct from all phenomenal change ; or we may endeavour, with Heraclitus, to conceive the universe as a system of incessant changes, immutable only in the law of its own mutability: and these two systems may be regarded as the type of all subsequent attempts. Yet both alike aim at an object which is beyond positive conception,

---

[1] Contemp. Rev. i. 46.

and which can be accepted only as something to be *believed in*, spite of its inconceivability.'[1] See also Martineau, 'A Word for Speculative Theology,' p. 20: 'We are made capable of knowing not only that which happens, but that which is; not only phenomena, but existences; not only laws, but causation. And this additional knowledge not only is *just as certain* as the other, but actually *underlies it as its condition*, and has to be assumed in every inductive proposition.'

---

## NOTE IV.

### Page 17.

This argument of Plato is worth stating out at length: 'The oracle enjoins us, "Know thyself," and only as we obey this can we take proper care of ourselves. But to know myself I must find out what my very self (αὐτοτοαυτό) is.

'1. Now this my very self is a somewhat distinct, first, from my *words and sentiments*. For I, talking with you, am making use of reasoned words; but he who makes use of a thing must be distinct from the thing made use of. As a shoemaker is different from his leather, a musician from his harp.

'2. And it is distinct, secondly, from my *body* also. A shoemaker makes use, not only of his material and his tools, but of his eyes to see them, and of his hands to handle them. And similarly a musician. The shoemaker, therefore, and the musician, are distinct from the eyes and hands which they make use of. Just so we make use of our whole body, in all its members and particles. We therefore are, in like manner, distinct from the body we make use of, and from all its members and particles. A man is somewhat other than his body.

When, therefore, we are enjoined to know our self, the self spoken of must be our very self, distinct from our body. Whosoever has attained to the knowledge of his body only, has become acquainted with not himself, but simply a something

---

[1] Contemp. Rev. i. 45.

which *belongs* to himself. Physicians, therefore, and gymnasts, with all their knowledge of the body, may know nothing of *the man*. Artisans, with all their technical acquirements, know not *the man*, nor even his belongings, but only the belongings of his belongings. Whence it is that we regard their arts as "base, mechanical," and not liberal. And further, to take proper care of your body is not necessarily to take proper care of your very self. You may enrich your body and yet starve your self.' (Just as our Lord says, 'A man's life consisteth not in the abundance of the things that he possesseth.') 'And so, when you are in love, you may be loving, not *the man*, but only something that belongs to the man. Whence it is that love fixed on the *person* (the mere mask of the soul) fades with the fading of this person; while love fixed on the *soul* endures as long as this soul maintains its culture and development.

But more than this; without the knowledge of our very self—our soul, we not only must be ignorant how to take proper care of our self, but how to take proper care of the body which belongs to ourself. For only in the light of our true nature can we see what is best for our belongings also. It is one and the same person who must know himself, and his belongings, and the belongings of these belongings. He who is ignorant of himself must be ignorant also of other men, and of groups of men such as families and states, and therefore be ignorant equally of what is best for them. No one can make himself happy, or make others happy, who is not wise and good. Before all things, therefore, strive to be good; and to be wise in order to goodness.' Compare, again, our Lord: 'Seek ye first God's righteousness, and all other blessings shall be added to you.' 'Strive, i.e. for that wisdom which consists in recognising your soul as the image of God, and God as the prototype of your soul.'

## NOTE V.

*Page* 19.

In no way can we rid ourselves of our ever present self. And yet how dexterously this irrepressible Thinker of all our thoughts and Observer of all our inward states may be *ignored*, is shown in Dr. Hake's Tract on 'Vital Force.' He there says (p. 54): 'Force ranges within an ever-changing series of phenomena.' Well! But 'phenomena' imply, by the very term, a some one beholding them; ᾧ φαίνονται. Again: 'Every form of force, from its coarsest manifestation to its most refined, is due to a scale through which the agent ascends.' But here, again, look at the very words. 'Forms' imply an observer before whom they are formed. And 'manifestations' imply a some one to whom they manifest themselves. Again (p. 55), 'Motion is one salient form of force.' But what is 'motion?' It is simply a change of position. And a change of position is a something *observable*, and observed by a some one to whom the change is apparent. Again, 'chemical action,' 'electricity,' 'heat,' 'magnetism,' 'light,'—these (says Dr. Hake) are all 'salient forms of force,' presenting 'a variety of behaviour.' Where the question recurs, 'forms,' to whom? 'salient,' before whom? presenting 'a variety of behaviour,' to whose cognizance? All the expressions imply a *beholder* different from the things beheld. Look again at what he says concerning 'cerebral force.' Its 'manifestations,' its 'phenomena,' its 'forms' are all, by the very force of the terms, manifestations, phenomena, forms *to* a some one beholding them, experiencing them. The observation and the experience lie not in the phenomena themselves, any more than the colours of the rainbow lie in the rainbow, but must lie in a somewhat distinct from them. If 'cerebral force' does (as Dr. Hake asserts, p. 47) 'become metamorphosed into thoughts, emotions, and will,' it must become so metamorphosed (i.e. literally made to take *new forms*) to *a some one*, a *me*, who becomes conscious of these metamorphoses. The 'cerebral force' does not, in any of these changes, *make* this some one, this me. It simply *presents* to this some one, this me, the differing *phenomena* of thought, emotion, and will. As well might we affirm that the transformations in a kaleidoscope *make* the *observer* of these transformations, the eye to which they present themselves, the being beyond the eye *to whom* that organ, in its turn, presents them. So that this some one, this observant **I**, is in no way accounted for by all this play of words; is in no way shown to be the product of this cerebral force, which is thus 'transformed' before it. Ever must this '**I**' be *pre*-supposed as *pre*-existent, in order to any 'manifestation,' in any 'form,' by any 'transformation' of this cerebral force. And this '**I**,' therefore, must be *accepted* by us as thus *pre*-existent, unless we *surreptitiously* ignore it. So impossible is it for materialism to account for, what Fichte terms, that 'duplicity of subject and object in all conscious conception, never to be explained by any workings of a force, seeing that such force, like everything organic, can never do more than generate products simply *objective*.'[1]

Dr. Hake's ignoration, therefore, must be amended thus: 'Oxygen and carbon combine to produce in the lungs the phenomena' which *I*, the *observer* of these phenomena, *to whom* they are phenomena, call 'chemical force.' This again, 'when the blood-cells are normal, produces a metamorphosis of chemical into electric or subvital force,' which *I*, the *observer* of this metamorphosis, call, on account of this new form *observed by me*, electric, or subvital force. This again, 'taking the track of the fibres of the brain, is metamorphosed into thought, emotion, and will;' i.e. *I* become conscious of it as taking the *form* of thought, emotion, and will. In all these stages, the last as much as the first, that of mental force as much as of chemical and vital force, the question incessantly recurs, and in vain you would drive it off your mind, To what are these transformations phenomena? By what are they experienced? What takes cognizance of them and gives them name? Not any of the other forces of the system. Not the sum total of those forces. But a some one distinct from the phenomena of each force separately and of all combined, whom you can neither make nor unmake by all your 'transformations' of force, and whom I call 'I myself I.'

[1] See I. H. Fichte, Anthropologie, 89.

For, further still, these 'transformations' not only take place to, or before, or in the consciousness of, a some one different from them; they take place only by the *concurrence* of this some one. It may be shown from the very nature of being, i.e. of atoms, or simple entities, that for any movements in other entities to become present to me, phenomena to me, they must *affect* me. Those entities must not merely change in themselves, and in their relations to each other; they must cause changes *in me* correspondent with the transformations of force without me. For observation is no mere passive *impression* as of a seal on wax; it is an active *conception* (con-capio) taking up and appropriating the change before me. And this conception could never take place if there were no 'I' to conceive; to take up the changes in the elements before me. It involves a re-action of the element 'I' on the other elements brought into contact with this 'I.' So that the 'thought, emotion and will,' supposed to be simply changes in the brain, must be the co-product of a somewhat *not* the brain, affected by the brain, re-acting on the brain. Nay, these changes, ascribed exclusively to the chemical, vital, electric, and cerebral forces, are, after all, changes of which we know nothing but from the changes in the *mental force*. While the materialists make the mind the product of the phenomena, the fact is that these phenomena are the product of the mind. The changes which we are supposed to *observe* are really changes which we *experience* in our self. 'The personality remains always shut up within the sphere of its own consciousness.'[1] And this personality, this mental force, productive of mental changes in co-incidence with the changes of the chemical, vital, electrical, and cerebral forces, has this peculiarity utterly absent from all those, that it is cognisant of its own action and interaction, cognisant of the changes set up in itself by means of other forces; *self-cognisant* therefore, or *self-conscious*.

And it is this self-conscious entity which must be recognised as constituting our *proper self*. 'Since consciousness,' says Bishop Butler, 'is a single and indivisible power, it should seem that the subject in which it resides must be so too.

[1] See on this Herbart, Hauptpunkte der Metaphys. 22.

Since the perception or consciousness which we have of our own existence is indivisible, so as that it is a contradiction to suppose one part of it should be here and the other there, the perceptive *power*, or the *power* of consciousness, is indivisible too; and consequently the *subject* in which this power resides; i.e. the conscious *being*.'[1]

See also Pfleiderer: 'Our thoughts are no mere product of the bodily senses, and the impressions which these receive from the world without us, but they include an à priori element,—that of conferring *form* on these impressions—which element can never have accrued to us from without, but must be of inward origin. And in this particular, at least, we must concede to the personality of man an independence of merely sensuous life. Self-consciousness and self-determination are the two aboriginal *facts* of our inward experience which materialism can never in anywise explain by the mere mechanism of influential forces; for these facts constitute the actual self-differentiation of the personal *self* from all mere *things*.'[2]

It is painful to find Dr. Maudsley's book on 'Body and Mind' full of the same confusion of thought as Dr. Hake's. The title should have been simply 'Body,' for all notion of *mind*, as other than a function of the higher nervous tissues, is dispensed with. Thus, he says (p. 110), 'I know not why the Power which created matter and its properties should be thought not to have endowed it with the functions of reason, feeling, and will.' And again (p. 125), 'To those who cannot conceive that any *organisation of matter*, however complex, should be capable of such exalted functions as those which are called mental, is it really more conceivable that any organisation of matter can be the mechanical instrument of the complex manifestations of an immaterial mind?' No, certainly! but then there is no such thing as 'matter' in your sense of a mere 'mechanical instrument.' The juggle is the same as with Büchner. All turns on, *what is* matter? If matter be the 'material' of existence, then to assume the sense in which these writers use it, is simply to beg the whole question. But if matter be only the phenomenal manifestation in space of im-

---

[1] Butler, Analogy, p. 21.   [2] Pfleiderer, Die Religion, i. 334.

material *forces* or atoms, reciprocally affecting each other, then the immaterial atom, *mind*, can affect the immaterial atoms which form the base of 'matter,' and be affected by them, in their own super-sensuous sphere. And as to Dr. Maudsley's theistic views, they repeatedly contradict themselves. Thus, in p. 131, he says: 'The wonder is that human intelligence should ever have grown to the height of either affirming or denying the existence of God' (mark the Comtean sing-song), 'for certainly the denial implies, even if the affirmation does not also, the assumption of the attributes of a God by him who makes it.' Where he confounds *ap*prehension (affirmation) with *com*prehension. The wonder is that a dog should presume to apprehend the *existence* of a man, seeing that he has not the attributes of a man!

And yet in another place he quotes Bacon's celebrated dictum on Providence and Deity apparently with approval, and adds, 'It is not easy to perceive how modern science, which makes its inductions concerning natural forces from observation of their manifestations, and arrives at generalisations of different forces, can, after observation of nature, avoid the generalisation of *an intelligent mental force*, linked in harmonious association and essential relations with other forces, but leading and constraining them to higher aims of evolution.' And yet 'the nature, *aim*, and power of this supreme intelligent force it is plainly impossible that man, a finite and transient part of nature, should comprehend' (p. 134). True as to the *essence* of the supreme, for we know not the essence of even our fellow men, but untrue as to the *aim*. For you know a man's aims by his doings; you know the *character* of this incomprehensible essence by the signs of this character which his acts supply you with; you *ap*prehend him, by these signs, to have reason, feeling, purpose, will; you see him to be clever, tasteful, powerful. And why not from *similar manifestations* obtain a similar apprehension of the supreme mental force? Nay, you have already taken this step, just immediately before, for you have allowed that we '*cannot avoid* the generalisation' (of course from the manifestations before us), not simply of a force, but ' of an *intelligent mental* force.' That is, you judge of the divine force as you judge of a human force, by *his works and ways*. Again (p. 133), 'Encompassing us and transcending our ken, is a universe of energies; how can man, then, the feeble atom of an hour, presume to affirm *whose* glory the heavens declare, whose handiwork the firmament showeth?' Why, surely, the glory and handiwork of 'the *intelligent mental force* which is in essential relation with these forces, and *leads and constrains* them to higher *aims*' (the writer's *own* word) 'of evolution.'

## NOTE VI.

*Page* 24.

HALF the confusion in the controversy of matter *v.* spirit results from the failure on both sides to settle what matter is. 'Every philosophic mind,' says Janet, 'in studying the system of Büchner, will be struck at once with a strange omission in it. Namely, that while he explains all being by matter, he has entirely forgotten to tell us what matter is. His system is thus rotten at the very core.'[1] And, in fact, the only true conception of matter is that which is supplied to us by the original word for it. Matter is properly 'materies,'[2] the *stuff* whereof anything is made, from mater, the mother of things; because it is to bodies what a mother is to her children.[3] Matter is *materials*; the sum total of the substances of which all the phenomena of body are but the form. Whence Herbart says: 'To conceive matter as merely a something extended, and yet as something real, is an absurdity. For extension itself has no reality; and therefore predicates derived from it have simply no meaning. Forces, such as weight, cohesion, and so on, which have reference merely to relations of space are simply

---

[1] Janet, Materialisme Contemp. 34.
[2] In the sense in which Ovid says, 'Materiem superabat opus.' And Seneca (Epist. lxv.): 'Faciens, hic Deus est; *ex quo fit*, hæc *materia* est. . . Potentius autem ac pretiosius est quod facit, quod est Deus, quam *materia* patiens Dei.'
[3] See Ainsworth in verbo.

phenomenal, and these phenomena must have *deeper bases underlying* them. Therefore the phenomena which men usually designate as " matter " can be the offspring only of what Leibnitz calls *monads,* that is, of such *materials,* or *elements* of things, as are in their very nature perfectly without extension.'[1] And hence the current distinction between matter and spirit is delusory. The only real distinction is that between things visible and things invisible, which things invisible must be sub-posed as the ground of these things visible. See more on this in Note XIV.

## NOTE VII.

### *Page* 30.

So much depends on a full conviction of this substantiality of the somewhat which I call my self, that I collect here some of the chief authorities on the point.

The question is not, whether there be individual realities at the base of all phenomena, for even Büchner admits ' matter *and force,*' a system of constants underlying all variables: but the question is, whether what I call my Self is a resultant only of those constants hitherto known and catalogued, oxygen, hydrogen, &c., or whether it be itself a constant, an ' elementary substance,' different in kind from those.

And the answer is, the *phenomena* ascribable to this unknown self are essentially different from the phenomena ascribed to the known ' elementary substances.' This ' self' therefore deserves and demands to be catalogued as an additional ' elementary substance,' begetting the phenomena of thought, in like manner as the acknowledged ' elementary substances' beget the phenomena of acidity, of water, &c. Whence it should be catalogued by a name analogous to those others, expressive of the phenomena to which it gives rise, as *noerogen.*

Now that this essential difference in the phenomena demands the recognition of an essentially different *base* for these phenomena, is thus insisted on by Coleridge: ' How the *esse*

---

[1] Herbart, Encycl. der Phil. 219–226.

assumed as originally distinct from the *scire* can ever unite itself with it; how *being* can transform itself into a *knowing*, becomes conceivable only on one condition, namely, if it can be shown that the vis representativa, or the sentient, is itself a *species of being*; either as a property or attribute, or as an hypostasis or self-subsistence. The former is the assumption of materialism' (when it says, thought is a property of brain-tissue). 'But how any affection from without can metamorphose itself into perception or will, the materialist has hitherto left not only as incomprehensible as he found it, but has aggravated it into a comprehensible absurdity. For grant that an object from without could act upon the conscious self as on a consubstantial object, yet such an affection could only engender something homogeneous with itself. Motion could only propagate motion. Matter has no inward. We remove one surface but to meet another. We can but divide a particle into particles; and each atom comprehends in itself the properties of the material universe. Try the experiment of explaining to yourself the evidence of your sensuous intuitions from the hypothesis that in any given perception there is a something which has been communicated to it by an impact or an impression *ab extra*. In the first place, by the impact on the percipient or ens representans, not the object itself but only its action or effect will pass into the same. Not the iron tongue, but its vibrations only, pass into the metal of the bell. Now, in our immediate perception it is not the mere power or act of the object, but the object itself which is immediately present. Or, would we explain this supervention of the object to the sensation by a productive faculty set in motion by an impulse; still the transition into the percipient of the object itself from which the impulse proceeded, assumes a power that can permeate and wholly possess the soul, "And like a God, by spiritual art, Be all in all, and all in every part." And how came the percipient here? And what is become of the wonder-promising matter that was to perform all these marvels by mere figure, weight, and motion? Materialism owes all its proselytes to the propensity to mistake distinct images for clear conceptions, and (*vice versâ*) to reject as inconceivable whatever from its own nature is unimaginable. But as soon as it becomes intelligible it ceases to be materialism. Priestley (e.g.) stripped matter of all its material properties, substituted spiritual powers, and when we expected to find a body, behold we had nothing but its ghost, the apparition of a defunct substance.'[1]

Similarly Mr. Bain (in 'Macmillan's Mag.' Sept. 1867): 'Mental states and bodily states are utterly contrasted. They cannot be compared. They have nothing in common except the most general of all attributes, degree, and order in time. Our mental experience, our feelings, our thoughts, have no extension, no place, no form or outline, no mechanical division of parts; and we are incapable of attending to anything mental until we shut off the view of all that. This, then, is the only real difficulty of the physical and mental relationship. There is an *alliance* with matter, with the object, or extended world; but the thing allied, the mind proper, has itself no extension and cannot be joined in local union.'

This 'only difficulty' is met by I. H. Fichte, with his theory that *all* elementary substances are of the same kind—all intellective. Only, in those which underlie *matter* the intelligence remains *instinctive* merely (according to Droxler's phrase: 'Nihil in sensu quod non prius *in instinctu*'); while in *mind* it rises to the higher powers of consciousness and self-consciousness; i.e. of knowing (cognising) the ends towards which it moves, and of cognising (moreover) our *self*, as consciously aiming at these ends.

And Sir John Herschel seems to have the same view when he says: 'The notion of the atom—the indivisible, the *thing* that has place, being, and power—is an absolute necessity of the human thinking mind, and is of all ages and nations. . . . And these atoms have their idiosyncrasies. They comport themselves according to their primary constitution. They conform to the fixed rule implanted in them. They act and react on each other according to the rigorously exact, mathematically determinate, relations laid down for them. They work out the pre-

---

[1] Coleridge, Biographia Literaria, 63.

conceived scheme of the universe.' And 'the presence of *mind* is what solves the whole difficulty.'[1]

But as to the reality and self-subsistence of the mental atom which I call myself, as distinguished from the other atoms with which it comes in contact, I. H. Fichte thus writes: 'That real substratum, the soul, which lies at the base of the phenomena of consciousness must be of an altogether different *kind* from the entities which give birth to the phenomena of material bodies. It is sui generis. Nay, the spirit of exact investigation of nature requires us to accept it as such. For nothing does science more insist on than the *separation and distinction of all specific marks* in the phenomena presented to us; and consequently it must equally insist on the separation and distinction of the real substrata which lie at the base, respectively, of these distinct phenomena.'[2] That is, plainly: As the *phenomena* of thought are distinct from those of body, so for the *base* of these phenomena we must accept a somewhat, equally distinct from the bases of those of body. As scientifically as we recognise oxygen, hydrogen, &c. as the bases of these latter, so scientifically must we recognise noerogen as the base of those former.

And that the phenomena of mind cannot be the product merely of the elementary substances which produce the phenomena of body, he thus argues: 'Never can the body, the nerves of sense, the brain, themselves feel, think, and be self-conscious. They cannot *cause* these phenomena; they only *occasion* them. We must, indeed, as the ground of every act of thought, admit a corresponding change in the bodily organism, yet this change in the bodily organism is translated into conception and consciousness by the *co-operatve force* of the soul. Thus, a child magnetised by Puysegur, though in his ordinary senses he lacked both mind and memory, yet in the magnetic state displayed both in a high degree. And this shows that the apparatus of consciousness could not lie within the brain, but on the contrary that the soul had power to emancipate itself from the fatuity of its ordinary condition into another region. And this other

---

[1] Herschel, Familiar Lectures, 454–458.
[2] I. H. Fichte, Anthropologie, 80.

region must lie behind that diseased state of consciousness, since the result of its supervening was a higher memory of its own past life. "This fact," says Passavant, "proves by *experience* that the nature of our soul is not dependent on its workings; that the injury or destruction of an organ *by means of which* our soul acts, can do no more than hinder the *manifestation* of the spiritual faculty in the world of phenomena, and has no power over this faculty itself. Nay, it proves that the soul can have a freer activity when deprived of this organ of manifestation; and, in a condition in which it is less dependent on its instruments, can unfold itself in a different manner from when it had them."'[1]

To the same effect Martineau: 'It is impossible to form a steady conception of thought, except as originating *behind* even the innermost bodily structures, and intrinsically different from them. However much you refine and attenuate the living organism, yet, after all, thought is something quite unlike the whitest and the thinnest tissue; and the most delicate of fibres, woven if you please in fairy loom, can never be spun out into emotions. Nor is it at all easier to imagine ideas and feelings to be the *results* of organisation, and to constitute one of the physical *relations* of atoms. If anyone affirms that the juxtaposition of a number of particles makes a hope, and that an aggregation of curious textures forms veneration, he affirms a proposition to which I can attach no idea. Agitate and affect these structures as you will, pass them through every imaginable change, let them vibrate and flow and take a thousand hues, still you can get nothing but motion and temperature and colour; fit marks and curious signals, of thought behind themselves, but no more to be confounded with it than are written characters to be mistaken for the genius and knowledge which may record themselves in language. The corporeal frame, then, is but the mechanism for making thoughts and affections *apparent*, the signal-house with which God has covered us, the electric telegraph by which quickest intimation flies abroad of the *spiritual force* within us.'[2]

---

[1] I. H. Fichte, Anthropologie, 387-391.

[2] Martineau, Sermons, i. 177.

The argument for an immediate conviction of self is ably put by Professor Calderwood: 'The simple fact of consciousness may be thus expressed, "I am thinking." Now this declaration, as Professor Huxley states, involves these three assertions—something called I exists; something called thought exists; and the thought is the result of the action of the I. Of these three, Professor Huxley regards the second as the only certain proposition. The other two, he thinks, are only hypotheses, or at best inferences, which have not the same certainty as the second. Let us see whether this be really the case. "I am thinking." Here the fact of which I am conscious is not merely that *there is a thinking process*, but that *I myself* am engaged in an exercise of thinking. We cannot express the fact of which we are conscious without some term which stands for our personality. We have no consciousness of *thought in the abstract*. If thought is known to me with a certainty which cannot be doubted, it is with the same certainty known as *my thought*. Or, take the thoughts of other men, which they communicate to others. The one distinction between these and the thoughts to which I refer when I say "I am thinking" is this, that these last are known to me as *my* thoughts. We all admit that we have the greatest amount of certainty as to our own thoughts simply because we know them *as our own*. But further. There is not merely a distinction in the *manner* of knowing, and consequently in the degree of *certainty* pertaining to the knowledge, but a distinction between one *form* of thinking known in one way, and another form of thinking known in a different way. This is the distinction between thinking which is *produced*, and thinking which is merely *received*. It is the distinction between mine and thine. That other men are thinkers is known to a man only by inference, not by immediate knowledge of their thinking. But that he himself is a thinker is known to each man *in the exercise* of his thinking power.'[1]

---

[1] Calderwood, in Cont. Rev. Sep. 1870.

## NOTE VIII.

*Page* 36.

ALL thought is differentiation. 'We *think* only relations of things. *Sensation* is singular and particular. Thought transcends this by the bringing down on the singular a universal. The two elements essential to all *thought* are the particular and the universal.' Ferrier, Lect. i. p. 337.

'Every effort of *thought*, from the least to the greatest, any the faintest twitch of consciousness is an act of *comparison*. There is no *thought* in the mind but has two factors, one to be compared with the other. To compare is the first glimmer of intelligence in the infant; to compare is the utmost splendour of reason in the sage. No comparison, no thought.'—Dallas, the 'Gay Science,' i. 266.

Whence all attempts to represent *creation* (which are but the development of *thought* concerning its process) turn on this same principle of *differentiation*. The first creative act, as symbolised by Moses, was the differentiation of light from darkness: 'God *divided* the light from the darkness,' Gen. i. 4. The second creative act was the differentiation of the under waters from the upper: 'God said, Let there be a firmament in the midst of the waters, and let it *divide* the waters from the waters,' Gen. i. 6. And the third creative act was the differentiation of water from land. 'God said, Let the waters be *gathered together* to one place, and let the dry land appear,' Gen. i. 9. And so on.

## NOTE IX.

*Page* 38.

THE carrying on through all its stages this process of differentiation constitutes the whole business of philosophy. For this business, on whatever subject of knowledge it be exercised, is simply the *clarifying of our notions* on that subject—the defecating them from the sediment of popular thought, and separating them from the accretions with which they are incrusted. 'Philosophy,' says Herbart, 'consists in the elaboration of notions;'[1] i.e. the working them out of their incrustations into complete refinement. Whence Sir W. Hamilton calls 'the faculty which *operates* on the raw material furnished by perception, the *elaborative* faculty.'[2] And M. Ferrier says: 'Philosophy exists only to correct the inadvertencies of man's ordinary thinking. She has no other mission to fulfil; no other object to overtake; no other business to do.'[3] And therefore, when Cicero begins to 'philosophise' about death, he sets out with examining, *revising*, and *clarifying* the popular notion of it: 'Mors igitur, quæ *videtur* notissima res esse, *quid sit*, primum est videndum.'[4] And Dr. Whewell says: 'Men, in seeking and obtaining scientific knowledge' (which is philosophy, or, as Ferrier terms it, 'reasoned truth,'), 'have always shown that they found the *formation of right conceptions* in their own minds to be an essential part of the process.'[5] And again: 'Man is the *interpreter* of nature, not the *spectator* merely, but the *interpreter* of nature; and this study of the language of nature is to be pursued by *examining ideas* as well as mere phenomena; Mr. Mill, indeed, says, "a conception is not furnished *by* the mind till it has been furnished *to* the mind." But it is furnished *to* the mind by *its own activity* operating according to its own laws. No doubt the conception may be formed, and in cases of discovery must be formed, by the suggestion and excitement which the facts themselves produce, and must be *so moulded as to agree with the facts*. But this does not make it superfluous to examine out of what *materials* such conceptions are formed, and how they are capable of being *moulded* and modified so as to agree with nature.

> It is the mind that sees; the outward eyes
> Present the object, but the mind descries.'[6]

[1] Herbart, Lehrb. der Phil. iv. p. 2.
[2] Hamilton, Lectures on Metaphysics, ii. 14.
[3] Ferrier, Instit. of Metaph. 32. Comp. his Tract on Scottish Philosophy, p. 12.
[4] Cicero, Tusc. Disp. i. 9. [5] Whewell on Induction, 32. [6] Ibid. 35, 37.

## NOTE X.

*Page* 40.

SEE on this subject **Ferrier** ('Lectures' i. 332): '*Thought* begins by regarding a particular sensation as one of a *class*; begins by thinking something more than the particular itself; and this something more is a class, a genus, a conception, a *universal*, or, in the language of Plato, an *idea*.' And again (p. 337): 'The *universal* element is called by Plato an *idea*. Take a tree: it is an *instance*: but of what? Not of the particular tree before us? Certainly not. The particular tree is before us, but that of which it is an instance is not before us, not before us as a particular, is not visible to our sense, though present to the mind as an idea, a universal.' Here we find the elements of all thought, the particular and the universal; the instance, and that of which the instance is an instance. As this cannot be an instance without being an instance of something, in so far as it is an instance it is a particular. The something of which it is an instance is a *universal*, an *idea*. Plato calls it also παράδειγμα.

But then, though Plato's 'Ideas' are manifestly what we call universal notions, and consider as the ultimate product of the process of differentiation, he did not satisfy himself with them as merely such. He would not accept them as products of our own ratiocination; he required them to be looked at as objects out of the mind, and independent of the mind, to the discovery of which it reaches by climbing up the ladder of special and general notions, to its very summit. These ideas indicate, indeed, the qualities of actual things; but these qualities in their native purity, entirely separated from the things themselves, which are only more or less imperfect shadows of them. And lest these qualities should be thought to change and perish with the changes of the things which yield to us some faint shadow of them, Plato transfers them into the region of pure, absolute *being*, as simple unchangeable essences. So that what we call universals, and regard as thoughts of the mind, Plato regards as ὄντως ὄντα, and objects presented to these thoughts.[1] Whence Cicero describes them as 'id, quod semper est simplex, et uniusmodi, et tale quale est,' and affirms that the mind *discerns* them (cernit); looks out upon them as objects revealed to it.[2] Consequently they are not our own thoughts, however abstract, but objects presented to our cognition; objects which form the *contrast* to all sensuous objects, inasmuch as these by their fluxional character betray their unreality. Think away, then, the contradictions in these sensuous objects; look at their *qualities* in their simple purity; refer these qualities to their *universal notions*; consider these universal notions as only cognitions of real objects; then these real objects are what Plato means by 'ideas.'[3] Compare Ritter, Historia Philosophiæ, 233: 'Εἶδος et ἰδέα proprie significat formam s. speciem, quæ cernitur oculis, translate id quod mente cernitur. Apud Platonem idea nonnunquam dicitur eodem sensu quo *notio*. In quo tamen cavendum ne *in animo tantum ejus qui cogitat* existere ideas putemus, quod ipse Plato negat Parmen. p. 132 B. Imo hoc quam maxime Platonis doctrina a Socratis distabat quod ille ideas separatim a rebus existere docebat. Quapropter Plato, imaginibus, ut assolet, rem persequens, ideas tanquam in alio mundo existere, neque tam *cogitari* quam mente pura *adspici*.'

---

[1] See Herbart, De Pl. Syst. fund. 35: 'Ne hæsitemus affirmare illa ipsa esse Platonis ὄντως ὄντα quæ nos quarumcunque rerum *notiones generales*, nec quicquam nisi animi cogitationes, dicere solemus.' And 49: 'Qualitates, nude positæ, segregatæ a rebus in δόξης regionem detrusis, ipsæ, ne una cum rebus pereant, per se stare, adeoque *esse* dicendæ sunt.' Compare Degerando, Histoire de Phil. ii. 246, who quotes from Aristotle (Met. xiii. 2), 'Socrate ne séparait point les universaux des choses particulières. Après lui on les sépara, on leur donna le nom d'*idées*; ainsi on considéra comme idée tout ce qui peut être exprimé par *un terme universel*;' (πάντων ἰδέας εἶναι τῶν καθόλου λεγομένων).

[2] Cicero, Acad. Post. i. 8, 30.

[3] See Herbart, *Lehrbuch der Phil.* § 121, p. 178-181; und De Platon. Systematis fundamento, passim.

## NOTE XI.

*Page 56.*

THE objection often made to the immediateness of the æsthetic judgments, drawn from their seeming variableness, and their acknowledged growth, is thus met by Mr. Lecky ('Europ. Morals,' i. 101): 'A bad *intellectual* education will produce not only erroneous or imperfect information, but also a false ply or habit of judgment. A bad *æsthetical* education will produce false canons of taste. Systematic abuse will pervert even some of our *physical* perceptions. In each case the experience of *many* minds under *many* conditions must be appealed to, to determine the standard of right and wrong' (that is, we must appeal from the imperfect 'reason' of the individual to that 'universal reason' which, when called forth, is recognised by all). 'We may decide particular moral questions by reasoning, but our reasoning itself is an appeal to certain moral *principles* which are revealed to us by intuition.' 'The conscience is not some mysterious agent, like the demon of Socrates, which gives specific and infallible information on particular cases. All that is affirmed is—first, that our will is not governed exclusively by the law of pleasure and pain, but also by the law of duty; secondly, that the basis of our conception of duty is an intuitive perception that among the various feelings, tendencies, and impulses that constitute our emotional being, there are some which are *essentially* good and ought to be encouraged, and some which are *essentially* bad, and ought to be repressed. As a psychological *fact* we are intuitively conscious that our benevolent affections are superior to our malevolent ones; truth to falsehood, justice to injustice, gratitude to ingratitude, chastity to sensuality; and that in all ages and countries the path of virtue has been towards the higher and not towards the lower feelings. "La loi fondamentale de la morale" (says Voltaire) "agit sur toutes les nations. Il y a mille différences dans les interprétations de cette loi en mille circonstances, mais le fond subsiste toujours le même, et ce fond c'est l'idée du juste et de l'injuste."'

And again (Ibid. 125): 'The eye of the mind, like the eye of the body, may be closed. Man is like a plant which requires a favourable soil for the full expansion of its natural and innate powers (see Reid, ' Active Powers,' iii. 8, p. 4). Yet those powers both rational and moral *are there*, and when quickened into action each will discharge its appointed functions. If it could be proved that there are savages who are absolutely destitute of the progressive energy which distinguishes reason from instinct, and of the moral aspiration which constitutes virtue, this would not prove that rational or moral faculties form no part of their nature. If you could show that there is a stage of barbarism in which man knows and feels and does nothing that might not be known, felt, and done by an ape, you would not have reduced him to the level of the brute; there would still be this broad distinction between them—the one possesses a *capacity for development* which the other does not possess. Under favourable circumstances the savage will become a reasoning, progressive, and moral man. Under no circumstances can a similar transformation be effected in the ape. It may be as difficult to detect the oakleaf in the acorn as in the stone. Yet the acorn may be converted into an oak. The stone will always continue to be a stone.'

## NOTE XII.

### Page 75.

FLECK has supplied a very exhaustive investigation of the word *religio*, and his conclusions are:

1. That *religio*, though not derivable direct from religare, must be accepted as coming from *legere*, in its sense of *binding together*, tying up, which afterwards expressed itself by the cognate word *ligare*; and is therefore equivalent to *religatio*, *religamentum, vinculum religans*.

2. That we must therefore receive the word *religare* as lying at the base of *religio*, and conveying to it its own proper sense. But *religare* means *revincire*, to bind back, restrain, anything

which presses forwards; as in '*naves ad terram religare;*' '*folia lactucæ religare;*' '*comas religare;*' '*manus post terga religare.*'

3. And hence *religio* is a binding back, a restraining of men; an arrest of their natural impulse and desire. And this in a twofold sense. An *objective* one, expressing a something which wards off approach and invasion; e.g. *religio templi*, jurisjurandi, officii, deorum. And a *subjective* one, denoting the *feeling* of abstinence and self-restraint, which hinders men from 'rushing in where angels fear to tread.' This feeling expresses itself in the meanings connected with *religion*, of consideration, carefulness, fear, awe. And its contrary is indicated in the phrase, '*homo sine religione*,' a man to whom nothing is sacred, who has no sense of restraint or reverence. Of these two senses, the objective one is the primary; the subjective the secondary. And we find this meaning pervading innumerable phrases in Roman writers. Nothing is more common with them than to conceive religion under the image of a restraining bond. Thus Cicero says: 'quod fœdus quum magis fide illius populi, quam aliquo publico *vinculo religionis* teneretur.' *Religio* is here conceived as *vinculum tenens* which assures to the fœdus its inviolability. So Livy: 'exsolvamus religione populum, si qua obligavimus;' Lucretius: 'animum religionum nodis exsolvere.' Cicero, again: 'tanta religione obstricta tota provincia est.' 'Hac ego religione non sum ab hoc conatu repulsus;' where *religio* comes before us as *repellens conatum.*

From all which Gellius rightly says: 'religiosus pro casto atque *observanti, cohibentique sese certis legibus finibusque* dici est cœptus.' And Servius: 'religio, i.e. metus ab eo, quod mentem *religet*, dicta religio.' And Arnobius: 'religio sæpissime est horror, qui objectus nobis ab aliquo signo *coercet nos*, et quasi *religatos* tenet.'—Fleck, 'System der Christl. Dogmatik,' 1–10.

## NOTE XIII.

*Page* 96.

THIS argument, from the *worth* of the soul to its permanency, is the one specially relied on by both Lotze and Rückert. Lotze says: 'That alone will last for ever which constitutes, on account of its *worth*, a permanent element in the organism of God's world. That will go to nothing which lacks this worth. Therefore we must repose ourselves on this simple faith, that God will deal with every creature according to what is fit and proper for it.'[1] And Rückert: 'If we admit the possible prolongation of existence beyond the present stage of being, the question still recurs, for what substance is such prolongation to be expected? And the answer is, plainly for *that* alone which, in this present stage of being, does not reach to the accomplishment of its idea, and, therefore, seems in contradiction with itself. Now this substance is not the body, nor the animal life, but only the SOUL, the force within us which is capable of choosing good, and whose very idea it is to make unconditionally this choice. For this idea we find it accomplishing either not at all, or at the most very imperfectly. We know nothing about the substance in which this force resides, but we do know the force itself, from actual experience. And my argument is this: in the realm of the ideal, such a force must be conceived as fulfilling its idea at every instant, as being at every instant a manifestation of God, and as contributing at every instant whatever it should towards this fulfilment; the problem is being perpetually solved. But in the realm of the actual this idea of the spirit is *not* fulfilled; the problem is never solved. If, then, this spirit goes to nothing along with the body and the animal life, then these two latter will have realised their idea, have accomplished their destiny; but the *former not*. But God is an all-gracious God, and the very idea of such graciousness demands for all the products of this grace an eternal possibility of raising the actual to the level of the ideal, of becoming what they were

---

[1] Lotze, Mikrokosmus, 425.

created to be. Therefore, I cannot but believe the eternal possibility of my deliverance from what is contrary to my ideal, sin; and, consequently, I cannot but believe, as the condition of this possibility, the eternal existence of my soul, in order to the fulfilment of this its destination; that is, I cannot but believe this eternal existence as a thing which God has destined for me; whether I can *prove* such existence upon other grounds or not, I *must believe* an eternal life, because I cannot admit the thought that man should not accomplish the high destiny assigned to him.'[1]

## NOTE XIV.

### *Page* 109.

This line of argument saves us from endless speculation about the *nature* of the forces which present themselves to us as *facts*. It renders quite unnecessary any decision of the question about 'matter' and 'spirit,' 'soul' and 'body.' For its validity lies in this simple conviction: *whatsoever* I myself may be, *whatsoever* other selfs may be, *whatsoever* the ultimate all-comprehending Self may be, each must BE, each is proved by its *manifestations* to BE. Whence Holbeach affirms (ii. 216): 'I can conceive as possible only one science, the science of *being*, of the things which *are*. Any scheme which does not take into account a controlling $\mathring{\eta}\theta o s$ as a constant element, seems to me purely arbitrary and false; a forging of the balance sheet by the mere exclusion of a certain *quantitas*—a mere hanging up of a curtain, and saying, "We don't know what's inside," when the air you breathe is both within and without.' 'Physical and metaphysical science are both on the same footing. The condition of well-being, nay, the condition (in the end) of being itself, is perpetual adjustment of oneself to the thing which IS, as it is afresh discerned from time to time. Science is no more and no less; religion is no more and no less; morality is no more and no less.' 'You say

[1] Rückert, Theologie, i. 232.

we can only know phenomena, we can never know things in themselves. Be it so. There are phenomena *and* phenomena; and I can know the infinite phenomenon just as assuredly as the finite.' (Which is Herbart's argument: 'As much as by human phenomena in daily life we know a man, so much, by divine phenomena in nature and events, we know God.') 'For if precisely the same arguments may be employed to make impossible the proof of the seen, if there is no argument which may be used to show that the *infinite* cannot be proved to have an objective existence, which may not equally be used so as to show that the *finite* has no objective existence, then *both* become *phenomenal* to logic.'

The futility of the distinctions between 'matter' and 'spirit,' 'soul' and 'body,' is now pretty generally acknowledged. 'Descartes' (says Coleridge, 'Biogr. Lit.' 62) 'was the first who introduced the absolute and essential heterogeneity of mind and matter. But since impenetrability is intelligible only as a mode of *resistance*, its admission places the essence of *matter* in an act or power which it possesses *in common with spirit*; and body and spirit are therefore no longer absolutely heterogeneous, but may be supposed to be different modes of a common substratum.' And so Dr. Huxley, in 'Lay Sermons,' 370: 'According to Descartes' view the soul is a mathematical point, having place but not extension. And not only has it place but it must exert force, for it is competent to change the course of the animal spirits, which consist of matter in motion. Thus, the soul becomes *a centre of force*. But then the distinction between spirit and matter vanishes; inasmuch as matter, according to a tenable hypothesis, may be nothing but *a multitude of centres of force*.' So also Spencer ('First Principles,' 223): 'The materialist and spiritualist controversy is a mere war of words, in which the disputants are equally absurd.' And Carpenter ('Physiology,' 797): 'The whole tendency of philosophical investigation at the present day is to show the utter futility of all the controversies with regard to the relation of mind and matter.' And Cornill ('Materialismus und Idealismus'): 'Materialism and spiritualism are empty abstractions, indicating only, at the utmost, *contrasted phenomena*.' And Leibnitz: 'The essence of all being, whether mind or matter, is *force*. Matter is simply an assemblage of simple *forces*.' And Dr. Huxley again, 'Lay Sermons,' 373: 'When materialists begin to talk about there being nothing else in the universe but matter and force and necessary laws, I decline to follow them. For all our knowledge is a knowledge of states of consciousness. " Matter " and " force " are, so far as we can know, mere names for certain forms of consciousness. " Necessary " means that of which we cannot conceive the contrary. " Law " means a rule which we have always found to hold good, and which we expect always will hold good. Thus, what we call the material world is only known to us under the forms of the ideal world; and, as Descartes tells us, our knowledge of the soul is more intimate and certain than our knowledge of the body.' 'The differences between metaphysics and physics are *complementary and not antagonistic*; and thought will never be completely fruitful until the one unites with the other' (371).

## NOTE XV.

*Page* 110.

THIS argument, from the organic unity of the world, seems to me the only perfectly satisfactory demonstration of God. For,

1. The argument from *effect to cause* is either insufficient or suicidal. It is insufficient if we keep to the narrower notion, 'All effects must have a cause,' for we know of no effects which are not also causes, and of no causes which are not also effects; and so we cannot reach to the conception of an absolute cause. And if we seek to cure this insufficiency by making the proposition more general, 'All being must have a ground of being,' then this ground also, since it is itself being, must have a ground of itself; and so on ad infinitum. And thus you get no first cause, or first being, but only an infinite series of causes or beings.

2. The argument from *show to substance*—i.e. from existence, or phenomenal being, to entity, or non-phenomenal

being—is more valid, and is employed in Heb. xi. 3, and Rom. i. 20. But still, this argument brings you only to substances in general, or substances in particular, not to a one individual substance. It is certain, indeed, that 'things which are seen have not their last ground in things that do appear' (Heb. xi. 3); and that 'invisible things, eternal power and divinity, are deducible from the consideration of the things that are made' (all the facts of the world prove a superhuman power), Rom. i. 20. But then, the One to whom this power belongs, of whom it is the attribute, is still left not fully reached.

3. The argument from *force to force*, or will to will, goes even further in its validity. And it has been well put by Mr. Kirkman ('Matter, Force, and Atheism,' p. 68): 'What these dread forces are whose constant presence and action we experience I know not; but every moment that I live under their untiring, unchanging, and beneficent teaching, they more and more appear to *be*. I meet them not, I have never met them, but as *equivalents or multiples of my own will-force*. I must compare them, therefore, with this my conscious will-force. This balances them here, overcomes them there, and combines itself with them, in ways innumerable, into one homogeneous result. But what can balance will but will? What can combine and harmonise with will but will? What can have equivalence and real relation in thought and act to will but will? I glory therefore in believing that all these forces are manifestations of the conscious present working *will* of the God in whom I live and move and have my being. F-o-r-c-e spells WILL.' But even here we reach wills, but not necessarily and undeniably a ONE single, sovereign will.

4. And this One can be reached only by the argument of *parts co-ordinated as a whole*. For such co-ordination as a whole demands from you the recognition of a one mental force pervading, unifying, and adjusting, towards determinate ends, this whole. And thus you arrive at both the existence and the character of God. His existence, because, the world being confessedly a *universe*—multiplicity concatenated into unity, and unity dominating multiplicity—there must be a living centre of this unity, *of* which all organisation is 'the continuous manifestation' (see Carpenter on Cell Force, 'Human

Phys.' 108) *out of* which all things must unfold themselves; *by* which they must be co-ordinated, and *to* which, with constantly increasing perfectionment, they must return. There must be One, in short, ' of whom, and through whom, and to whom, are all things, to whom be glory for ever ! ' Rom. xi. 36. And with the existence of this One you also get his *nature and character*: for all the things that you observe being interactive towards a pre-determined end, and this end being manifestly their ultimate *good*, the One of whom they are the manifestation, and by whom they are incessantly actuated and adjusted, must have a *mind* to devise such interaction; a *heart* to purpose the good to which it tends; and a *will*, of infinite force, to accomplish by such interaction this good. God must be intelligence, love, and power.

All, therefore, in our truest and surest conceptions of God, must run up into this idea of Him as *the author of an organised universe*. 'The one thing wonderful,' says Herbart, 'and that which surpasses all comprehension, is, and must ever continue to be, *the commencement of an organised world* (das Beginnen eines zweckmässigen Naturlaufes).'[1] And similarly J. S. Mill: 'If ignorance is, with Sir W. Hamilton, a necessary condition of wonder, can he find nothing to wonder at in the *origin* of the system of which Newton discovered the laws?'[2] And so a writer in the ' British Quarterly Review:' ' Even those who maintain the development theory, and even if they hold the co-eternity of matter, must rest their theory of the universe on *a primal miracle*, by which the first substance was endowed with energies and laws that would unfold into all the varieties of animate and inanimate nature.'[3] Compare I. H. Fichte: 'That interaction of the forces of the universe which observation assures us of, does of itself indicate a ground of their unity, which must (in fact if not in time) be antecedent to the things which it thus regulates and unites into a whole.'[4] And 'Blackwood's Magazine' for June 1867: 'When science presents to us things as a whole, the conviction immediately follows that this whole existed in thought and idea before it was developed as a reality in time and space.'

---

[1] Herbart, Lehrbuch der Phil. 211.
[2] J. S. Mill, Review of Hamilton, 544.
[3] British Quarterly for Jan. 1861.
[4] I. H. Fichte, Psychologie, i. 24.

## NOTE XVI.

### Page 122.

In all departments of knowledge the same distinction holds. 'If,' asks Mr. Dallas, 'the field of art be the unknown and unknowable, where is there room for a science of art?' And his answer is: 'If we cannot tear the secret from art, we can at any rate lay bare the conditions under which it passes current. There is a science of biology, though no one can define what is life. The science of life is but a science of the laws and conditions under which life is *manifested*. So, again, is it essential to the science of electricity that we should know for certain what is electricity? We know not what it is; we see only its effects. And yet, relating to these *effects of an unknown power*, there has been built up a great science. Again, we can trace the orbits of comets and reckon upon their visits, though of themselves, their what, their why, their wherefore, we know almost nothing. And so there may be a science of the fine arts, though the theme of art is the unknown, and its motive power is the hidden soul.'—'The Gay Science,' i. 334. And just similarly, I say, there may be a science concerning God, a theology, though God Himself in Himself is 'unknown and unknowable.' God is not more 'unknowable' than man, than any elementary substance. All are, in their essence, inscrutable, yet in their workings scrutable.

---

## NOTE XVII.

### Page 124.

On the truth, though insufficiency of representative terms, see Mr. Dallas, 'The Gay Science,' ii. 214-18: 'Fiction is not falsehood; it is the best approximation to truth. "The legitimate end of fiction," says Dr. Johnson, "is the conveyance of truth." Neither in word nor in thought do we ever reach the perfect grasp and exact rendering of truth. All our efforts are but approximations. A residue of error cleaves to all knowledge, all expression. There is no more falsehood in the fictions of art and of poetry than in those of philosophy, of religion, of law, of grammar, of mathematics. The mathematician tells us that a line is length without breath, and that a point has position but no magnitude. But there is no such thing in nature; this whole science is built on this impossible fiction. So in grammar; do you utter falsehoods in using the plural for the singular pronoun? In philosophy, what fictions are abstract ideas! The abstract idea of a triangle is not a reality, nor is it the mental image of a reality, since all three-sided figures in nature must be scalene, isosceles, or equilateral, and the ideal triangle is none of the three. So the general idea of man answers to no individual in existence. But are these abstract ideas false? On the contrary, it is in these fictions that the philosopher expresses the highest truths which the mind of man can grasp. Look, again, at the fictions of sense. I see at the end of my table a book; I know that it is rectangular, but I see it as a rhomboid, and if I were a painter I should paint it as a rhomboid. The rhomboid is a fiction of the eye; but is it false? The whole theory of foreshortening is based on the fictions of perspective, but it is only in these fictions that the truth of drawing can be rendered. The steel grate in my room blushes with the reflected colour of the hearthrug. You who talk of the falsehoods of fiction decide whether it is better for an artist to paint that grate the colour of steel or the colour of the crimson rug; which would be the truer tint? And, again, decide which is truer, to say that the sun is just now setting, or that the earth is wheeling from the sun. Nay, look to religion itself, and see the fictions to which we are reduced. We speak of the Most High God as if He were like ourselves, with the same passions and the same limits; irascible, affectionate, jealous, with feet upon a footstool, with hand outstretched, with arm laid bare, with bowels that sound like a harp for Moab, and inward parts for Kir-haresh. Is all this false? And if we discard these fictions, can we find other terms in which to express, with equal force and clearness, the truths which the fictions convey? In all the above cases, the fictions are more or less short of the truth, but still are *charged with truth,* and mean truth; they are the poor, faltering human expressions of truth, which cannot be half so well conveyed in other forms.' See a similar train of thought in the Rev. G. W. Cox's 'Mythology of the Aryan Nations,' i. 46.

## NOTE XVIII.

*Page* 125.

COMPARE Tissandier, 'Théodicée,' pp. 28–31 : 'Quand je dis *je pense, j'aime, je veux,* je ne déclare point qu'il y a *hors de moi* des objets, des êtres, des phénomènes, qui répondent à mes conceptions, à mes idées. Cette question est distincte de la première, n'est point comprise dans la première, et ce n'est qu'après la première qu'elle doit être abordée. Je commence par *me renfermer dans le moi,* et *sans en sortir,* je déclare que je pense, etc. . . . La langue, image exacte de la pensée, a toujours un mot qui représente *l'être* ; affirmant de lui un *état,* ou une opération. Quand je dis "je doute," cette proposition implique la plus rigoureuse affirmation, *non pas en égard aux choses étrangères à ma personne,* mais relativement à *moi,* et au doute qui n'est qu'une *manière d'être de moi.* . . . Dans chacun des actes de la conscience nous sont donnés un être et une modification de cet être. . . . Un être particulier et l'inépuisable variété de ses phénomènes, de ses manifestations, de ses actes, voilà ce que nous connaissons d'abord.'

## NOTE XIX.

*Page* 129.

ON the right and necessity we have to ascribe 'feelings and sentiments' to God, see a beautiful passage in Martineau's Essays, ii. 315 : 'Plotinus questions (says Kingsley) "Why should the absolute goodness be like our goodness? and generally whether virtues can be predicated of the divine nature. And thus, by setting up a different standard of morality for the divine and for the human, he gradually arrives at the conclusion that virtue is not the end but the means; not the *divine nature itself* as the Christian schools held, but only the purgative process by which man was to ascend to heaven and to arrive at that nature; that nature itself being *what*?" Now this will be found to be the great fundamental difference between monism and monotheism; between the metaphysic evolution of the universe from one *principle*, and the moral recognition in it and beyond it of one *God*. The latter doctrine retains without fear the *human analogy* in its conception of the divine nature, and places there whatever is venerable and holy in character. The former, often doubting whether its deity really *thinks*, can never persuade itself that he *feels*. The source of all can be recipient of nothing; and he abides behind the impressions which he only gives. In nothing does the contrast of this idea with the Christian appear more striking than in its application to the theory of worship. The question is raised by Jamblichus: "How, if the gods are impassible, can they be accessible to prayer?" The answer is intensely heathen. "It is not that the gods descend to the soul of the suppliant, but that he lifts his soul to them. Nor is it change of place only that must be denied to them; there is no change of *feeling* in relation to the worshippers; for the gods are insusceptible of joy or grief, of anger or love. Do we speak sometimes of their anger? We mean only that the soul withdraws from them. Of their propitiation? We mean that the soul draws nigh to them. Prayer is simply a means of rendering oneself like the gods; whatever resembles them has them present in essence." Let this be compared with the passage, "If any man love me *my Father will love him*, and we will *come to him* and *make our abode with him*," and the difference between the genius of heathen theosophy and Christian faith is exhibited in its very essence.'

## NOTE XX.

*Page* 160.

Such is the universal *feeling* of the religious sense that God cannot be the author of evil. And yet the objections of Cotta, in Cicero, 'De Nat. Deorum,' iii. 30, are not easily to be answered: 'Hanc igitur tantam à Dis immortalibus arbitramur malorum sementem esse factam? Si enim *rationem* hominibus Di dederunt, malitiam dederunt; est enim malitia versuta et fallax *ratio* nocendi. Iidem etiam Di fraudem dederunt, facinus ceteraque quorum nihil nec suscipi sine *ratione* nec effici potest. Utinam igitur istam calliditatem hominibus Di ne dedissent! *qua perpauci benè utuntur, innumerabiles autem inprobè utuntur*; ut donum hoc divinum *rationis et consilii* ad *fraudem* hominibus non ad *bonitatem* impertitum esse videatur! Sed urgetis identidem *hominum* esse istam culpam, non Deorum. Ut si medicus gravitatem morbi, gubernator vim tempestatis accuset. . . . Si homines rationem bono consilio à Dis immortalibus datam in fraudem malitiamque convertunt; non dari illam quam dari humano generi melius fuit. Ut, si medicus sciat, eum ægrotum qui jussus sit vinum sumere, meracius sumpturum, statimque periturum; magna sit in culpa: sic vestra ista providentia reprehendenda, quæ *rationem* dederit iis *quos scieret ea perversè et improbè usuros*.' At least such objections can be answered only on the principles thrown out by I. H. Fichte—1. That the only source of *good* to man is that endowment which is abused by him to *evil* ('die Möglichkeit des Bösen liegt in dem was zugleich der Quelle seiner Vollkommenheit ist,' 2,391). 2. That man, to be man and not a machine, must be *self-developing*, and therefore liable to *fail in* this his self-development through weakness, or to *fall from* it through wilfulness. And 3. That this original endowment, capable for a time of being misused, must ultimately, and even through this misuse, attain its full perfectionment. 'The eternal purpose which pervades the universe can never be frustrated by either the failures or the antagonisms of the creature's freedom; though, during the process of development, it may be delayed by the intervening elements of created weakness or wilfulness.'[1] 'The very power of wrong is but a mistaken power of right. The larger venture of such power, in man particularly, is liable indeed to worse contingencies of evil, but yet is destined to produce a higher resultant of bliss. The nodding of a schoolboy's top is not the measure for the oscillations of a world. And by the greatness of man's aberration I measure the greatness of his orbit and his orb.'[2]

---

## NOTE XXI.

*Page* 163.

This great principle that the so-called 'Fall' is no unlooked-for frustration of God's intention, but a stage towards the accomplishment of it, finds for itself expression in the saying of St. Paul (Rom. viii. 20), that 'the creation was made subject to corruption, though against its own feeling, yet by the will of God.' ('Non sua sponte sed Dei qui subjecit auctoritate.'—*Fritzche*.) And the same surmise of this truth lies at the base of the supralapsarian form of Calvinism; for Calvin is perfectly justified in arguing: 'People say that it is nowhere asserted, in so many words, that God willed Adam's fall; as if it were possible that the Supreme, whom Scripture sets forth as doing all things after the counsel of his own will, could have made the noblest of his creatures without any prevision and provision as to what should become of him! How can anyone deny that God must have known what should happen to Adam before He made him; and, moreover, must have known this, because he had predestined his whole career?'[3] And Augustin still more justly says: 'God, the Lord of all things, who made

---

[1] I. H. Fichte, Spec. Theol. ii. 391.     [2] Parker, Theism, 250.

[3] 'Disertis verbis hoc extare negant, decretum fuisse a Deo ut sua defectione periret Adam. Quasi vero idem ille Deus quem Scriptura prædicat facere quæcunque vult, *ambiguo fine* condiderit nobilissimam ex suis creaturis . . . . Inficiari nemo poterit quin præsciverit Deus quem exitum esset habiturus homo, antequam ipsum conderet; *et ideo præsciverit quia decreto suo sic ordinarat.*'—Calvin, *Instit.* iii. 23–7.

every creature very good, and foresaw that nevertheless evils would develope themselves out of this good, and knew also that it pertained more to his omnipotent goodness to *bless the world* by *means of evil* rather than altogether to preclude evil—He it was who so ordained the course of angels and of men as to show therein, first, what is inseparable from a freely acting creature, and next, what further benefit his grace could bring out of this.'[1] Whence he exclaims elsewhere : 'O happy fall, whence we obtain so glorious a rise!'

The one error on this subject, of Augustin, of Calvin, and of so many others, lies in assigning as the *motive* of this predestination, God's glory rather than his creatures' good; whereas it is the ordering all things for his creatures' good which alone constitutes God's glory. The primary motive, in Him whose essence is *love*, must be, not *self* in any form, but the good of others; not an 'égoïsme,' however lofty and imperial, but an 'altruisme,' which is never satisfied without diffusing through other beings the divine perfections, and therewith the divine blessedness. The Calvinistic view of God is like the Hegelian; *self* is its centre. In the first, *self-glorification*; in the second, *self-culture*. Against which latter view see the eloquent protest of Herbart : 'We must beat down Spinosism and idealism, which rob us altogether of any Being distinct from this world, and from ourselves as issuing from Him into separate personality, and so preclude all possibility of *love* in Him devoting itself to us as objects of his care. We must never conceive the divine beneficence under the form of a *nepotism*, contemplating only its own belongings. For love which turns back into itself as *self-love* has lost all the worth of love. There can be no religion if the world be regarded as only one vast system of self-development, wherein the one only *real* Being educates himself up to perfection. Religion can exist only when we regard God as our *Father*, who, having graciously

---

[1] 'Deum, Dominumque rerum omnium, qui creavit omnia bona valde, et *mala ex bonis oritura* praescivit ; et scivit magis ad suam *omnipotentissimam bonitatem* pertinere, etiam *de malis benefacere quam mala esse* **non sinere**; sic ordinasse angelorum et hominum **vitam, ut** in ea prius ostenderet quid posset liberum arbitrium deinde quid posset *gratiæ suæ beneficium.*'—Augustin, *Enchir. ad Laurentium.*

provided for our self-development in order to our good, takes none of that selfish interest in us which results from zeal for his own perfectionment or his own glory.'[1] With which compare the remarkable confession of poor Heine: 'I have indeed returned to God, like the prodigal son, after long tending of swine. The yearning for heaven came upon me and urged me forth through forests and ambushed passes, over the giddiest mountains of logical bewilderment. On my course I discovered the God of the pantheist, but *he could not help me*. This poor visionary being has interwoven and incorporated himself with the world, and become so imprisoned in it that he can do nothing but gape at you powerlessly and without purpose. No! To have a *will* on our side we must have a *personality*; and in order to his manifesting this will in our behalf he must have elbow-room. When you need a God, one that can help you (*for that is* the *principal point*), you must accept also his identity and oneness; his superhumanity, his *all-goodness* and *all-wisdom*. And then the immortality of the soul, our deathlessness after death, will be immediately conceded to us into the bargain. But as to the God of the pantheist! at bottom he is no god at all, even as pantheists themselves are nothing but atheists under a mask.'—Heine, '*Romanzen*,' as quoted in 'Frazer's Mag.' for January, 1854.

## NOTE XXII.

*Page* 170.

The immanence of God throughout the universe is as essential an idea as that of his distinction from this universe. 'Whither,'

---

[1] Herbart, *Lehrbuch der Phil.* 215. The strange misapprehension of this passage in Mansel's *Bampton Lectures* (first edition) obliges me to remind you that Herbart's theism—his childlike confiding theism—is everywhere manifest. See the whole section of which the above passage is part. See the famous fourth chapter of his *Encycl. der Phil.* See his *Pädagogik.* See his *Kleine Schriften*, iii. 169 and 173: 'We all believe in one God, and in Him we recognise the ideal of perfect *Love*; of one distinct from ourselves yet akin to us as our *Father*, and ever providing, not for his own interests, but for ours. He is our infinitely-exalted Friend.'

says the Psalmist, 'shall I go from thy Spirit, and whither shall I flee from thy presence? If I ascend up into heaven' (the highest conceivable point above me) 'thou art there! If I make my bed in the underworld' (the lowest conceivable point beneath me), 'behold thou art there! If I take the wings of the morning' (fly to the furthest east, on one side) 'or dwell in the uttermost parts of the sea' (in the furthest west, on the other side), 'even there shall thy hand lead me, and thy right hand shall hold me.'[1] And with this accords the great question of the Lord by his prophet: 'Am I a God at hand, saith the Lord, and not a God afar off? Can any hide himself in secret places that I shall not see him? saith the Lord. Do not I fill heaven and earth? saith the Lord.'[2] Nor less the declaration of the Apostle: 'He is not far from any one of us, for in him we live and move and have our being.'[3]

But then we must never push this notion of the divine immanence in all things to that of God's *identity* with all things. 'The Christian,' says Nitzch, 'can never for a moment conceive of God without reference to a world which is not itself God, but only from God and for God.'[4] And so Schenkel: 'As certainly as we cannot conceive God fully without reference to the world which He has made, so certainly must we conceive Him as absolutely distinct from this his world.'[5] Yet Tennyson, in one single short piece ('The Higher Pantheism') not only confounds the two ideas, but contradicts himself in his enunciation of them. For while he begins,

> The sun, the moon, the stars, the seas, the hills and the plains,
> Are not these, O soul, the *vision* of Him who reigns?

He goes on—

> Is not the vision *He*? Tho' He be not that which He seems;
> Is He not all but Thou, that hast power to feel 'I am I.'

---

[1] Ps. cxxxix. 7–10.  [2] Jer. xxiii. 23, 24.  [3] Acts xvii. 27.
[4] Christl. Lehre. § 85.  [5] Christl. Dogm. ii. 20.

## NOTE XXIII.

*Page* 191.

This great principle of the insufficiency, though necessity, of conventional *conceptions*, for the hinting rather than expressing the eternal *ideas* which underlie all thought; and of the consequent danger that imagination, which shapes the concrete, will often usurp the place of ideality, which simply contemplates the abstract, and thus will misrepresent what it attempts to illustrate, is well put by Professor Ferrier ('Lect.' i. 338): 'Ideas cannot be *individualised*. You cannot form any sort of *representation* of the idea, or universal, or paradeigma. It cannot be *pictured* to the imagination, for this would at once reduce it to the particular, and convert it into only an *instance*. An idea is diametrically opposed to an image.'

And the extent to which Milton has permitted this intrusion of the imagination into the sphere of the ideal, is well shown by Professor Seeley: ' How **strange an inconsistency lies in the** very construction of **" Paradise Lost."** A Puritan has rebelled against sensuous worship. He has risen in indignation against a scheme of religion which **was** too material, which degraded invisible and awful realities **by** too near an association with what was visible and familiar. But, in the meanwhile, a poet, who is the same person, having a mind *inveterately plastic and creative*, is quite unable to think, even on religious subjects, without *forms distinctly conceived*. And therefore, while with one hand he throws down forms, with the other he raises them up. The iconoclast is at the same time an idolater. **For one of the** most striking features of " Paradise Lost " is the daring materialism that runs through it, the boldness with which divine persons are introduced, the distinctness **with which theological doctrines are pragmatised. Milton the Puritan** is not much less sensuous **than Dante the Catholic. He does not, indeed, crowd his description with** details intended simply to produce illusion, as Dante does, almost in the manner of Defoe ; **but his pictures will** always be found to be curiously distinct. Nothing **daunts him,** nothing **overawes**

T

him; his style never becomes tremulous, the eye of his imagination is never dazzled, he looks straight before him where the seraphim cover their faces; "the living throne, the sapphire blaze, where angels tremble as they gaze," he *sees* and describes with unfailing distinctness. Thus the Puritan becomes to the full as mythological in his religious conceptions as the mediæval Catholic had been.'[1]

Now contrast with this that sublime vision in the fourth chapter of the Book of Revelation. There, while imagination is allowed full play on all the accessories of the scene, observe how the essential idea is carefully withdrawn from her; how she folds her wings, and pauses in sacred awe, and yields her place to the purest ideality when she nears the thought of the inscrutable Supreme. The writer does not venture (to use the words of Mr. Seeley) to 'look straight before him, undaunted, where seraphim vail their faces.' He never '*sees*' God. In that splendid picture the *accessory* images are all drawn from the temple and its services. You are led through its outer courts along the marble pavement (like 'a sea of glass'), past the seven-branched lights up to the mystic vail, resplendent with the rainbow tints brought out from it by the light of the holiest place gleaming through its blue and purple and scarlet, and fine twined linen of cunning work. And so you reach the throne of the Most High. But if you ask, Who sits upon this throne? Whom does the seer see there? Under what form does he depicture Him? You find that he feels like the prophet of old, 'To whom can I liken God, and with what likeness shall I compare him?' And so he at once transcends the region of the sensuous, and rises into the ideal. He leaves description and takes refuge in analogy. He ventures on no comparison of *things*, but only on comparison of *terms*. All that he can say is, As the *relation* of brilliant jewels to the dazzled eye, so was the *relation* of the Undiscernible to my mind; it was '*as if* I looked upon a jasper and a sardine stone!' And thus the utterance of the most imaginative of writers concerning the Supreme is simply just the same as the idealisation of Him by

---

[1] Seeley, Lectures and Essays, 136.

St. Paul, 'Who dwelleth in the light which no man can approach unto; whom no man hath seen nor can see.'

Hence, therefore, the important rule which we must ever carefully apply to our interpretation of Scripture: Take the concrete conceptions with which it abounds only for what they are worth—only as *hints*, for the time, of those eternal *ideas* which they conventionally and imperfectly represent. For all particulars which bring out these ideas to the sense, all images which give them temporary shape, must ever fall short of the purity, and so of the certainty, of the ideas themselves. And they must, moreover, vary in their truthfulness and force with the country, the age, and the people to which these ideas, through their instrumentality, are revealed. They must, therefore, give place, where needful, to other images and other conceptions more accordant with the age, and place, and people down to which these ideas are conveyed. To require that the thoughts of prophets and apostles of a time gone by should be expressed throughout all ages, in forms appropriate only to that time gone by, is the same as to require that they should be brought before us still in no other *tongue* than that in which they were first enunciated; it is to enforce a sacred language, like the vulgate Latin, never to be departed from, for our religious reading, for our religious services, for our creeds, for our prayers. To say that modern thought should never translate the *conceptions* of the sacred writers into forms more suitable *to us* for clothing their ideas, is the same thing as to say, You must not venture to translate their *words* into your mother tongue, but go on always gabbling Hebrew and Greek (the 'ipsissima verba' of inspiration) as a mystic charm. No! The grand ideas of truth can never change; they die not, they know no decay; but the conceptions which represent these ideas must, *in order to* the preservation of these ideas unchanged, be ever changing with a changing world. Bacon's rule applies here as everywhere. Permanency can be secured only by progression. 'The business of the minister of religion is not accomplished even when he has translated Greek and Hebrew into the language of his people; there remains still the duty that the ideas which glimmer in the far-off depths of ancient history be brought home to their bosoms, to become the source of **warmth,** and healing, and nourishment for their *present* daily life.'[1]

---

## NOTE XXIV.

### *Page* 197.

THIS view of inspiration Rothe establishes by appeal to the ex- **perience of all** devout minds : 'Everyone who claims to be **heard** in this matter should be reminded to bring with him some ***experience*** of the quickening influences of the Divine Spirit in the depths of his own soul. What we call "a genial thought" has a close analogy to this inspiration. And to such 'genial thoughts' every accomplished mind cannot but ascribe the best part of its spiritual **acquisitions. Such** will confess, as Perthes does, that "much more has come to him, throughout his life, by sudden immission, than by the laborious processes of reflection and meditation." Just as Baader also says, "When Claudius asserts that our discoveries are not found by us, but find us, he expresses a profound truth. Think only of those rare moments of illumination in which a new truth, like a new **star, emerges** on the horizon of your consciousness, or flames forth into sight. You feel it to be a stranger, and yet already **known** within you; what has been often sought for, surmised, but yet now starts up so entirely new, so unexpected, so full of a sweet astonishment to your mind, that its appearance throws **you** back on the remembrance of your erroneous guesses, and you exclaim, 'This, then, and not (as I imagined) that or the other—*this* **is the** true thought for me! for now my soul is altogether warmth **and light.'** Yet, while you are rejoicing, the vision vanishes. **It comes** like spirits, and so departs; it has shone forth on you like an angelic messenger, and leaves you glowing and glorified by its light." Now such moments of illumination I can call by no other term than moments of poetic inspiration; and as surely as this inspiration comes and

---

[1] Herbart, Ency. Phil. 62.

departs without our co-operation, as clearly as our mind perceives that the gift of it is like the breath imparted to infant life, so certain is it that everything true and great and beautiful in our thoughts and actions must be referred, not to what is commonly called labour and investigation, but to similar inspirations from on high. All that we can claim as our own work is the utterance, the communication of the treasures which have been confided to us, the becoming echoes of the voice within.'[1]

Of such sudden illuminations Leithead gives a physical explanation which, however, will be found to go no further than one step in the countless links of secondary causes, by means of which the First Cause works in us. 'Who,' he says, 'has not experienced that peculiar, that indescribable sensation which accompanies the process of intense thought, whilst engaged in the study of some abstruse subject? Do we not feel that, during the first efforts, the brain seems as it were to be scarcely at all acted upon? By degrees, we become sensible of the influence of some new power, or at least we are conscious of the increase of the perceptive faculty, until at length we are enabled to overcome the difficulty by which we were so long baffled. And, what is remarkable, this result occurs frequently, if not invariably, with almost a startling *suddenness*, the truth flashing upon the mind with the velocity of light; and we then begin to wonder at the tedious perceptive process which has thus enabled the "mind's eye" to see more distinctly. The electrophysiological theory furnishes us with a ready explanation of this phenomenon. During the first efforts of thinking, but a small portion of the electric fluid is transmitted to the brain; gradually, the ganglions become charged with it, until the accumulation is such that the brain is immediately and intensely acted upon; hence the result, as above described, in the increased perceptive power. . . . . Whence also in dreaming: tasks which to one, during his wakeful moments, appeared replete with difficulties, have been accomplished by him with astonishing facility during sleep.'

[1] Rothe, Dogmatik, 71.

## NOTE XXV.

### Page 204.

In this mere outline of religious truth, I cannot go into the great question of the Church and the Churches; but I think it well to remind you that by a Christian brotherhood I do not mean simply a school of thought, a sect of thinkers. There is not only a Christianity, but a Christendom. And this Christendom organises itself into religious societies of various extent and constitution; from 'the Church in the house,' which St. Paul commemorates in four several places (Rom. xvi. 5; 1 Cor. xvi. 19; Col. iv. 15; Philemon 2), to the larger bodies of Congregational, Presbyterian, Episcopalian, and National Churches. Nor can it do otherwise, as M. Guizot has shown in his fifth lecture on 'European Civilisation.' For religion (he says) is not a mere *sentiment* of dependence and adoration; it involves in itself doctrines to be believed, duties to be performed, and an authority of some kind bearing witness to these doctrines and promoting these duties. Therefore religion is a fruitful principle of *association*: for (1) as a system of principles, truth belongs to no one exclusively; it is universal, it is common property, and so men need to avow and hold it in common. (2) As a system of precepts, law obligatory on one is obligatory on all. Such law therefore must be published for all, held up before all, confessed, honoured, and promoted by all. (3) There must therefore be *sanctions* of some kind for such principles and precepts. And to supply these sanctions by an authority superior to individual fancy—the authority of a common spirit, common beliefs, and common obligations—this is the object of a religious society.

And just these conditions you find existing in the three great stages of development of sacred society. In the sacred *family*, constituted in Abraham, the distinguishing dogma is, God as the head of family life (Gen. xvii. 8, 9 : 'I will be the God of thee and thy seed after thee, therefore thou shalt keep my covenant, thou and thy seed after thee in their generations'). The corresponding duty is the 'keeping the way of this God,' the 'doing justice and judgment' (Gen. xviii. 19). And the corresponding authority by which this dogma and this duty are to be watched over and promoted, is *patriarchal*: 'I know *Abraham* that he will command his *children* and his *household after him* that they keep the way of the Lord.'

Then, in the sacred *nation*, the dogma is, God as the sovereign in national life: 'Ye said to me, a king shall reign over us, when *the Lord your God was your king.*'[1] The corresponding duty is, 'These words which I command thee this day' (i.e. the statutes of my realm) 'shall be in thine heart, and thou shalt teach them diligently to thy children.'[2] And the corresponding authority is *priestly*, for though God reigns, it is by the instrumentality of his ministers of state, the priests. For the rule in this society is the rule of *law*. And the priests were appointed to expound the law, to restrain transgressors of the law from the worship of the great King, and to restore them to this worship by sacrifice. 'The priest's lips should keep knowledge, and men should seek the law at his mouth, for he is the messenger' (the communicator of the will[3]) 'of the Lord of hosts.'[4]

And next in the sacred *brotherhood*, as the distinguishing dogma is God as the father of men, coming down to dwell in them by his Spirit; so the corresponding duty is the cherishing this spirit, walking in this spirit, diffusing everywhere this spirit; and the corresponding authority which is to rule in this brotherhood is the authority of this Spirit residing in the community, and coming forth with utterance, and life, and power in those members of the community who have the largest measure of his presence: 'Where two or three are gathered together in my name, there am I in the midst of them.'[5] 'I will pray the Father, and he shall give you another Guardian, and he shall abide with you for ever; he shall teach you all things and bring all things to your remembrance whatsoever I have said to you!'[6] 'They were *all* filled with the Holy Ghost.' 'And Peter stood up with the eleven' (as exponents of the Spirit that was in all), 'and lifted up his

---

[1] 1 Sam. xii. 12.   [2] Deut. vi. 6, 7.   [3] See Haggai i. 13.
[4] Malachi ii. 7.   [5] Matt. xviii. 20.   [6] John xiv. 16, 26.

voice.'¹ 'Look ye out among you seven men **of** blameless character, *full of the Holy Ghost and wisdom*, whom we may appoint over this business.'² '**Take** heed to the flock over which *the Holy Ghost hath made you overseers*, to tend the church of God.'³ 'Do you trust that you are inwardly moved *by the Holy Ghost* to take upon you this office and ministration, to serve God for the promoting of his glory, and the edifying of his people?'⁴ '*Receive the Holy Ghost* for **the** office and work of a bishop in the church of God. And remember that thou stir up *the grace of God* which is given thee by this imposition of our hands.'⁵

As, then, the first authority was patriarchal, and the **second** priestly, so this in the Christian brotherhood may be termed *prophetic*. It is the authority of prophets, or men filled with **the Spirit of God,** deliberating, speaking, and acting as the utterance of this Spirit in the community of which they are the representatives. And, as the nature of the authority, so must be its exercise; not patriarchal, not legal, but in a *prophetic* manner, by mental, moral, and spiritual influence. 'Holding fast the faithful word as you have been taught, by *sound teaching* exhort and convince the gainsayers.'⁶ 'Speak then the things which become *sound teaching.*' '*Exhort* young men to be sober-minded.' '*Exhort* servants to be obedient to their masters.' '*Put them in mind* to be subject to principalities and powers, to be ready to every good work.'⁷ '**Of** these things *put them in remembrance*, charging them before the Lord.'⁸ 'Them that sin *rebuke* before all, that others also may fear.'⁹ 'A man that is an heretic, after the first **and** second *admonition*, reject.'¹⁰ But then this rejection, or displacement **from** the society, must be the act of the society itself, after **due deliberation.** '**In the** name of our Lord Jesus Christ when ye are gathered together with my spirit . . . put away from among yourselves that evil person.'¹¹

But such being the nature of the Christian brotherhood, and

---

¹ Acts ii. 4, 14.  ² Ibid. vi. 3.  ³ Ibid. xx. 28.
⁴ The Ordering of Deacons.  ⁵ The Consecration of Bishops.
⁶ Titus i. **9.**  ⁷ Titus ii. 1, 6, **9**; iii. 1.  ⁸ 2 Tim. ii. 14.
⁹ 1 Tim. **v. 20.**  ¹⁰ Titus iii. 10.  ¹¹ 1 Cor. v. 4, 13.

such its government, you see at once wherein must consist its unity. This unity must ever be spiritual and not legal; not uniformity but unanimity; a unity of the spirit maintained by the bonds of peace. Closely mixed up as were Churchmen of old with the Roman polity, it was natural that they should be seduced into aping this polity and strive to erect a spiritual imperialism. But they fell by this entirely away from the essential idea of the universal brotherhood in Christ. This brotherhood is federal, not monarchical. It constitutes the United States of Christendom. It is a confederation of visible churches, whether large or small, under an invisible Head. This invisible Head alone forms the point of union of the whole body, joined together and compacted in Him. He alone is in the midst of the seven candlesticks, which represent the seven churches. And we are one body in proportion only as we are filled with one Spirit, one hope, one Lord, one faith, one baptism, one God and Father of all, above all, through all, and in all. 'The third essential character of the Church of Christ is the absence of any visible head; the non-existence, nay the utter preclusion, of any local or personal centre of unity, of any single source of universal power. Kepler and Newton, substituting the *idea* of the infinite for the *conception* of a finite and determined world, and finding a centre in every point of matter and an absolute circumference nowhere, explained at once the unity and the distinction that co-exist throughout the creation, by focal instead of central bodies; the attractive and restraining power of the sun, or focal orb, in each particular system, supposing and resulting from an actual power present in all and over all, throughout an interminable multitude of systems; and this we rightly name the true system of the heavens. Even such is the true scheme and idea of the Christian Church.'[1]

[1] Coleridge, **Church and State**, 137.

LONDON: PRINTED BY
SPOTTISWOODE AND CO., NEW-STREET SQUARE
AND PARLIAMENT STREET

*By the same Author,*

## THE FATHERHOOD OF GOD.

Price 4s. 6d.

## THE SPIRITUAL LIFE.

Eighth Edition, price 4s.

## LIVE WHILE YOU LIVE.

Seventh Edition, price 1s. 6d.

39 Paternoster Row, E.C.
London: *January* 1871.

# GENERAL LIST OF WORKS

PUBLISHED BY

Messrs. LONGMANS, GREEN, READER, and DYER.

---

| | |
|---|---|
| Arts, Manufactures, &c. ............... 12 | Index ........................... 21—24 |
| Astronomy, Meteorology, Popular Geography, &c. ...................... 7 | Miscellaneous Works and Popular Metaphysics ........................ 6 |
| Biographical Works ................. 3 | Natural History & Popular Science 8 |
| Chemistry, Medicine, Surgery, and the Allied Sciences .................. 9 | Periodical Publications ............... 20 |
| | Poetry and The Drama ............... 18 |
| Commerce, Navigation, and Mercantile Affairs ......................... 19 | Religious and Moral Works ......... 14 |
| | Rural Sports, &c. ..................... 19 |
| Criticism, Philology, &c. .............. 4 | Travels, Voyages, &c. ................. 16 |
| Fine Arts and Illustrated Editions 11 | Works of Fiction ...................... 17 |
| History, Politics, and Historical Memoirs ........................... 1 | Works of Utility and General Information ......................... 20 |

---

## *History, Politics, Historical Memoirs, &c.*

**The History of England from** the fall of Wolsey to the Defeat of the Spanish Armada. By JAMES ANTHONY FROUDE, M.A.

CABINET EDITION, 12 vols. cr. 8vo. £3 12s.
LIBRARY EDITION, 12 vols. 8vo. £8 18s.

**The History of England from** the Accession of James II. By Lord MACAULAY.

LIBRARY EDITION, 5 vols. 8vo. £4.
CABINET EDITION, 8 vols. post 8vo. 48s.
PEOPLE'S EDITION, 4 vols. crown 8vo. 16s.

**Lord Macaulay's Works.** Complete and uniform Library Edition. Edited by his Sister, Lady TREVELYAN. 8 vols. 8vo. with Portrait, price £5 5s. cloth, or £8 8s. bound in tree-calf by Rivière.

**An Essay on the History of the** English Government and Constitution, from the Reign of Henry VII. to the Present Time. By JOHN EARL RUSSELL. Fourth Edition, revised. Crown 8vo. 6s.

**Selections from Speeches of Earl** Russell, 1817 to 1841, and from Despatches, 1859 to 1865; with Introductions. 2 vols. 8vo. 28s.

**Varieties of Vice-Regal Life.** By Major-General Sir WILLIAM DENISON, K.C.B. late Governor-General of the Australian Colonies, and Governor of Madras. With Two Maps. 2 vols. 8vo. 28s.

**On Parliamentary Government** in England its Origin, Development, and Practical Operation. By ALPHEUS TODD, Librarian of the Legislative Assembly of Canada. 2 vols. 8vo. price £1 17s.

**The Constitutional History of** England since the Accession of George III. 1760—1860. By Sir THOMAS ERSKINE MAY, K.C.B. Second Edit. 2 vols. 8vo. 33s.

**A Historical Account of the Neu**trality of Great Britain during the American Civil War. By MONTAGUE BERNARD, M.A. Royal 8vo. price 16s.

**The History of England,** from the Earliest Times to the Year 1866. By C. D. YONGE, Regius Professor of Modern History in the Queen's University, Belfast. New Edition. Crown 8vo. 7s. 6d.

**A History of Wales,** derived from Authentic Sources. By JANE WILLIAMS, Ysgafell, Author of a Memoir of the Rev. Thomas Price, and Editor of his Literary Remains. 8vo. 14s.

A

**Lectures on the History** of England, from the Earliest Times to the Death of King Edward II. By WILLIAM LONGMAN. With Maps and Illustrations. 8vo. 15s.

**The** History of the Life and Times of Edward the Third. By WILLIAM LONGMAN. With 9 Maps, 8 Plates, and 16 Woodcuts. 2 vols. 8vo. 28s.

**History of Civilization in England** and France, Spain and Scotland. By HENRY THOMAS BUCKLE. New Edition of the entire work, with a complete INDEX. 3 vols. crown 8vo. 24s.

**Realities of Irish Life.** By W. STEUART TRENCH, Land Agent in Ireland to the Marquess of Lansdowne, the Marquess of Bath, and Lord Digby. Fifth Edition. Crown 8vo. 6s.

**The Student's Manual of the** History of Ireland. By M. F. CUSACK, Authoress of the 'Illustrated History of Ireland, from the Earliest Period to the Year of Catholic Emancipation.' Crown 8vo. price 6s.

**A Student's Manual of the** History of India, from the Earliest Period to the Present. By Colonel MEADOWS TAYLOR, M.R.A.S. M.R.I.A. Crown 8vo. with Maps, 7s. 6d.

**The History of India,** from the Earliest Period to the close of Lord Dalhousie's Administration. By JOHN CLARK MARSHMAN. 3 vols. crown 8vo. 22s. 6d.

**Indian Polity:** a View of the System of Administration in India. By Lieut.-Col. GEORGE CHESNEY. Second Edition, revised, with Map. 8vo. 21s.

**Home Politics:** being a Consideration of the Causes of the Growth of Trade in relation to Labour, Pauperism, and Emigration. By DANIEL GRANT. 8vo. 7s.

**Democracy in America.** By ALEXIS DE TOCQUEVILLE. Translated by HENRY REEVE. 2 vols. 8vo. 21s.

**Waterloo Lectures:** a Study of the Campaign of 1815. By Colonel CHARLES C. CHESNEY, R.E. late Professor of Military Art and History in the Staff College. Second Edition. 8vo. with Map, 10s. 6d.

**The Military Resources of Prussia** and France, and Recent Changes in the Art of War. By Lieut.-Col. CHESNEY, R.E. and HENRY REEVE, D.C.L. Crown 8vo. 7s. 6d.

**The Overthrow of the** Germanic Confederation by Prussia in 1866. By Sir A. MALET, Bart. K.B.C. late H.B.M. Envoy and Minister at Frankfort. With 5 Maps. 8vo. 18s.

**The Oxford Reformers**—John Colet, Erasmus, and Thomas More; being a History of their Fellow-Work. By FREDERIC SEEBOHM. Second Edition. 8vo. 14s.

**History of the** Reformation in Europe in the Time of Calvin. By J. H. MERLE D'AUBIGNÉ, D.D. VOLS. I. and II. 8vo. 28s. VOL. III. 12s. VOL. IV. price 16s. and VOL. V. price 16s.

**Chapters from French History;** St. Louis, Joan of Arc, Henri IV. with Sketches of the Intermediate Periods. By J. H. GURNEY, M.A. New Edition. Fcp. 8vo. 6s. 6d.

**The History of Greece.** By C. THIRLWALL, D.D. Lord Bishop of St. David's. 8 vols. fcp. 28s.

**The Tale of the Great Persian** War, from the Histories of Herodotus. By GEORGE W. COX, M.A. late Scholar of Trin. Coll. Oxon. Fcp. 3s. 6d.

**Greek History from Themistocles** to Alexander, in a Series of Lives from Plutarch. Revised and arranged by A. H. CLOUGH. Fcp. with 44 Woodcuts, 6s.

**Critical History of the Language** and Literature of Ancient Greece. By WILLIAM MURE, of Caldwell. 5 vols. 8vo. £3 9s.

**History of the** Literature of Ancient Greece. By Professor K. O. MÜLLER. Translated by LEWIS and DONALDSON. 3 vols. 8vo. 21s.

**The History of Rome.** By WILHELM IHNE. Translated and revised by the Author. VOLS. I. and II. 8vo. [Just ready.

**History of the City of Rome from** its Foundation to the Sixteenth Century of the Christian Era. By THOMAS H. DYER, LL.D. 8vo. with 2 Maps, 15s.

**History of the Romans under** the Empire. By Very Rev. CHARLES MERIVALE, D.C.L. Dean of Ely. 8 vols. post 8vo. price 48s.

**The Fall of the Roman Republic;** a Short History of the Last Century of the Commonwealth. By the same Author. 12mo. 7s. 6d.

Historical and Chronological Encyclopædia; comprising Chronological Notices of all the Great Events of Universal History, including Treaties, Alliances, Wars, Battles, &c.; Incidents in the Lives of Eminent Men, Scientific and Geographical Discoveries, Mechanical Inventions, and Social, Domestic, and Economical Improvements. By the late B. B. WOODWARD, B.A. and W. L. R. CATES. 1 vol. 8vo.
[In the press.

History of European Morals from Augustus to Charlemagne. By W. E. H. LECKY, M.A. 2 vols. 8vo. price 28s.

History of the Rise and Influence of the Spirit of Rationalism in Europe. By the same Author. Cabinet Edition (the Fourth). 2 vols. crown 8vo. price 16s.

God in History; or, the Progress of Man's Faith in the Moral Order of the World. By the late Baron BUNSEN. Translated from the German by SUSANNA WINKWORTH; with a Preface by Dean STANLEY. 3 vols. 8vo. 42s.

Socrates and the Socratic Schools. Translated from the German of Dr. E. ZELLER, with the Author's approval, by the Rev. OSWALD J. REICHEL, B.C.L. and M.A. Crown 8vo. 8s. 6d.

The Stoics, Epicureans, and Sceptics. Translated from the German of Dr. E. ZELLER, with the Author's approval, by OSWALD J. REICHEL, B.C.L. and M.A. Crown 8vo. 14s.

The History of Philosophy, from Thales to Comte. By GEORGE HENRY LEWES. Third Edition, rewritten and enlarged. 2 vols. 8vo. 30s.

The Mythology of the Aryan Nations. By GEORGE W. COX, M.A. late Scholar of Trinity College, Oxford. 2 vols. 8vo. price 28s.

The English Reformation. By F. C. MASSINGBERD, M.A. Chancellor of Lincoln. 4th Edition, revised. Fcp. 7s. 6d.

Maunder's Historical Treasury; comprising a General Introductory Outline of Universal History, and a Series of Separate Histories. Fcp. 6s.

Critical and Historical Essays contributed to the *Edinburgh Review* by the Right Hon. Lord MACAULAY:—

CABINET EDITION, 4 vols. 24s.
LIBRARY EDITION, 3 vols. 8vo. 36s.
PEOPLE'S EDITION, 2 vols. crown 8vo. 8s.
STUDENT'S EDITION, crown 8vo. 6s.

History of the Early Church, from the First Preaching of the Gospel to the Council of Nicæa, A.D. 325. By the Author of 'Amy Herbert.' New Edition. Fcp. 4s. 6d.

Sketch of the History of the Church of England to the Revolution of 1688. By the Right Rev. T. V. SHORT, D.D. Lord Bishop of St. Asaph. Eighth Edition. Crown 8vo. 7s. 6d.

History of the Christian Church, from the Ascension of Christ to the Conversion of Constantine. By E. BURTON, D.D late Regius Prof. of Divinity in the University of Oxford. Fcp. 3s. 6d.

*Biographical Works.*

The Life of Isambard Kingdom Brunel, Civil Engineer. By ISAMBARD BRUNEL, B.C.L. of Lincoln's Inn, Chancellor of the Diocese of Ely. With Portrait, Plates, and Woodcuts. 8vo. 21s.

The Life and Letters of the Rev. Sydney Smith. Edited by his Daughter, Lady HOLLAND, and Mrs. AUSTIN. New Edition, complete in One Volume. Crown 8vo. price 6s.

A Memoir of G. E. L. Cotton, D.D. late Lord Bishop of Calcutta; with Selections from his Journals and Letters. Edited by Mrs. COTTON. With Portrait. 8vo. [Just ready.

Some Memorials of R. D. Hampden, Bishop of Hereford. Edited by his Daughter, HENRIETTA HAMPDEN. With Portrait. 8vo. [Just ready.

The Life and Travels of George Whitefield, M.A. of Pembroke College, Oxford, Chaplain to the Countess of Huntingdon. By J. P. GLEDSTONE. Post 8vo. [Just ready.

Memoir of Pope Sixtus the Fifth. By Baron HÜBNER. Translated from the Original in French, with the Author's sanction, by HUBERT E. H. JERNINGHAM. 2 vols. 8vo. [In the press.

**The Life and Letters of Faraday.** By Dr. BENCE JONES, Secretary of the Royal Institution. Second Edition, with Portrait and Woodcuts. 2 vols. 8vo. 28s.

**Faraday as a Discoverer.** By JOHN TYNDALL, LL.D. F.R.S. Professor of Natural Philosophy in the Royal Institution. New and Cheaper Edition, with Two Portraits. Fcp. 8vo. 3s. 6d.

**Lives of the Lord Chancellors** and Keepers of the Great Seal of Ireland, from the Earliest Times to the Reign of Queen Victoria. By J. R. O'FLANAGAN, M.R.I.A. Barrister. 2 vols. 8vo. 30s.

**Dictionary of General Biography;** containing Concise Memoirs and Notices of the most Eminent Persons of all Countries, from the Earliest Ages to the Present Time. Edited by WILLIAM L. R. CATES. 8vo. price 21s.

**Memoirs of Baron Bunsen,** drawn chiefly from Family Papers by his Widow, FRANCES Baroness BUNSEN. Second Edition, abridged; with 2 Portraits and 4 Woodcuts. 2 vols. post 8vo. 21s.

**The Letters of the Right Hon.** Sir George Cornewall Lewis to various Friends. Edited by his Brother, the Rev. Canon Sir G. F. LEWIS, Bart. 8vo. with Portrait, 14s.

**Life of the Duke of Wellington.** By the Rev. G. R. GLEIG, M.A. Popular Edition, carefully revised; with copious Additions. Crown 8vo. with Portrait, 5s.

**Father Mathew: a Biography.** By JOHN FRANCIS MAGUIRE, M.P. Popular Edition, with Portrait. Crown 8vo. 3s. 6d.

**History of my Religious Opinions.** By J. H. NEWMAN, D.D. Being the Substance of Apologia pro Vitâ Suâ. Post 8vo. price 6s.

**Letters and Life of Francis** Bacon, including all his Occasional Works. Collected and edited, with a Commentary, by J. SPEDDING. VOLS. I. & II. 8vo. 24s. VOLS. III. & IV. 24s. VOL. V. 12s.

**Felix Mendelssohn's Letters from** *Italy and Switzerland,* and *Letters* from 1833 to 1847, translated by Lady WALLACE. With Portrait. 2 vols. crown 8vo. 5s. each.

**Memoirs of Sir Henry Havelock,** K.C.B. By JOHN CLARK MARSHMAN. People's Edition, with Portrait. Crown 8vo. price 3s. 6d.

**Essays in Ecclesiastical Biography.** By the Right Hon. Sir J. STEPHEN, LL.D. Cabinet Edition. Crown 8vo. 7s. 6d.

**The Earls of Granard:** a Memoir of the Noble Family of Forbes. Written by Admiral the Hon. JOHN FORBES, and Edited by GEORGE ARTHUR HASTINGS, present Earl of Granard, K.P. 8vo. 10s.

**Vicissitudes of Families.** By Sir J. BERNARD BURKE, C.B. Ulster King of Arms. New Edition, remodelled and enlarged. 2 vols. crown 8vo. 21s.

**Lives of the Tudor Princesses,** including Lady Jane Grey and her Sisters. By AGNES STRICKLAND. Post 8vo. with Portrait, &c. 12s. 6d.

**Lives of the Queens of England.** By AGNES STRICKLAND. Library Edition, newly revised; with Portraits of every Queen, Autographs, and Vignettes. 8 vols. post 8vo. 7s. 6d. each.

**Maunder's Biographical Treasury.** Thirteenth Edition, reconstructed and partly re-written, with above 1,000 additional Memoirs, by W. L. R. CATES. Fcp. 6s.

---

## *Criticism, Philosophy, Polity, &c.*

**The Subjection of Women.** By JOHN STUART MILL. New Edition. Post 8vo. 5s.

**On Representative Government.** By JOHN STUART MILL. Third Edition. 8vo. 9s. crown 8vo. 2s.

**On Liberty.** By the same Author. Fourth Edition. Post 8vo. 7s. 6d. Crown 8vo. 1s. 4d.

**Principles of Political Economy.** By the same. Sixth Edition. 2 vols. 8vo. 30s. or in 1 vol. crown 8vo. 5s.

**Utilitarianism.** By the same. 3d Edit. 8vo. 5s.

**Dissertations and Discussions.** By the same Author. Second Edition. 3 vols. 8vo. 36s.

**Examination of Sir W. Hamilton's** Philosophy, and of the principal Philosophical Questions discussed in his Writings. By the same. Third Edition. 8vo. 16s.

**Inaugural Address** delivered to the University of St. Andrews. By JOHN STUART MILL. 8vo. 5s. Crown 8vo. 1s.

**Analysis of the Phenomena of the Human Mind.** By JAMES MILL. A New Edition, with Notes, Illustrative and Critical, by ALEXANDER BAIN, ANDREW FINDLATER, and GEORGE GROTE. Edited, with additional Notes, by JOHN STUART MILL. 2 vols. 8vo. price 28s.

**The Elements of Political Economy.** By HENRY DUNNING MACLEOD, M.A. Barrister-at-Law. 8vo. 16s.

**A Dictionary of Political Economy;** Biographical, Bibliographical, Historical, and Practical. By the same Author. VOL. I. royal 8vo. 30s.

**Lord Bacon's Works,** collected and edited by R. L. ELLIS, M.A. J. SPEDDING, M.A. and D. D. HEATH. New and Cheaper Edition. 7 vols. 8vo. price £3 13s. 6d.

**A System of Logic, Ratiocinative** and Inductive. By JOHN STUART MILL. Seventh Edition. 2 vols. 8vo. 25s.

**Analysis of Mr. Mill's System of Logic.** By W. STEBBING, M.A. New Edition. 12mo. 3s. 6d.

**The Institutes of Justinian;** with English Introduction, Translation, and Notes. By T. C. SANDARS, M.A. Barrister-at-Law. New Edition. 8vo. 15s.

**The Ethics of Aristotle;** with Essays and Notes. By Sir A. GRANT, Bart. M.A. LL.D. Second Edition, revised and completed. 2 vols. 8vo. price 28s.

**The Nicomachean Ethics of Aristotle.** Newly translated into English. By R. WILLIAMS, B.A. Fellow and late Lecturer Merton College, Oxford. 8vo. 12s.

**Bacon's Essays, with Annotations.** By R. WHATELY, D.D. late Archbishop of Dublin. Sixth Edition. 8vo. 10s. 6d.

**Elements of Logic.** By R. WHATELY, D.D. late Archbishop of Dublin. New Edition. 8vo. 10s. 6d. crown 8vo. 4s. 6d.

Elements of Rhetoric. By the same Author. New Edition. 8vo. 10s. 6d. Crown 8vo. 4s. 6d.

English Synonymes. By E. JANE WHATELY. Edited by Archbishop WHATELY. 5th Edition. Fcp. 3s.

**An Outline of the Necessary Laws of Thought:** a Treatise on Pure and Applied Logic. By the Most Rev. W. THOMSON, D.D. Archbishop of York. Ninth Thousand. Crown 8vo. 5s. 6d.

**The Election of Representatives,** Parliamentary and Municipal; a Treatise. By THOMAS HARE, Barrister-at-Law. Third Edition, with Additions. Crown 8vo. 6s.

**Speeches of the Right Hon. Lord** MACAULAY, corrected by Himself. People's Edition, crown 8vo. 3s. 6d.

**Lord Macaulay's Speeches on** Parliamentary Reform in 1831 and 1832. 16mo. price ONE SHILLING.

**Walker's Pronouncing Dictionary** of the English Language. Thoroughly revised Editions, by B. H. SMART. 8vo. 12s. 16mo. 6s.

**A Dictionary of the English Language.** By R. G. LATHAM, M.A. M.D. F.R.S. Founded on the Dictionary of Dr. S. JOHNSON, as edited by the Rev. H. J. TODD, with numerous Emendations and Additions. 4 vols. 4to. price £7.

**Thesaurus of English Words and** Phrases, classified and arranged so as to facilitate the expression of Ideas, and assist in Literary Composition. By P. M. ROGET, M.D. New Edition. Crown 8vo. 10s. 6d.

**The Debater;** a Series of Complete Debates, Outlines of Debates, and Questions for Discussion. By F. ROWTON. Fcp. 6s.

**Lectures on the Science of Language,** delivered at the Royal Institution. By MAX MÜLLER, M.A. &c. Foreign Member of the French Institute. 2 vols. 8vo. price 30s.

**Chapters on Language.** By F. W. FARRAR, M.A. F.R.S. late Fellow of Trin. Coll. Cambridge. Crown 8vo. 8s. 6d.

**A Book about Words.** By G. F. GRAHAM. Fcp. 8vo. 3s. 6d.

**Southey's Doctor,** complete in One Volume, edited by the Rev. J. W. WARTER, B.D. Square crown 8vo. 12s. 6d.

**Historical and Critical Commentary** on the Old Testament; with a New Translation. By M. M. KALISCH, Ph.D. Vol. I. *Genesis,* 8vo. 18s. or adapted for the General Reader, 12s. Vol. II. *Exodus,* 15s. or adapted for the General Reader, 12s. Vol III. *Leviticus,* Part I. 15s. or adapted for the General Reader, 8s.

A Hebrew Grammar, with Exercises. By the same. Part I. *Outlines with Exercises,* 8vo. 12s. 6d. KEY, 5s. Part II. *Exceptional Forms and Constructions,* 12s. 6d.

**Manual of English Literature,**
Historical and Critical: with a Chapter on English Metres. By THOMAS ARNOLD, M.A. Second Edition. Crown 8vo. 7s. 6d.

**A Latin-English Dictionary.** By J. T. WHITE, D.D. of Corpus Christi College, and J. E. RIDDLE, M.A. of St. Edmund Hall, Oxford. Third Edition, revised. 2 vols. 4to. pp. 2,128, price 42s.

White's College Latin-English Dictionary (Intermediate Size), abridged from the Parent Work for the use of University Students. Medium 8vo. pp. 1,048, price 18s.

**White's Junior** Student's Complete Latin-English and English-Latin Dictionary. Revised Edition. Square 12mo. pp. 1,058, price 12s.

Separately { ENGLISH-LATIN, 5s. 6d.
{ LATIN-ENGLISH, 7s. 6d.

**An English-Greek Lexicon,** containing all the Greek Words used by Writers of good authority. By C. D. YONGE, B.A. New Edition. 4to. 21s.

**Mr. Yonge's New Lexicon, En-**glish and Greek, abridged from his larger work (as above). Square 12mo. 8s. 6d.

**The Mastery of Languages;** or, the Art of Speaking Foreign Tongues Idiomatically. By THOMAS PRENDERGAST, late of the Civil Service at Madras. Second Edition. 8vo. **6s.**

**A Greek-English Lexicon.** Compiled by H. G. LIDDELL, D.D. Dean of Christ Church, and R. SCOTT, D.D. Dean of Rochester. Sixth Edition. Crown 4to. price 36s.

**A Lexicon, Greek and English,** abridged for Schools from LIDDELL and SCOTT's *Greek-English Lexicon*. Twelfth Edition. Square 12mo. 7s. 6d.

**A Practical Dictionary of the** French and English Languages. By Professor LÉON CONTANSEAU, many years French Examiner for Military and Civil Appointments, &c. New Edition, carefully revised. Post 8vo. 10s. 6d.

**Contanseau's Pocket Dictionary,** French and English, abridged from the Practical Dictionary, by the Author. **New Edition.** 18mo. price 3s. **6d.**

**A Sanskrit-English Dictionary.** The Sanskrit words printed both in **the** original Devanagari and in Roman letters; with References to the Best Editions of Sanskrit Authors, and with Etymologies **and** comparisons of Cognate Words chiefly in Greek, **Latin,** Gothic, and Anglo-Saxon. Compiled by T. BENFEY. 8vo. 52s. 6d.

**New Practical Dictionary of the** German Language; German-English, and English-German. By the Rev. W. L. BLACKLEY, M.A. and Dr. CARL MARTIN FRIEDLÄNDER. Post 8vo. 7s. 6d.

**Staff College Essays.** By Lieutenant EVELYN BARING, Royal Artillery. 8vo. with Two Maps, 8s. 6d.

---

## *Miscellaneous Works* and *Popular Metaphysics.*

The Essays and Contributions of A. K. H. B. Author of 'The Recreations of a Country Parson.' Uniform Editions:—

Recreations **of a** Country Parson. FIRST and SECOND SERIES, 3s. 6d. each.

The Commonplace Philosopher **in** Town and Country. Crown 8vo. 3s. 6d.

Leisure Hours in Town; Essays Consolatory, Æsthetical, Moral, Social, and Domestic. Crown **8vo. 3s.** 6d.

The **Autumn** Holidays of a Country Parson. Crown 8vo. 3s. 6d.

The Graver Thoughts of a Country Parson. FIRST and SECOND SERIES, crown 8vo. 3s. 6d. each.

Critical Essays of a Country Parson, selected from Essays contributed to *Fraser's Magazine.* Crown 8vo. 3s. 6d.

Sunday Afternoons at the Parish Church of a Scottish University City. Crown 8vo. 3s. 6d.

Lessons of Middle Age, with some Account of various Cities and Men. Crown 8vo. 3s. 6d.

Counsel and Comfort Spoken from a City Pulpit. Crown 8vo. 3s. 6d.

Changed Aspects of Unchanged Truths; Memorials of St. Andrews Sundays. Crown 8vo. 3s. 6d.

Present-Day Thoughts; Memorials of St. Andrews Sundays. Crown 8vo. 3s. 6d.

**Short Studies on Great Subjects.** By JAMES ANTHONY FROUDE, M.A. late Fellow of Exeter College, Oxford. Third Edition. 8vo. 12s.

**Lord Macaulay's Miscellaneous Writings:—**
LIBRARY EDITION, 2 vols. 8vo. Portrait, 21s.
PEOPLE'S EDITION, 1 vol. crown 8vo. 4s. 6d.

**The Rev. Sydney Smith's Miscellaneous Works;** including his Contributions to the *Edinburgh Review*. 1 vol. crown 8vo. 6s.

**The Wit and Wisdom of the Rev. SYDNEY SMITH: a Selection of the most memorable Passages in his Writings and Conversation. Crown 8vo. 3s. 6d.

**The Silver Store.** Collected from Mediæval Christian and Jewish Mines. By the Rev. S. BARING-GOULD, M.A. Crown 8vo. 3s. 6d.

**Traces of History in the Names** of Places; with a Vocabulary of the Roots out of which Names of Places in England and Wales are formed. By FLAVELL EDMUNDS. Crown 8vo. 7s. 6d.

**The Eclipse of Faith;** or, a Visit to a Religious Sceptic. By HENRY ROGERS. **Twelfth Edition. Fcp. 5s.**

Defence of the Eclipse of Faith, by its Author. Third Edition. Fcp. 3s. 6d.

Selections from the Correspondence of R. E. H. Greyson. By the same Author. Third Edition. Crown 8vo. 7s. 6d.

**Families of Speech,** Four Lectures delivered at the Royal Institution of Great Britain. By the Rev. F. W. FARRAR, M.A. F.R.S. Post 8vo. with 2 Maps, 5s. 6d.

**Chips from a German Workshop;** being Essays on the Science of Religion, and on Mythology, Traditions, and Customs. By MAX MÜLLER, M.A. &c. Foreign Member of the French Institute. 3 vols. 8vo. £2.

**Word Gossip;** a Series of Familiar Essays on Words and their Peculiarities. By the Rev. W. L. BLACKLEY, M.A. Fcp. 8vo. 5s.

**An Introduction to Mental Philosophy,** on the Inductive Method. By J. D. MORELL, M.A. LL.D. 8vo. 12s.

Elements of Psychology, containing the Analysis of the Intellectual Powers. By the same Author. Post 8vo. 7s. 6d.

**The Secret of Hegel:** being the Hegelian System in Origin, **Principle, Form,** and Matter. By JAMES HUTCHISON STIRLING. 2 vols. 8vo. 28s.

Sir William Hamilton; being the Philosophy of Perception: an Analysis. By the same Author. 8vo. 5s.

**The Senses and the Intellect.** By ALEXANDER BAIN, LL.D. Prof. of Logic in the Univ. of Aberdeen. Third Edition. 8vo. 15s.

The Emotions and the Will, by the same Author. Second Edition. 8vo. 15s.

On the Study of Character, including an Estimate of Phrenology. By the same Author. 8vo. 9s.

**Mental and Moral Science:** a Compendium of Psychology and Ethics. By the same Author. Second Edition. Crown **8vo.** 10s. 6d.

**Strong and Free;** or, First Steps towards Social Science. By the Author of 'My Life and What shall I do with it?' 8vo. 10s. 6d.

**The Philosophy of Necessity; or,** Natural Law as applicable to Mental, Moral, and Social Science. By CHARLES BRAY. **Second Edition.** 8vo. 9s.

The Education of the Feelings and Affections. By the same Author. Third Edition. 8vo. 3s. 6d.

On Force, its Mental and Moral Correlates. By the same Author. 8vo. 5s.

**Time and Space;** a Metaphysical Essay. By SHADWORTH H. HODGSON. (This work covers the whole ground of Speculative Philosophy.) 8vo. price 16s.

**The Theory of Practice;** an Ethical Inquiry. By the same Author. (This work, in conjunction with the foregoing, completes a system of Philosophy.) 2 vols. 8vo. price 24s.

**A Treatise on Human Nature;** being an Attempt to Introduce the Experimental Method of Reasoning into Moral Subjects. By DAVID HUME. Edited, with Notes, &c. by T. H. GREEN, Fellow, and T. H. GROSE, late Scholar, of Balliol College, Oxford. [*In the press.*

**Essays Moral, Political, and Literary.** By DAVID HUME. By the same Editors. [*In the press.*

\*\*\* The above will form a new edition of DAVID HUME'S *Philosophical Works*, complete in Four Volumes, but to be had in Two separate Sections as announced.

## Astronomy, Meteorology, Popular Geography, &c.

**Outlines of Astronomy.** By Sir J. F. W. HERSCHEL, Bart. M.A. New Edition, revised; with Plates and Woodcuts. 8vo. 18s.

**Other Worlds than Ours;** the Plurality of Worlds Studied under the Light of Recent Scientific Researches. By R. A. PROCTOR, B.A. F.R.A.S. Second Edition, revised and enlarged; with 14 Illustrations. Crown 8vo. 10s. 6d.

**The Sun; Ruler,** Light, Fire, and Life of the Planetary System. By the same Author. With 10 Plates (7 coloured) and 107 Woodcuts. Crown 8vo. price 14s.

**Saturn and its System.** By the same Author. 8vo. with 14 Plates, 14s.

**The Handbook of the Stars.** By the same Author. Square fcp. 8vo. with 3 Maps, price 5s.

**Celestial Objects for Common** Telescopes. By T. W. WEBB, M.A. F.R.A.S. Second Edition, revised and enlarged, with Map of the Moon and Woodcuts. 16mo. price 7s. 6d.

**Navigation and Nautical As**tronomy (Practical, Theoretical, Scientific) for the use of Students and Practical Men. By J. MERRIFIELD, F.R.A.S. and H. EVERS. 8vo. 14s.

**A General Dictionary** of Geography, Descriptive, Physical, Statistical, and Historical; forming a complete Gazetteer of the World. By A. KEITH JOHNSTON, F.R.S.E. New Edition. 8vo. price 31s. 6d.

**M'Culloch's Dictionary, Geogra**phical, Statistical, and Historical, of the various Countries, Places, and principal Natural Objects in the World. Revised Edition, with the Statistical Information throughout brought up to the latest returns By FREDERICK MARTIN. 4 vols. 8vo. with coloured Maps, £4 4s.

**A Manual of Geography,** Physical, Industrial, and Political. By W. HUGHES, F.R.G.S. Prof. of Geog. in King's Coll. and in Queen's Coll. Lond. With 6 Maps. Fcp. 7s. 6d.

**The States of the River Plate:** their Industries and Commerce, Sheep Farming, Sheep Breeding, Cattle Feeding, and Meat Preserving; the Employment of Capital, Land and Stock and their Values, Labour and its Remuneration. By WILFRID LATHAM, Buenos Ayres. Second Edition. 8vo. 12s.

**Maunder's Treasury of Geogra**phy, Physical, Historical, Descriptive, and Political. Edited by W. HUGHES, F.R.G.S. With 7 Maps and 16 Plates. Fcp. 6s.

---

## Natural History and Popular Science.

**Ganot's Elementary Treatise on** Physics, Experimental and Applied, for the use of Colleges and Schools. Translated and Edited with the Author's sanction by E. ATKINSON, Ph.D. F.C.S. New Edition, revised and enlarged; with a Coloured Plate and 620 Woodcuts. Post 8vo. 15s.

**The Elements of Physics or** Natural Philosophy. By NEIL ARNOTT, M.D. F.R.S. Physician-Extraordinary to the Queen. Sixth Edition, re-written and completed. 2 Parts, 8vo. 21s.

**The Forces of the Universe.** By GEORGE BERWICK, M.D. Post 8vo. 5s.

**Dove's Law of Storms,** considered in connexion with the ordinary Movements of the Atmosphere. Translated by R. H. SCOTT, M.A. T.C.D. 8vo. 10s. 6d.

**Sound:** a Course of Eight Lectures delivered at the Royal Institution of Great Britain. By Professor JOHN TYNDALL, LL.D. F.R.S. New Edition, with Portrait and Woodcuts. Crown 8vo. 9s.

**Heat a Mode of Motion.** By Professor JOHN TYNDALL, LL.D. F.R.S. Fourth Edition. Crown 8vo. with Woodcuts, price 10s. 6d.

**Researches on Diamagnetism** and Magne-Crystallic Action; including the Question of Diamagnetic Polarity. By Professor TYNDALL. With 6 Plates and many Woodcuts. 8vo. 14s.

**Notes of a Course of Nine Lec**tures on Light, delivered at the Royal Institution, A.D. 1869. By Professor TYNDALL. Crown 8vo. 1s. sewed, or 1s. 6d. cloth.

Notes of a Course of Seven Lectures on Electrical Phenomena and Theories, delivered at the Royal Institution, A.D. 1870. By Professor TYNDALL. Crown 8vo. 1s. sewed, or 1s. 6d. cloth.

Professor Tyndall's Essays on the Use and Limit of the Imagination in Science. Being the Second Edition, with Additions, of a Discourse on the Scientific Use of the Imagination. 8vo. 3s.

Light: its Influence on Life and Health. By FORBES WINSLOW, M.D. D.C.L. Oxon. (Hon.) Fcp. 8vo. 6s.

A Treatise on Electricity, in Theory and Practice. By A. DE LA RIVE, Prof. in the Academy of Geneva. Translated by C. V. WALKER, F.R.S. 3 vols. 8vo. with Woodcuts, £3 13s.

The Correlation of Physical Forces. By W. R. GROVE, Q.C. V.P.R.S. Fifth Edition, revised, and Augmented by a Discourse on Continuity. 8vo. 10s. 6d. The *Discourse*, separately, price 2s. 6d.

The Beginning: its When and its How. By MUNGO PONTON, F.R.S.E. Post 8vo. with very numerous Illustrations.

Manual of Geology. By S. HAUGHTON, M.D. F.R.S. Fellow of Trin. Coll. and Prof. of Geol. in the Univ. of Dublin. Second Edition, with 66 Woodcuts. Fcp. 7s. 6d.

Van Der Hoeven's Handbook of ZOOLOGY. Translated from the Second Dutch Edition by the Rev. W. CLARK, M.D. F.R.S. 2 vols. 8vo. with 24 Plates of Figures, 60s.

Professor Owen's Lectures on the Comparative Anatomy and Physiology of the Invertebrate Animals. Second Edition, with 235 Woodcuts. 8vo. 21s.

The Comparative Anatomy and Physiology of the Vertebrate Animals. By RICHARD OWEN, F.R.S. D.C.L. With 1,472 Woodcuts. 3 vols. 8vo. £3 13s. 6d.

The Origin of Civilisation and the Primitive Condition of Man; Mental and Social Condition of Savages. By Sir JOHN LUBBOCK, Bart. M.P. F.R.S. Second Edition, revised, with 25 Woodcuts. 8vo. price 16s.

The Primitive Inhabitants of Scandinavia. Containing a Description of the Implements, Dwellings, Tombs, and Mode of Living of the Savages in the North of Europe during the Stone Age. By SVEN NILSSON. 8vo. Plates and Woodcuts, 18s.

Homes without Hands: a Description of the Habitations of Animals, classed according to their Principle of Construction. By Rev. J. G. WOOD, M.A. F.L.S. With about 140 Vignettes on Wood. 8vo. 21s.

Bible Animals; being a Description of Every Living Creature mentioned in the Scriptures, from the Ape to the Coral. By the Rev. J. G. WOOD, M.A. F.L.S. With about 100 Vignettes on Wood. 8vo. 21s.

The Harmonies of Nature and Unity of Creation. By Dr. G. HARTWIG. 8vo. with numerous Illustrations, 18s.

The Sea and its Living Wonders. By the same Author. Third Edition, enlarged, 8vo. with many Illustrations, 21s.

The Tropical World. By the same Author. With 8 Chromoxylographs and 172 Woodcuts. 8vo. 21s.

The Polar World: a Popular Description of Man and Nature in the Arctic and Antarctic Regions of the Globe. By the same Author. With 8 Chromoxylographs, 3 Maps, and 85 Woodcuts. 8vo. 21s.

A Familiar History of Birds. By E. STANLEY, D.D. late Lord Bishop of Norwich. Fcp. with Woodcuts, 3s. 6d.

**Kirby and Spence's Introduction** to Entomology, or Elements of the Natural History of Insects. Crown 8vo. 5s.

**Maunder's** Treasury of Natural History, or Popular Dictionary of Zoology. Revised and corrected by T. S. CONNOLD, M.D. Fcp. with 900 Woodcuts, 6s.

The Elements of Botany for Families and Schools. Tenth Edition, revised by THOMAS MOORE, F.L.S. Fcp. with 154 Woodcuts, 2s. 6d.

The Treasury of Botany, or Popular Dictionary of the Vegetable Kingdom; with which is incorporated a Glossary of Botanical Terms. Edited by J. LINDLEY, F.R.S. and T. MOORE, F.L.S. assisted by eminent Contributors. Pp. 1,274, with 274 Woodcuts and 20 Steel Plates. TWO PARTS, fcp. 8vo. 12s.

The British Flora; comprising the Phænogamous or Flowering Plants and the Ferns. By Sir W. J. HOOKER, K.H. and G. A. WALKER-ARNOTT, LL.D. 12mo. with 12 Plates, 14s.

**The Rose Amateur's Guide.** By THOMAS RIVERS. New Edition. Fcp. 4s.

**Loudon's Encyclopædia of Plants;** comprising the Specific Character, Description, Culture, History, &c. of all the Plants found in Great Britain. With upwards of 12,000 Woodcuts. 8vo. 42s.

Maunder's Scientific and Literary Treasury; a Popular Encyclopædia of Science, Literature, and Art. New Edition, thoroughly revised and in great part re-written, with above 1,000 new articles, by J. Y. JOHNSON, Corr. M.Z.S. Fcp. 6s.

A Dictionary of Science, Literature, and Art. Fourth Edition, re-edited by the late W. T. BRANDE (the Author) and GEORGE W. COX, M.A. 3 vols. medium 8vo. price 63s. cloth.

## Chemistry, Medicine, Surgery, and *the* Allied Sciences.

A Dictionary of Chemistry and the Allied Branches of other Sciences. By HENRY WATTS, F.C.S. assisted by eminent Scientific and Practical Chemists. 5 vols. medium 8vo. price £7 3s.

Elements of Chemistry, Theoretical and Practical. By WILLIAM A. MILLER, M.D. LL.D. Professor of Chemistry, King's College, London. Fourth Edition. 3 vols. 8vo. £3.
PART I. CHEMICAL PHYSICS, 15s.
PART II. INORGANIC CHEMISTRY, 21s.
PART III. ORGANIC CHEMISTRY, 24s.

A Manual of Chemistry, Descriptive and Theoretical. By WILLIAM ODLING, M.B. F.R.S. PART I. 8vo. 9s. PART II. nearly ready.

A Course of Practical Chemistry, for the use of Medical Students. By W. ODLING, M.B. F.R.S. New Edition, with 70 new Woodcuts. Crown 8vo. 7s. 6d.

Outlines of Chemistry; or, Brief Notes of Chemical Facts. By the same Author. Crown 8vo. 7s. 6d.

Lectures on Animal Chemistry Delivered at the Royal College of Physicians in 1865. By the same Author. Crown 8vo. 4s. 6d.

Lectures on the Chemical Changes of Carbon, delivered at the Royal Institution of Great Britain. By the same Author. Crown 8vo. 4s. 6d.

Chemical Notes for the Lecture Room. By THOMAS WOOD, F.C.S. 2 vols. crown 8vo. I. on Heat, &c. price 3s. 6d. II. on the Metals, price 5s.

A Treatise on Medical Electricity, Theoretical and Practical; and its Use in the Treatment of Paralysis, Neuralgia, and other Diseases. By JULIUS ALTHAUS, M.D. &c. Second Edition, revised and partly re-written; with Plate and 62 Woodcuts. Post 8vo. price 15s.

The Diagnosis, Pathology, and Treatment of Diseases of Women; including the Diagnosis of Pregnancy. By GRAILY HEWITT, M.D. &c. President of the Obstetrical Society of London. Second Edition, enlarged; with 116 Woodcuts. 8vo. 24s.

Lectures on the Diseases of Infancy and Childhood. By CHARLES WEST, M.D. &c. Fifth Edition. 8vo. 16s.

On the Surgical Treatment of Children's Diseases. By T. HOLMES, M.A. &c. late Surgeon to the Hospital for Sick Children. Second Edition, with 9 Plates and 112 Woodcuts. 8vo. 21s.

A System of Surgery, Theoretical and Practical, in Treatises by Various Authors. Edited by T. HOLMES, M.A. &c. Surgeon and Lecturer on Surgery at St. George's Hospital, and Surgeon-in-Chief to the Metropolitan Police. Second Edition, thoroughly revised, with numerous Illustrations. 5 vols. 8vo. £5 5s.

Lectures on the Principles and Practice of Physic. By Sir THOMAS WATSON, Bart. M.D. Physician-in-Ordinary to the Queen. New Edition in the press.

Lectures on Surgical Pathology. By JAMES PAGET, F.R.S. Third Edition, revised and re-edited by the Author and Professor W. TURNER, M.B. 8vo. with 131 Woodcuts, 21s.

Cooper's Dictionary of Practical Surgery and Encyclopædia of Surgical Science. New Edition, brought down to the present time. By S. A. LANE, Surgeon to St. Mary's Hospital, &c. assisted by various Eminent Surgeons. VOL. II. 8vo. completing the work. [*Early in* 1871.

On Chronic Bronchitis, especially as connected with Gout, Emphysema, and Diseases of the Heart. By E. HEADLAM GREENHOW, M.D. F.R.C.P. &c. 8vo. 7s. 6d.

The Climate of the South of France as Suited to Invalids; with Notices of Mediterranean and other Winter Stations. By C. T. WILLIAMS, M.A. M.D. Oxon. Assistant-Physician to the Hospital for Consumption at Brompton. Second Edition. Crown 8vo. 6s.

**Pulmonary Consumption;** its Nature, Treatment, and Duration exemplified by an Analysis of One Thousand Cases selected from upwards of Twenty Thousand. By C. J. B. WILLIAMS, M.D. F.R.S. Consulting Physician to the Hospital for Consumption at Brompton; and C. T. WILLIAMS, M.A. M.D. OXON.
[*Nearly ready.*

**Clinical Lectures on Diseases of** the Liver, Jaundice, and Abdominal Dropsy. By C. MURCHISON, M.D. Physician and Lecturer on the Practice of Medicine, Middlesex Hospital. Post 8vo. with 25 Woodcuts, 10s. 6d.

**Anatomy, Descriptive and Surgical.** By HENRY GRAY, F.R.S. With about 410 Woodcuts from Dissections. Fifth Edition, by T. HOLMES, M.A. Cantab. With a New Introduction by the Editor. Royal 8vo. 28s.

**Clinical Notes on Diseases of** the Larynx, investigated and treated with the assistance of the Laryngoscope. By W. MARCET, M.D. F.R.S. Crown 8vo. with 5 Lithographs, 6s.

**The House I Live in;** or, Popular Illustrations of the Structure and Functions of the Human Body. Edited by T. G. GIRTIN. New Edition, with 25 Woodcuts. 16mo. price 2s. 6d.

**Outlines of Physiology,** Human and Comparative. By JOHN MARSHALL, F.R.C.S. Professor of Surgery in University College, London, and Surgeon to the University College Hospital. 2 vols. crown 8vo. with 122 Woodcuts, 32s.

**Physiological Anatomy and Physiology of Man.** By the late R. B. TODD, M.D. F.R.S. and W. BOWMAN, F.R.S. of King's College. With numerous Illustrations. VOL. II. 8vo. 25s.

VOL. I. New Edition by Dr. LIONEL S. BEALE, F.R.S. in course of publication; PART I. with 8 Plates, 7s. 6d.

**Copland's Dictionary of Practical Medicine,** abridged from the larger work, and throughout brought down to the present state of Medical Science. 8vo. 36s.

**A Manual of Materia Medica** and Therapeutics, abridged from Dr. PEREIRA's *Elements* by F. J. FARRE, M.D. assisted by R. BENTLEY, M.R.C.S. and by R. WARINGTON, F.R.S. 1 vol. 8vo. with 90 Woodcuts, 21s.

**Thomson's Conspectus of the** British Pharmacopœia. Twenty-fifth Edition, corrected by E. LLOYD BIRKETT, M.D. 18mo. 6s.

**Essays on Physiological Subjects.** By GILBERT W. CHILD, M.A. F.L.S. F.C.S. Second Edition. Crown 8vo. with Woodcuts, 7s. 6d.

## *The Fine* Arts, *and Illustrated Editions.*

**In Fairyland;** Pictures from the Elf-World. By RICHARD DOYLE. With a Poem by W. ALLINGHAM. With Sixteen Plates, containing Thirty-six Designs printed in Colours. Folio, 31s. 6d.

**Life of John Gibson, R.A.** Sculptor. Edited by Lady EASTLAKE. 8vo. 10s. 6d.

**Materials for a History of Oil** Painting. By Sir CHARLES LOCKE EASTLAKE, sometime President of the Royal Academy. 2 vols. 8vo. 30s.

**Albert Durer, his Life and** Works; including Autobiographical Papers and Complete Catalogues. By WILLIAM B. SCOTT. With Six Etchings by the Author and other Illustrations. 8vo. 16s.

**Half-Hour Lectures on the History** and Practice of the Fine and Ornamental Arts. By. W. B. SCOTT. Second Edition. Crown 8vo. with 50 Woodcut Illustrations, 8s. 6d.

**The Lord's Prayer Illustrated** by F. R. PICKERSGILL, R.A. and HENRY ALFORD, D.D. Dean of Canterbury. Imp. 4to. 21s.

**The Chorale Book for England:** the Hymns Translated by Miss C. WINKWORTH; the Tunes arranged by Prof. W. S. BENNETT and OTTO GOLDSCHMIDT. Fcp. 4to, 12s. 6d.

**Six Lectures on Harmony.** Delivered at the Royal Institution of Great Britain. By G. A. MACFARREN. 8vo. 10s. 6d.

**Lyra Germanica,** the Christian Year. Translated by CATHERINE WINKWORTH; with 125 Illustrations on Wood drawn by J. LEIGHTON, F.S.A. Quarto, 21s.

**Lyra Germanica,** the Christian Life. Translated by CATHERINE WINKWORTH; with about 200 Woodcut Illustrations by J. LEIGHTON, F.S.A. and other Artists. Quarto, 21s.

**The New Testament**, illustrated with Wood Engravings after the Early Masters, chiefly of the Italian School. Crown 4to. 63s. cloth, gilt top; or £5 5s. morocco.

**The Life of Man Symbolised by the Months of the Year** in their Seasons and Phases. Text selected by RICHARD PIGOT. 25 Illustrations on Wood from Original Designs by JOHN LEIGHTON, F.S.A. Quarto, 42s.

**Cats' and Farlie's Moral Emblems**; with Aphorisms, Adages, and Proverbs of all Nations; comprising 121 Illustrations on Wood by J. LEIGHTON, F.S.A. with an appropriate Text by R. PIGOT. Imperial 8vo. 31s. 6d.

**Shakspeare's Midsummer Night's Dream**, illustrated with 24 Silhouettes or Shadow Pictures by P. KONEWKA, engraved on Wood by A. VOGEL. Folio. 31s. 6d.

**Sacred and Legendary Art.** By Mrs. JAMESON. 6 vols. square crown 8vo. price £5 15s. 6d.

Legends of the Saints and Martyrs. Fifth Edition, with 19 Etchings and 187 Woodcuts. 2 vols. price 31s. 6d.

Legends of the Monastic Orders. Third Edition, with 11 Etchings and 88 Woodcuts. 1 vol. price 21s.

Legends of the Madonna. Third Edition, with 27 Etchings and 165 Woodcuts. 1 vol. price 21s.

The History of Our Lord, with that of His Types and Precursors. Completed by Lady EASTLAKE. Revised Edition, with 13 Etchings and 281 Woodcuts. 2 vols. price 42s.

---

## *The Useful Arts, Manufactures, &c.*

**Gwilt's Encyclopædia of Architecture**, with above 1,600 Woodcuts. Fifth Edition, with Alterations and considerable Additions, by WYATT PAPWORTH. 8vo. 52s. 6d.

**A Manual of Architecture**: being a Concise History and Explanation of the principal Styles of European Architecture, Ancient, Mediæval, and Renaissance; with their Chief Variations and a Glossary of Technical Terms. By THOMAS MITCHELL. With 150 Woodcuts. Crown 8vo. 10s. 6d.

**Italian Sculptors**: being a History of Sculpture in Northern, Southern, and Eastern Italy. By C. C. PERKINS. With 30 Etchings and 13 Wood Engravings. Imperial 8vo. 42s.

**Tuscan Sculptors, their Lives, Works, and Times.** By the same Author. With 45 Etchings and 28 Woodcuts from Original Drawings and Photographs. 2 vols. imperial 8vo. 63s.

**Hints on Household Taste in** Furniture, Upholstery, and other Details. By CHARLES L. EASTLAKE, Architect. Second Edition, with about 90 Illustrations. Square crown 8vo. 18s.

**The Engineer's Handbook**; explaining the principles which should guide the young Engineer in the Construction of Machinery. By C. S. LOWNDES. Post 8vo. 5s.

**Lathes and Turning, Simple, Mechanical, and Ornamental.** By W. HENRY NORTHCOTT. With about 240 Illustrations on Steel and Wood. 8vo. 18s.

**Principles of Mechanism**, designed for the use of Students in the Universities, and for Engineering Students generally. By R. WILLIS, M.A. F.R.S. &c. Jacksonian Professor in the Univ. of Cambridge. Second Edition, enlarged; with 374 Woodcuts. 8vo. 18s.

**Handbook of Practical Telegraphy**, published with the sanction of the Chairman and Directors of the Electric and International Telegraph Company, and adopted by the Department of Telegraphs for India. By R. S. CULLEY. Third Edition. 8vo. 12s. 6d.

**Ure's Dictionary of Arts, Manufactures, and Mines.** Sixth Edition, re-written and greatly enlarged by ROBERT HUNT, F.R.S. assisted by numerous Contributors. With 2,000 Woodcuts. 3 vols. medium 8vo. £4 14s. 6d.

**Treatise on Mills and Millwork.** By Sir W. FAIRBAIRN, Bart. With 18 Plates and 322 Woodcuts. 2 vols. 8vo. 32s.

Useful Information for Engineers. By the same Author. FIRST, SECOND, and THIRD SERIES, with many Plates and Woodcuts. 3 vols. crown 8vo. 10s. 6d. each.

The Application of Cast and Wrought Iron to Building Purposes. By the same Author. Fourth Edition, with 6 Plates and 118 Woodcuts. 8vo. 16s.

**Iron Ship Building, its History** and Progress, as comprised in a Series of Experimental Researches. By W. FAIRBAIRN, Bart. F.R.S. With 4 Plates and 130 Woodcuts, 8vo. 18s.

Encyclopædia of Civil Engineering, Historical, Theoretical, and Practical. By E. CRESY, C.E. With above 3,000 Woodcuts. 8vo. 42s.

A Treatise on the Steam Engine, in its various Applications to Mines, Mills, Steam Navigation, Railways, and Agriculture. By J. BOURNE, C.E. New Edition; with Portrait, 37 Plates, and 546 Woodcuts. 4to. 42s.

Catechism of the Steam Engine, in its various Applications to Mines, Mills, Steam Navigation, Railways, and Agriculture. By JOHN BOURNE, C.E. New Edition, with 89 Woodcuts. Fcp. 6s.

Recent Improvements in the Steam-Engine. By JOHN BOURNE, C.E. being a SUPPLEMENT to his 'Catechism of the Steam-Engine.' New Edition, including many New Examples, with 124 Woodcuts. Fcp. 8vo. 6s.

Bourne's Examples of Modern Steam, Air, and Gas Engines of the most Approved Types, as employed for Pumping, for Driving Machinery, for Locomotion, and for Agriculture, minutely and practically described. In course of publication, to be completed in Twenty-four Parts, price 2s. 6d. each, forming One Volume, with about 50 Plates and 400 Woodcuts.

A Treatise on the Screw Propeller, Screw Vessels, and Screw Engines, as adapted for purposes of Peace and War. By JOHN BOURNE, C.E. Third Edition, with 54 Plates and 287 Woodcuts. Quarto, 63s.

Handbook of the Steam Engine. By JOHN BOURNE, C.E. forming a KEY to the Author's Catechism of the Steam Engine. With 67 Woodcuts. Fcp. 9s.

A History of the Machine-Wrought Hosiery and Lace Manufactures. By WILLIAM FELKIN, F.L.S. F.S.S. With several Illustrations. Royal 8vo. 21s.

Mitchell's Manual of Practical Assaying. Third Edition for the most part re-written, with all the recent Discoveries incorporated. By W. CROOKES, F.R.S. With 188 Woodcuts. 8vo. 28s.

Reimann's Handbook of Aniline and its Derivatives; a Treatise on the Manufacture of Aniline and Aniline Colours. Revised and edited by WILLIAM CROOKES, F.R.S. 8vo. with 5 Woodcuts, 10s. 6d.

On the Manufacture of Beet-Root Sugar in England and Ireland. By WILLIAM CROOKES, F.R.S. With 11 Woodcuts. 8vo. 8s. 6d.

Practical Treatise on Metallurgy, adapted from the last German Edition of Professor KERL'S *Metallurgy* by W. CROOKES, F.R.S. &c. and E. RÖHRIG, Ph.D. M.E. 3 vols. 8vo. with 625 Woodcuts, price £4 19s.

The Art of Perfumery; the History and Theory of Odours, and the Methods of Extracting the Aromas of Plants. By Dr. PIESSE, F.C.S. Third Edition, with 53 Woodcuts. Crown 8vo. 10s. 6d.

Chemical, Natural, and Physical Magic, for Juveniles during the Holidays. By the same Author. With 38 Woodcuts. Fcp. 6s.

Loudon's Encyclopædia of Agriculture: comprising the Laying-out, Improvement, and Management of Landed Property, and the Cultivation and Economy of the Productions of Agriculture. With 1,100 Woodcuts. 8vo. 21s.

Loudon's Encyclopædia of Gardening: comprising the Theory and Practice of Horticulture, Floriculture, Arboriculture, and Landscape Gardening. With 1,000 Woodcuts. 8vo. 21s.

Bayldon's Art of Valuing Rents and Tillages, and Claims of Tenants upon Quitting Farms, both at Michaelmas and Lady-Day. Eighth Edition, revised by J. C. MORTON. 8vo. 10s. 6d.

## *Religious* and *Moral Works.*

An Exposition of the 39 Articles, Historical and Doctrinal. By E. HAROLD BROWNE, D.D. Lord Bishop of Ely. Eighth Edition. 8vo. 16s.

Examination-Questions on Bishop Browne's Exposition of the Articles. By the Rev. J. GORLE, M.A. Fcp. 3s. 6d.

The Life and Epistles of St. Paul. By the Rev. W. J. CONYBEARE, M.A. and the Very Rev. J. S. HOWSON, D.D. Dean of Chester.

LIBRARY EDITION, with all the Original Illustrations, Maps, Landscapes on Steel, Woodcuts, &c. 2 vols. 4to. 48s.

INTERMEDIATE EDITION, with a Selection of Maps, Plates, and Woodcuts. 2 vols. square crown 8vo. 31s. 6d.

STUDENT'S EDITION, revised and condensed, with 46 Illustrations and Maps. 1 vol. crown 8vo. 9s.

**The Voyage and Shipwreck of St. Paul**; with Dissertations on the Ships and Navigation of the Ancients. By JAMES SMITH, F.R.S. **Crown 8vo.** Charts, 10s. 6d.

**Evidence of the Truth of the** Christian Religion derived from the Literal Fulfilment of Prophecy. By ALEXANDER KEITH, D.D. 37th Edition, with numerous Plates, in square 8vo. 12s. 6d.; also the 39th Edition, in post 8vo. with 5 Plates, 6s.

**The History and Destiny of the World** and of the Church, according to Scripture. By the **same** Author. Square **8vo.** with 40 Illustrations, **10s.**

**The History and Literature of** the Israelites, according to the Old Testament and the Apocrypha. By C. DE ROTHSCHILD and A. DE ROTHSCHILD. With **2** Maps. 2 vols. post 8vo. price 12s. **6d.**
VOL. I. *The Historical Books*, 7s. 6d.
VOL. II. *The Prophetic and Poetical Writings*, price 5s.

**Ewald's History of Israel to the** Death of Moses. Translated from the German. Edited, with a Preface and an Appendix, by RUSSELL MARTINEAU, M.A. Second Edition. 2 vols. 8vo. 24s.

**History of the Karaite Jews.** By WILLIAM HARRIS RULE, D.D. Post 8vo. price 7s. 6d.

**The Life of Margaret Mary** Hallahan, better known in the religious world by the name of Mother Margaret. By her RELIGIOUS CHILDREN. Second Edition. **8vo.** with Portrait, 10s.

**The See of Rome in the Middle** Ages. By the Rev. OSWALD J. REICHEL, B.C.L. and M.A. **8vo.** 18s.

**The** Evidence for the Papacy as derived from the Holy Scriptures and from Primitive Antiquity. By the Hon. COLIN LINDSAY. **8vo.** 12s. 6d.

**The Pontificate of Pius the** Ninth; being the Third Edition, enlarged and continued, of 'Rome and its Ruler.' By J. F. MAGUIRE, M.P. Post 8vo. **Portrait,** price 12s. 6d.

Ignatius Loyola and the Early Jesuits. By STEWART ROSE. New Edition, **in the press.**

**An Introduction to the Study of** the New Testament, Critical, Exegetical, and Theological. By the Rev. S. DAVIDSON, D.D. LL.D. 2 vols. 8vo. 30s.

**A Critical** and Grammatical Commentary on **St. Paul's** Epistles. By C. J. ELLICOTT, D.D. Lord Bishop of Gloucester and Bristol. 8vo.
Galatians, Fourth Edition, 8s. **6d.**
Ephesians, Fourth Edition, 8s. 6d.
Pastoral Epistles, Fourth Edition, 10s. 6d.
Philippians, **Colossians,** and Philemon, Third Edition, **10s. 6d.**
Thessalonians, **Third Edition,** 7s. **6d.**

**Historical Lectures on the Life of** Our Lord Jesus Christ; being the Hulsean Lectures for 1859. By C. J. ELLICOTT, D.D. Lord Bishop of Gloucester and Bristol. Fifth Edition. 8vo. 12s.

**The Greek Testament; with Notes,** Grammatical and Exegetical. By the Rev. W. WEBSTER, M.A. and the Rev. W. F. WILKINSON, M.A. **2** vols. 8vo. £2 4s.

**Horne's Introduction to the Critical** Study and Knowledge of the Holy Scriptures. Twelfth Edition; with 4 Maps and 22 Woodcuts and Facsimiles. 4 vols. 8vo. 42s.

Compendious Introduction to **the** Study of the Bible. Edited by the Rev. **JOHN AYRE, M.A.** With Maps, &c. Post 8vo. **6s.**

**The** Treasury of Bible Knowledge; being a Dictionary of the Books, Persons, Places, Events, and other Matters of which mention **is** made in Holy Scripture. By Rev. **J.** AYRE, M.A. With Maps, 15 Plates, **and** numerous Woodcuts. Fcp. 6s.

**Every-day Scripture Difficulties** explained and illustrated. By J. E. PRESCOTT, M.A. VOL. I. *Matthew* and *Mark*; VOL. II. *Luke* and *John*. 2 vols. 8vo. price 9s. each.

**The Pentateuch and Book of** Joshua Critically Examined. By the Right Rev. J. W. COLENSO, D.D. Lord Bishop of Natal. Crown 8vo. price 6s.

**The Four Cardinal Virtues** (Fortitude, Justice, Prudence, Temperance) in relation to the Public **and** Private Life of Catholics: Six Sermons for the Day. With Preface, Appendices, &c. By the Rev. ORBY SHIPLEY, M.A. Crown 8vo. with Frontispiece, 7s. 6d.

**The Formation of Christendom.** By T. W. ALLIES. PARTS I. and II. 8vo. price 12s. each.

**Four Discourses of Chrysostom,** chiefly on the parable of the Rich Man and Lazarus. Translated by F. ALLEN, B.A. Crown **8vo.** 3s. **6d.**

**Christendom's Divisions**; a Philosophical Sketch of the Divisions of the Christian Family in East and West. By EDMUND S. FFOULKES. Post 8vo. 7s. 6d.

**Christendom's Divisions**, PART II. *Greeks and Latins.* By the same Author. Post 8vo. 15s.

**The Hidden Wisdom of Christ** and the Key of Knowledge; or, History of the Apocrypha. By ERNEST DE BUNSEN. 2 vols. 8vo. 28s.

**The Keys of St. Peter**; or, the House of Rechab, connected with the History of Symbolism and Idolatry. By the same Author. 8vo. 14s.

**The Power of the Soul over the** Body. By GEO. MOORE, M.D. M.R.C.P.L. &c. Sixth Edition. Crown 8vo. 8s. 6d.

**The Types of Genesis** briefly considered as Revealing the Development of Human Nature. By ANDREW JUKES. Second Edition. Crown 8vo. 7s. 6d.

**The Second Death and the Restitution** of All Things, with some Preliminary Remarks on the Nature and Inspiration of Holy Scripture. By the same Author. Second Edition. **Crown** 8vo. 3s. 6d.

**Thoughts for the Age.** By ELIZABETH M. SEWELL, Author of 'Amy Herbert.' New Edition. Fcp. 8vo. **price 5s.**

**Passing Thoughts on Religion. By the** same Author. Fcp. 5s.

**Self-examination before Confirmation. By** the same Author. 32mo. 1s. 6d.

**Thoughts for the Holy Week,** for Young Persons. By the **same** Author. New Edition. Fcp. 8vo. 2s.

**Readings for a Month** Preparatory to Confirmation from Writers of the Early and English Church. By the same. Fcp. 4s.

**Readings for Every Day in Lent,** compiled from the Writings of Bishop JEREMY TAYLOR. By the same Author. Fcp. 5s.

**Preparation for the Holy Communion:** the Devotions chiefly **from** the works of JEREMY TAYLOR. By the same. 32mo. 3s.

**Principles of Education** drawn from Nature and Revelation, and Applied **to** Female Education in the Upper Classes. By the same Author. 2 vols. fcp. 12s. 6d.

**Bishop Jeremy Taylor's Entire** Works: with Life by BISHOP HEBER. Revised and corrected by the Rev. C. P. EDEN. 10 vols. £5 5s.

**England and Christendom.** By ARCHBISHOP MANNING, D.D. Post 8vo. price 10s. 6d.

**The Wife's Manual**; or, Prayers, Thoughts, and Songs on Several Occasions of a Matron's Life. By the Rev. W. CALVERT, M.A. Crown 8vo. 10s. 6d.

**Singers and Songs of the Church**: being Biographical Sketches of the Hymn-Writers in all the principal Collections; with Notes on their Psalms and Hymns. By JOSIAH MILLER, M.A. Second Edition, enlarged. Post 8vo. 10s. 6d.

**'Spiritual Songs' for the Sundays** and Holidays throughout the Year. By J. S. B. MONSELL, LL.D. Vicar of Egham and Rural Dean. Fourth Edition, Sixth Thousand. Fcp. price 4s. 6d.

**The Beatitudes. By** the **same Author.** Third Edition, **revised.** Fcp. **3s. 6d.**

**His Presence not his Memory**, 1855. By the same Author, in memory of his SON. Sixth **Edition.** 16mo. 1s.

**Lyra** Germanica, translated from the German by Miss C. WINKWORTH. FIRST **SERIES,** the *Christian Year,* Hymns for the Sundays and Chief Festivals of the Church; SECOND SERIES, the *Christian Life.* Fcp. 8vo. price 5s. 6d. each SERIES.

**Lyra Eucharistica**: Hymns and Verses on the Holy Communion, Ancient and Modern: with other Poems. Edited by the Rev. ORBY SHIPLEY, M.A. Second Edition. Fcp. 5s.

**Shipley's Lyra Messianica.** Fcp. 5s.

**Shipley's Lyra Mystica.** Fcp. 5s.

**Endeavours after the Christian** Life: Discourses. By JAMES MARTINEAU. Fourth Edition, carefully revised. Post 8vo. 7s. 6d.

**Invocation of Saints and Angels**; for the use of Members of the English Church. Edited by the Rev. ORBY SHIPLEY, M.A. 24mo. 3s. 6d.

## Travels, Voyages, &c.

**The Playground of Europe.** By LESLIE STEPHEN, late President of the Alpine Club. Post 8vo. with Frontispiece. [*Just ready.*

**Westward by Rail**: the New Route to the East. By W. F. RAE. Post 8vo. with Map, price 10s. 6d.

**Travels in the Central Caucasus** and Bashan, including Visits to Ararat and Tabreez and Ascents of Kazbek and Elbruz. By DOUGLAS W. FRESHFIELD. Square crown 8vo. with Maps, &c., 18s.

**Cadore** or **Titian's Country.** By JOSIAH GILBERT, one of the Authors of the 'Dolomite Mountains.' With Map, Facsimile, and 40 Illustrations. Imp.8vo. 31s. 6d.

**Zigzagging amongst Dolomites;** with more than 300 Illustrations by the Author. By the Author of ' How we Spent the Summer.' Oblong 4to. price 15s.

**The Dolomite Mountains.** Excursions through Tyrol, Carinthia, Carniola, and Friuli. By J. GILBERT and G. C. CHURCHILL, F.R.G.S. With numerous Illustrations. Square crown 8vo. 21s.

**Pilgrimages in the Pyrenees and** Landes. By DENYS SHYNE LAWLOR. Crown 8vo. with Frontispiece and Vignette, price 15s.

**How we Spent the Summer; or,** a Voyage en Zigzag in Switzerland and Tyrol with some Members of the ALPINE CLUB. Third Edition, re-drawn. In oblong 4to. with about 300 Illustrations, 15s.

**Pictures in Tyrol and Elsewhere.** From a Family Sketch-Book. By the same Author. Second Edition. 4to. with many Illustrations, 21s.

**Beaten Tracks; or, Pen and Pencil** Sketches in Italy. By the same Author. With 42 Plates of Sketches. 8vo. 16s.

**The Alpine Club Map of the Chain** of Mont Blanc, from an actual Survey in 1863—1864. By A. ADAMS-REILLY, F.R.G.S. M.A.C. In Chromolithography on extra stout drawing paper 28in. × 17in. price 10s. or mounted on canvas in a folding case, 12s. 6d.

**England to Delhi;** a Narrative of Indian Travel. By JOHN MATHESON, Glasgow. With Map and 82 Woodcut Illustrations. 4to. 31s. 6d.

**History of Discovery in our** Australasian Colonies, Australia, Tasmania, and New Zealand, from the Earliest Date to the Present Day. By WILLIAM HOWITT. 2 vols. 8vo. with 3 Maps, 20s.

**The Capital of the Tycoon;** a Narrative of a 3 Years' Residence in Japan. By Sir RUTHERFORD ALCOCK, K.C.B. 2 vols. 8vo. with numerous Illustrations, 42s.

**Guide to the Pyrenees,** for the use of Mountaineers. By CHARLES PACKE. Second Edition, with Maps, &c. and Appendix. Crown 8vo. 7s. 6d.

**The Alpine Guide.** By JOHN BALL, M.R.I.A. late President of the Alpine Club. Post 8vo. with Maps and other Illustrations.

Guide to the Eastern Alps, price 10s. 6d.

Guide to the Western Alps, including Mont Blanc, Monte Rosa, Zermatt, &c. price 6s. 6d.

Guide to the Central Alps, including all the Oberland District, price 7s. 6d.

Introduction on Alpine Travelling in general, and on the Geology of the Alps, price 1s. Either of the Three Volumes or Parts of the *Alpine Guide* may be had with this INTRODUCTION prefixed, price 1s. extra.

**Roma Sotterranea;** or, an Account of the Roman Catacombs, especially of the Cemetery of San Callisto. Compiled from the Works of Commendatore G. B. DE ROSSI, by the Rev. J. S. NORTHCOTE, D.D. and the Rev. W. B. BROWNLOW. With Plans and numerous other Illustrations. 8vo. 31s. 6d.

**Memorials of London and London** Life in the 13th, 14th, and 15th Centuries; being a Series of Extracts, Local, Social, and Political, from the Archives of the City of London, A.D. 1276–1419. Selected, translated, and edited by H. T. RILEY, M.A. Royal 8vo. 21s.

**Commentaries on the History,** Constitution, and Chartered Franchises of the City of London. By GEORGE NORTON, formerly one of the Common Pleaders of the City of London. Third Edition. 8vo. 14s.

**The Northern Heights of London**; or, Historical Associations of Hampstead, Highgate, Muswell Hill, Hornsey, and Islington. By WILLIAM HOWITT. With about 40 Woodcuts. Square crown 8vo. 21s.

**The Rural Life of England.** By the same Author. With Woodcuts by Bewick and Williams. Medium, 8vo. 12s. 6d.

**Visits to Remarkable Places:** Old Halls, Battle-Fields, and Scenes illustrative of striking Passages in English History and Poetry. By the same Author. 2 vols. square crown 8vo. with Wood Engravings, 25s.

**Narrative of the Euphrates Expedition** carried on by Order of the British Government during the years 1835, 1836, and 1837. By General F. R. CHESNEY, F.R.S. With 2 Maps, 45 Plates, and 16 Woodcuts. 8vo. 24s.

## Works of Fiction.

**Lothair.** By the Right Hon. B. DISRAELI, Cabinet Edition (the Eighth), complete in One Volume, with a Portrait of the Author, and a new General Preface. Crown 8vo. price 6s.—By the same Author, Cabinet Editions, revised, uniform with the above:—

CONINGSBY, 6s.
SYBIL, 6s.
TANCRED, 6s.
VENETIA, 6s.
HENRIETTA TEMPLE, 6s.
CONTARINI FLEMING and RISE OF ISKANDER, 6s.
ALROY; IXION; the INFERNAL MARRIAGE; and POPANILLA. Price 6s.
YOUNG DUKE and COUNT ALARCOS, 6s.
VIVIAN GREY, 6s.

**The Modern Novelist's Library.** Each Work, in crown 8vo. complete in a Single Volume:—

MELVILLE'S GLADIATORS, 2s. boards; 2s. 6d. cloth.
―――― GOOD FOR NOTHING, 2s. boards; 2s. 6d. cloth.
―――― HOLMBY HOUSE, 2s. boards; 2s. 6d. cloth.
―――― INTERPRETER, 2s. boards; 2s. 6d. cloth.
―――― QUEEN'S MARIES, 2s. boards; 2s. 6d. cloth.
TROLLOPE'S WARDEN, 1s. 6d. boards; 2s. cloth.
―――― BARCHESTER TOWERS, 2s. boards; 2s. 6d. cloth.
BRAMLEY-MOORE'S SIX SISTERS OF THE VALLEYS, 2s. boards; 2s. 6d. cloth.

**Stories and Tales by the Author** of 'Amy Herbert,' uniform Edition:—

AMY HERBERT, 2s. 6d.
GERTRUDE, 2s. 6d.
EARL'S DAUGHTER, 2s. 6d.
EXPERIENCE OF LIFE, 2s. 6d.
CLEVE HALL, 3s. 6d.
IVORS, 3s. 6d.
KATHARINE ASHTON, 3s. 6d.
MARGARET PERCIVAL, 5s.
LANETON PARSONAGE, 4s. 6d.
URSULA, 4s. 6d.

**A Glimpse of the World.** Fcp. 7s. 6d.

**Journal of a Home Life.** Post 8vo. 9s. 6d.

**After Life;** a Sequel to the 'Journal of a Home Life.' Post 8vo. 10s. 6d.

**A Visit to my Discontented Cousin.** Reprinted, with some Additions, from *Fraser's Magazine*. Crown 8vo. price 7s. 6d.

**Ierne;** a Tale. By W. STEUART TRENCH, Author of 'Realities of Irish Life.' 2 vols post 8vo. [*Just ready.*

**Three Weddings.** By the Author of 'Dorothy,' &c. Fcp. 8vo. 5s.

**The Giant;** a Witch's Story for English Boys. Edited by ELIZABETH M. SEWELL, Author of 'Amy Herbert,' &c. Fcp. 8vo. price 5s.

**Uncle Peter's Fairy Tale for the XIXth Century.** By the same Author and Editor. Fcp. 8vo. 7s. 6d.

**Vikram and the Vampire;** or, Tales of Hindu Devilry. Adapted by RICHARD F. BURTON, F.R.G.S. &c. With 33 Illustrations. Crown 8vo. 9s.

**Becker's Gallus;** or, Roman Scenes of the Time of Augustus. Post 8vo. 7s. 6d.

**Becker's Charicles:** Illustrative of Private Life of the Ancient Greeks. Post 8vo. 7s. 6d.

**Tales of Ancient Greece.** By GEORGE W. COX, M.A. late Scholar of Trin. Coll. Oxford. Being a collective Edition of the Author's Classical Series and Tales, complete in One Volume. Crown 8vo. 6s. 6d.

**Cabinet Edition of Novels and Tales** by G. J. WHYTE MELVILLE:—

THE GLADIATORS, 5s. HOLMBY HOUSE, 5s.
DIGBY GRAND, 5s. GOOD FOR NOTHING, 6s.
KATE COVENTRY, 5s. QUEEN'S MARIES, 6s.
GENERAL BOUNCE, 5s. THE INTERPRETER, 5s.

**Our Children's Story.** By One of their Gossips. By the Author of 'Voyage en Zigzag,' &c. Small 4to. with Sixty Illustrations by the Author, price 10s. 6d.

**Wonderful Stories from Norway,** Sweden, and Iceland. Adapted and arranged by JULIA GODDARD. With an Introductory Essay by the Rev. G. W. COX, M.A. and Six Illustrations. Square post 8vo. 6s.

c

## *Poetry* and *The Drama*.

**Thomas Moore's Poetical Works,** the only Editions containing the Author's last Copyright Additions:—
Shamrock Edition, **price 3s. 6d.**
Ruby Edition, with **Portrait, 6s.**
Cabinet Edition, 10 vols. fcp. 8vo. **35s.**
People's Edition, **Portrait, &c. 10s. 6d.**
Library Edition, **Portrait & Vignette, 14s.**

**Moore's Lalla Rookh,** Tenniel's Edition, with 68 Wood Engravings from Original Drawings and other Illustrations. Fcp. 4to. 21s.

**Moore's** Irish Melodies, Maclise's Edition, with 161 Steel Plates from Original Drawings. Super-royal 8vo. 31s. 6d.

**Miniature** Edition of Moore's Irish *Melodies,* with Maclise's Illustrations (as above), reduced in Lithography. Imp. 16mo. **10s. 6d.**

**Southey's Poetical Works,** with the Author's last Corrections and copyright Additions. Library Edition. Medium 8vo. with Portrait and Vignette, 14s.

**Lays of Ancient Rome**; with *Ivry* and the *Armada*. By the Right Hon. LORD MACAULAY. 16mo. **4s. 6d.**

**Lord** Macaulay's **Lays of Ancient** Rome. With 90 **Illustrations on Wood, Original and** from the Antique, from **Drawings by** G. SCHARF. Fcp. 4to. **21s.**

**Miniature Edition of Lord** Macaulay's Lays of Ancient Rome, with Scharf's Illustrations (as above) reduced in Lithography. **Imp.** 16mo. 10s. 6d.

**Goldsmith's Poetical Works,** Illustrated with Wood Engravings from Designs by Members of the ETCHING CLUB. Imp. 16mo. **7s. 6d.**

**Poems of Bygone Years.** Edited by the Author of 'Amy Herbert.' Fcp. 8vo. 5s.

**Poems, Descriptive and Lyrical.** By THOMAS COX. New Edition. Fcp. 8vo. price 5s.

'**Show moral** propriety, mental culture, and no **slight acquaintance** with the technicalities of song.'
ATHENÆUM.

**Madrigals, Songs, and Sonnets.** By JOHN ARTHUR BLAIKIE and EDMUND WILLIAM GOSSE. Fcp. 8vo. price 5s.

**Poems.** By JEAN INGELOW. Fifteenth Edition. Fcp. 8vo. 5s.

**Poems by** Jean Ingelow. With nearly 100 Illustrations by Eminent Artists, engraved on Wood by DALZIEL Brothers. Fcp. 4to. 21s.

**Mopsa the Fairy.** By JEAN INGELOW. With Eight Illustrations engraved on Wood. Fcp. 8vo. 6s.

**A Story of Doom,** and other Poems. By JEAN INGELOW. Third Edition. Fcp. price 5s.

**Glaphyra, and other Poems.** By FRANCIS REYNOLDS, Author of 'Alice Rushton.' 16mo. 5s.

**Bowdler's Family Shakspeare,** cheaper Genuine Edition, complete in 1 vol large type, with 36 **Woodcut** Illustrations, price 14s. or in 6 pocket vols. 3s. 6d. each.

**Arundines Cami.** Collegit atque edidit H. DRURY, M.A. Editio Sexta, curavit H. J. HODGSON, M.A. Crown 8vo. price 7s. 6d.

**Horatii** Opera, Pocket Edition, with **carefully** corrected Text, Marginal References, **and** Introduction. Edited by the Rev. J. E. YONGE, M.A. Square 18mo. 4s. 6d.

**Horatii Opera,** Library Edition, with Copious English Notes, Marginal References and Various Readings. Edited by the Rev. J. E. YONGE, M.A. 8vo. 21s.

**The Æneid of Virgil** Translated into English Verse. By JOHN CONINGTON, M.A. Corpus Professor of Latin in the University of Oxford. New Edition. Crown 8vo. 9s.

**The Story of Sir Richard Whittington,** Thrice Lord Mayor of London, A.D. 1397, 1406-7, and 1419. Written in Verse and Illustrated by E. CARR. With Eleven Plates. Royal 4to. 21s.

**Hunting Songs** and Miscellaneous Verses. By R. E. EGERTON WARBURTON. Second Edition. Fcp. 8vo. 5s.

**Works by Edward Yardley**:—
FANTASTIC STORIES, fcp. 3s. 6d.
MELUSINE AND OTHER POEMS, fcp. 5s.
HORACE'S ODES TRANSLATED INTO ENGLISH VERSE, crown 8vo. 6s.
SUPPLEMENTARY STORIES AND POEMS, fcp. 3s. 6d.

## Rural Sports, &c.

**Encyclopædia of Rural Sports;** a Complete Account, Historical, Practical, and Descriptive, of Hunting, Shooting, Fishing, Racing, &c. By D. P. BLAINE. With above 600 Woodcuts (20 from Designs by JOHN LEECH). 8vo. 21s.

**The Dead Shot,** or Sportsman's Complete Guide; a Treatise on the Use of the Gun, Dog-breaking, Pigeon-shooting, &c. By MARKSMAN. Fcp. with Plates, 5s.

**A Book on Angling:** being a Complete Treatise on the Art of Angling in every branch, including full Illustrated Lists of Salmon Flies. By FRANCIS FRANCIS. Second Edition, with Portrait and 15 other Plates, plain and coloured. Post 8vo. 15s.

**Wilcocks's Sea-Fisherman;** comprising the Chief Methods of Hook and Line Fishing in the British and other Seas, a glance at Nets, and remarks on Boats and Boating. Second Edition, enlarged, with 80 Woodcuts. Post 8vo. 12s. 6d.

**The Fly-Fisher's Entomology.** By ALFRED RONALDS. With coloured Representations of the Natural and Artificial Insect. Sixth Edition, with 20 coloured Plates. 8vo. 14s.

**The Book of the Roach.** By GREVILLE FENNELL, of 'The Field.' Fcp. 8vo. price 2s. 6d.

**Blaine's Veterinary Art:** a Treatise on the Anatomy, Physiology, and Curative Treatment of the Diseases of the Horse, Neat Cattle, and Sheep. Seventh Edition, revised and enlarged by C. STEEL. 8vo. with Plates and Woodcuts, 18s.

**Horses and Stables.** By Colonel F. FITZWYGRAM, XV. the King's Hussars. Pp. 624; with 24 Plates of Illustrations, containing very numerous Figures engraved on Wood. 8vo. 15s.

**Youatt on the Horse.** Revised and enlarged by W. WATSON, M.R.C.V.S. 8vo. with numerous Woodcuts, 12s. 6d.

**Youatt on the Dog.** (By the same Author.) 8vo. with numerous Woodcuts, 6s.

**The Horse's Foot, and how to keep** it Sound. By W. MILES, Esq. Ninth Edition, with Illustrations. Imp. 8vo. 12s. 6d.

**A Plain Treatise on Horse-shoeing.** By the same Author. Sixth Edition, post 8vo. with Illustrations, 2s. 6d.

**Stables and Stable Fittings.** By the same. Imp. 8vo. with 13 Plates, 15s.

**Remarks on Horses' Teeth,** addressed to Purchasers. By the same. Post 8vo. 1s. 6d.

**Robbins's Cavalry Catechism;** or, Instructions on Cavalry Exercise and Field Movements, Brigade Movements, Out-post Duty, Cavalry supporting Artillery, **Artillery attached** to Cavalry. 12mo. 5s.

**The Dog in** Health and Disease. By STONEHENGE. With 70 Wood Engravings. New Edition. Square crown 8vo. 10s. 6d.

**The** Greyhound. By the same Author. Revised Edition, with 24 Portraits of Greyhounds. Square crown 8vo. 10s. 6d.

**The Ox,** his Diseases and their Treatment; with an Essay on Parturition in the Cow. By J. R. DOBSON, M.R.C.V.S. Crown 8vo. with Illustrations, 7s. 6d.

---

## Commerce, Navigation, and Mercantile Affairs.

**The** Elements of Banking. By HENRY DUNNING MACLEOD, M.A. of Trinity College, Cambridge, and of the Inner Temple, Barrister-at-Law. Post 8vo.
[*Nearly ready.*

**The Law of Nations Considered** as Independent Political Communities. By Sir TRAVERS TWISS, D.C.L. 2 vols. 8vo. 30s. or separately, PART I *Peace,* 12s. PART II. *War,* 18s.

**The Theory and Practice of** Banking. By HENRY DUNNING MACLEOD, M.A. Barrister-at-Law. Second Edition, entirely remodelled. 2 vols. 8vo. 30s.

**M'Culloch's Dictionary, Practical,** Theoretical, and Historical, of Commerce and Commercial Navigation. New Edition, revised throughout and corrected to the Present Time; with a Biographical Notice of the Author. Edited by H. G. REID, Secretary to Mr. M'Culloch for many **years.** 8vo. price 63s. cloth.

## Works of Utility and General Information.

**Modern Cookery for Private Families**, reduced to a System of Easy Practice in a Series of carefully-tested Receipts. By ELIZA ACTON. Newly revised and enlarged; with 8 Plates, Figures, and 150 Woodcuts. Fcp. 6s.

**A Practical Treatise on Brewing;** with Formulæ for Public Brewers, and Instructions for Private Families. By W. BLACK. Fifth Edition. 8vo. 10s. 6d.

**Chess Openings.** By F. W. LONGMAN, Balliol College, Oxford. Fcp. 8vo. 2s. 6d.

**The Cabinet Lawyer;** a Popular Digest of the Laws of England, Civil, Criminal, and Constitutional. 25th Edition; with Supplements of the Acts of the Parliamentary Session of 1870. Fcp. 10s. 6d.

**The Philosophy of Health;** or, an Exposition of the Physiological and Sanitary Conditions conducive to Human Longevity and Happiness. By SOUTHWOOD SMITH, M.D. Eleventh Edition, revised and enlarged; with 113 Woodcuts. 8vo. 7s. 6d.

**Maunder's Treasury of Knowledge** and Library of Reference: comprising an English Dictionary and Grammar, Universal Gazetteer, Classical Dictionary, Chronology, Law Dictionary, Synopsis of the Peerage, Useful Tables, &c. Fcp. 6s.

**Hints to Mothers on the Management** of their Health during the Period of Pregnancy and in the Lying-in Room. By T. BULL, M.D. Fcp. 5s.

**The Maternal Management of Children** in Health and Disease. By THOMAS BULL, M.D. Fcp. 5s.

**How to Nurse Sick Children;** containing Directions which may be found of service to all who have charge of the Young. By CHARLES WEST, M.D. Second Edition. Fcp. 8vo. 1s. 6d.

**Notes on Hospitals.** By FLORENCE NIGHTINGALE. Third Edition, enlarged; with 13 Plans. Post 4to. 18s.

**Pewtner's Comprehensive Specifier;** a Guide to the Practical Specification of every kind of Building-Artificer's Work; with Forms of Building Conditions and Agreements, an Appendix, Foot-Notes, and Index. Edited by W. YOUNG, Architect. Crown 8vo. 6s.

**Tidd Pratt's Law** relating to Benefit Building Societies; with Practical Observations on the Act and all the Cases decided thereon, also a Form of Rules and Forms of Mortgages. Fcp. 3s. 6d.

**Collieries and Colliers:** a Handbook of the Law and Leading Cases relating thereto. By J. C. FOWLER, of the Inner Temple, Barrister, Stipendiary Magistrate. Second Edition. Fcp. 8vo. 7s. 6d.

**Willich's Popular Tables** for Ascertaining the Value of Lifehold, Leasehold, and Church Property, Renewal Fines, &c.; the Public Funds; Annual Average Price and Interest on Consols from 1731 to 1867; Chemical, Geographical, Astronomical, Trigonometrical Tables, &c. Post 8vo. 10s.

**Coulthart's Decimal Interest Tables** at Twenty-four Different Rates not exceeding Five per Cent. Calculated for the use of Bankers. To which are added Commission Tables at One-eighth and One-fourth per Cent. 8vo. 15s.

## Periodical Publications.

**The Edinburgh Review, or Critical Journal**, published Quarterly in January, April, July, and October. 8vo. price 6s. each Number.

**Notes on Books:** An Analysis of the Works published during each Quarter by Messrs. LONGMANS & Co. The object is to enable Bookbuyers to obtain such information regarding the various works as is usually afforded by tables of contents and explanatory prefaces. 4to. Quarterly. Gratis.

**Fraser's Magazine.** Edited by JAMES ANTHONY FROUDE, M.A. New Series, published on the 1st of each Month. 8vo. price 2s. 6d. each Number.

**The Alpine Journal:** A Record of Mountain Adventure and Scientific Observation. By Members of the Alpine Club. Edited by LESLIE STEPHEN. Published Quarterly, May 31, Aug. 31, Nov. 30, Feb. 28. 8vo. price 1s. 6d. each No.

# INDEX.

| | |
|---|---|
| Acton's Modern Cookery | 20 |
| Alcock's Residence in Japan | 16 |
| Allies on Formation of Christendom | 14 |
| Allen's Discourses of Chrysostom | 14 |
| Alpine Guide (The) | 16 |
| ——— Journal | 20 |
| Althaus on Medical Electricity | 10 |
| Arnold's Manual of English Literature | 6 |
| Arnott's Elements of Physics | 8 |
| Arundines Cami | 18 |
| Autumn Holidays of a Country Parson | 6 |
| Ayre's Treasury of Bible Knowledge | 14 |
| | |
| Bacon's Essays by Whately | 5 |
| ——— Life and Letters, by Spedding | 4 |
| ——— Works | 5 |
| Bain's Mental and Moral Science | 7 |
| ——— on the Emotions and Will | 7 |
| ——— on the Senses and Intellect | 7 |
| ——— on the Study of Character | 7 |
| Ball's Guide to the Central Alps | 16 |
| ——— Guide to the Western Alps | 16 |
| ——— Guide to the Eastern Alps | 16 |
| Baring's Staff College Essays | 6 |
| Bayldon's Rents and Tillages | 13 |
| Beaten Tracks | 16 |
| Becker's Charicles and Gallus | 17 |
| Benfey's Sanskrit-English Dictionary | 6 |
| Bernard on British Neutrality | 1 |
| Berwick's Forces of the Universe | 8 |
| Black's Treatise on Brewing | 20 |
| Blackley's Word-Gossip | 7 |
| ——— German-English Dictionary | 6 |
| Blackie and Gosse's Poems | 18 |
| Blaine's Rural Sports | 19 |
| ——— Veterinary Art | 19 |
| Bourne on Screw Propeller | 13 |
| ——— 's Catechism of the Steam Engine | 13 |
| ——— Examples of Modern Engines | 13 |
| ——— Handbook of Steam Engine | 13 |
| ——— Treatise on the Steam Engine | 13 |
| ——— Improvements in the same | 13 |
| Bowdler's Family Shakspeare | 18 |
| Bramley-Moore's Six Sisters of the Valley | 17 |
| Brande's Dictionary of Science, Literature, and Art | 10 |
| Bray's (C.) Education of the Feelings | 7 |
| ——— Philosophy of Necessity | 7 |
| ——— On Force | 7 |
| Browne's Exposition of the 39 Articles | 13 |
| Brunel's Life of Brunel | 3 |
| Buckle's History of Civilisation | 2 |
| Bull's Hints to Mothers | 20 |
| ——— Maternal Management of Children | 20 |
| Bunsen's God in History | 3 |
| ——— Memoirs | 4 |

| | |
|---|---|
| Bunsen (E. De) on Apocrypha | 15 |
| ——— 's Keys of St. Peter | 15 |
| Burke's Vicissitudes of Families | 4 |
| Burton's Christian Church | 3 |
| ——— Vikram and the Vampire | 17 |
| | |
| Cabinet Lawyer | 20 |
| Calvert's Wife's Manual | 15 |
| Carr's Sir R. Whittington | 18 |
| Cates's Biographical Dictionary | 4 |
| Cats and Farlie's Moral Emblems | 12 |
| Changed Aspects of Unchanged Truths | 6 |
| Chesney's Euphrates Expedition | 17 |
| ——— Indian Polity | 2 |
| ——— Waterloo Campaign | 2 |
| Chesney's and Reeve's Military Essays | 2 |
| Child's Physiological Essays | 11 |
| Chorale Book for England | 11 |
| Clough's Lives from Plutarch | 2 |
| Colenso (Bishop) on Pentateuch and Book of Joshua | 14 |
| Commonplace Philosopher in Town and Country | 6 |
| Conington's Translation of Virgil's Æneid | 18 |
| Contanseau's Two French Dictionaries | 6 |
| Conybeare and Howson's Life and Epistles of St. Paul | 13 |
| Cooper's Surgical Dictionary | 10 |
| Copland's Dictionary of Practical Medicine | 11 |
| Cotton's (Bishop) Life | 3 |
| Coulthart's Decimal Interest Tables | 20 |
| Counsel and Comfort from a City Pulpit | 6 |
| Cox's (G. W.) Aryan Mythology | 3 |
| ——— Tale of the Great Persian War | 2 |
| ——— Tales of Ancient Greece | 17 |
| Cox's (T.) Poems | 18 |
| Cresy's Encyclopædia of Civil Engineering | 13 |
| Critical Essays of a Country Parson | 6 |
| Crookes on Beet-Root Sugar | 13 |
| Culley's Handbook of Telegraphy | 12 |
| Cusack's Student's History of Ireland | 2 |
| | |
| D'Aubigné's History of the Reformation in the time of Calvin | 2 |
| Davidson's Introduction to New Testament | 14 |
| Dead Shot (The), by Marksman | 19 |
| De la Rive's Treatise on Electricity | 8 |
| Denison's Vice-Regal Life | 1 |
| De Tocqueville's Democracy in America | 2 |
| Disraeli's Lothair | 17 |
| ——— Novels and Tales | 17 |
| Dobson on the Ox | 19 |
| Dove's Law of Storms | 8 |
| Doyle's Fairyland | 11 |
| Dyer's City of Rome | 2 |

| | |
|---|---|
| EASTLAKE'S Hints on Household Taste | 12 |
| ———— History of Oil Painting | 11 |
| ———— Life of Gibson | 11 |
| Edinburgh Review | 20 |
| EDMUNDS'S Names of Places | 7 |
| Elements of Botany | 9 |
| ELLICOTT'S Commentary on Ephesians | 14 |
| ———— Lectures on Life of Christ | 14 |
| ———— Commentary on Galatians | 14 |
| ———— Pastoral Epist. | 14 |
| ———— Philippians, &c. | 14 |
| ———— Thessalonians | 14 |
| EWALD'S History of Israel | 14 |
| | |
| FAIRBAIRN'S Application of Cast and Wrought Iron to Building | 12 |
| ———— Information for Engineers | 12 |
| ———— Treatise on Mills and Millwork | 12 |
| ———— Iron Shipbuilding | 12 |
| FARADAY'S Life and Letters | 4 |
| FARRAR'S Chapters on Language | 5 |
| ———— Families of Speech | 7 |
| FELKIN on Hosiery & Lace Manufactures | 13 |
| FENNEL'S Book of the Roach | 19 |
| FFOULKES'S Christendom's Divisions | 15 |
| FITZWYGRAM on Horses and Stables | 19 |
| FORBES'S Earls of Granard | 4 |
| FOWLER'S Collieries and Colliers | 20 |
| FRANCIS'S Fishing Book | 19 |
| FRASER'S Magazine | 20 |
| FRESHFIELD'S Travels in the Caucasus | 16 |
| FROUDE'S History of England | 1 |
| ———— Short Studies | 7 |
| | |
| GANOT'S Elementary Physics | 8 |
| GIANT (The) | 17 |
| GILBERT'S Cadore | 16 |
| ———— and CHURCHILL'S Dolomites | 16 |
| GIRTIN'S House I Live In | 11 |
| GLEDSTONE'S Life of WHITEFIELD | 3 |
| GODDARD'S Wonderful Stories | 17 |
| GOLDSMITH'S Poems, Illustrated | 18 |
| GOULD'S Silver Store | 7 |
| GRAHAM'S Book About Words | 5 |
| GRANT'S Ethics of Aristotle | 5 |
| ———— Home Politics | 2 |
| Graver Thoughts of a Country Parson | 6 |
| Gray's Anatomy | 11 |
| GREENHOW on Bronchitis | 10 |
| GROVE on Correlation of Physical Forces | 9 |
| GURNEY'S Chapters of French History | 2 |
| GWILT'S Encyclopædia of Architecture | 12 |
| | |
| HAMPDEN'S (Bishop) Memorials | 3 |
| Hare on Election of Representatives | 5 |
| HARTWIG'S Harmonies of Nature | 9 |
| ———— Polar World | 9 |
| ———— Sea and its Living Wonders | 9 |
| ———— Tropical World | 9 |
| HAUGHTON'S Manual of Geology | 9 |
| HERSCHEL'S Outlines of Astronomy | 8 |
| HEWITT on the Diseases of Women | 10 |
| HODGSON'S Time and Space | 7 |
| ———— Theory of Practice | 7 |
| HOLMES'S Surgical Treatment of Children | 10 |

| | |
|---|---|
| HOLMES'S System of Surgery | 10 |
| HOOKER and WALKER-ARNOTT'S British Flora | 9 |
| HORNE'S Introduction to the Scriptures | 14 |
| ———— Compendium of the Scriptures | 14 |
| How we Spent the Summer | 16 |
| HOWITT'S Australian Discovery | 16 |
| ———— Northern Heights of London | 16 |
| ———— Rural Life of England | 16 |
| ———— Visits to Remarkable Places | 17 |
| HÜBNER'S Pope Sixtus | 3 |
| HUGHES'S Manual of Geography | 8 |
| HUME'S Essays | 7 |
| ———— Treatise on Human Nature | 7 |
| | |
| IHNE'S History of Rome | 2 |
| INGELOW'S Poems | 18 |
| ———— Story of Doom | 18 |
| ———— Mopsa | 18 |
| | |
| JAMESON'S Legends of Saints and Martyrs | 12 |
| ———— Legends of the Madonna | 12 |
| ———— Legends of the Monastic Orders | 12 |
| ———— Legends of the Saviour | 12 |
| JOHNSTON'S Geographical Dictionary | 8 |
| JUKES on Second Death | 15 |
| ———— on Types of Genesis | 15 |
| | |
| KALISCH'S Commentary on the Bible | 5 |
| ———— Hebrew Grammar | 5 |
| KEITH on Destiny of the World | 14 |
| ———— Fulfilment of Prophecy | 14 |
| KERL'S Metallurgy, by CROOKES and RÖHRIG | 13 |
| KIRBY and SPENCE'S Entomology | 9 |
| | |
| LATHAM'S English Dictionary | 5 |
| ———— River Plate | 8 |
| LAWLOR'S Pilgrimages in the Pyrenees | 16 |
| LECKY'S History of European Morals | 3 |
| ———— Rationalism | 3 |
| Leisure Hours in Town | 6 |
| Lessons of Middle Age | 6 |
| LEWES'S Biographical History of Philosophy | 3 |
| LEWIS'S Letters | 4 |
| LIDDELL and SCOTT'S Greek-English Lexicon | 6 |
| ———— Abridged ditto | 6 |
| Life of Man Symbolised | 12 |
| ———— Margaret M. Hallahan | 14 |
| LINDLEY and MOORE'S Treasury of Botany | 9 |
| LINDSAY'S Evidence for the Papacy | 14 |
| LONGMAN'S Edward the Third | 2 |
| ———— Lectures on History of England | 2 |
| ———— Chess Openings | 20 |
| Lord's Prayer Illustrated | 11 |
| LOUDON'S Encyclopædia of Agriculture | 13 |
| ———— Gardening | 13 |
| ———— Plants | 9 |
| LOWNDES'S Engineer's Handbook | 12 |
| LUBBOCK'S Origin of Civilisation | 9 |
| Lyra Eucharistica | 15 |
| ———— Germanica | 11, 15 |
| ———— Messianica | 15 |

| | |
|---|---|
| Lyra Mystica | 15 |
| MACAULAY'S (Lord) Essays | 3 |
| ———— History of England | 1 |
| ———— Lays of Ancient Rome | 18 |
| ———— Miscellaneous Writings | 7 |
| ———— Speeches | 5 |
| ———— Works | 1 |
| MACFARREN'S Lectures on Harmony | 11 |
| MACLEOD'S Elements of Political Economy | 5 |
| ———— Dictionary of Political Economy | 5 |
| ———— Elements of Banking | 19 |
| ———— Theory and Practice of Banking | 19 |
| MCCULLOCH'S Dictionary of Commerce | 19 |
| ———— Geographical Dictionary | 8 |
| MAGUIRE'S Life of Father Mathew | 4 |
| ———— PIUS IX | 14 |
| MALET'S Overthrow of Germanic Confederation | 2 |
| MANNING'S England and Christendom | 15 |
| MARCET on the Larynx | 11 |
| MARSHALL'S Physiology | 11 |
| MARSHMAN'S History of India | 2 |
| ———— Life of Havelock | 4 |
| MARTINEAU'S Endeavours after the Christian Life | 15 |
| MASSINGBERD'S History of the Reformation | 3 |
| MATHESON'S England to Delhi | 16 |
| MAUNDER'S Biographical Treasury | 4 |
| ———— Geographical Treasury | 8 |
| ———— Historical Treasury | 3 |
| ———— Scientific and Literary Treasury | 10 |
| ———— Treasury of Knowledge | 20 |
| ———— Treasury of Natural History | 9 |
| MAY'S Constitutional History of England | 1 |
| MELVILLE'S Digby Grand | 17 |
| ———— General Bounce | 17 |
| ———— Gladiators | 17 |
| ———— Good for Nothing | 17 |
| ———— Holmby House | 17 |
| ———— Interpreter | 17 |
| ———— Kate Coventry | 17 |
| ———— Queen's Maries | 17 |
| MENDELSSOHN'S Letters | 4 |
| MERIVALE'S Fall of the Roman Republic | 2 |
| ———— Romans under the Empire | 2 |
| MERRIFIELD and EVERS'S Navigation | 8 |
| MILES on Horse's Foot and Horse Shoeing | 19 |
| ———— on Horses' Teeth and Stables | 19 |
| MILL (J.) on the Mind | 5 |
| MILL (J. S.) on Liberty | 4 |
| ———— Subjection of Women | 4 |
| ———— on Representative Government | 4 |
| ———— on Utilitarianism | 4 |
| ————'s Dissertations and Discussions | 4 |
| ———— Political Economy | 4 |
| MILL'S System of Logic | 5 |
| ———— Hamilton's Philosophy | 4 |
| ———— Inaugural Address at St. Andrew's | 4 |
| MILLER'S Elements of Chemistry | 10 |
| ———— Hymn Writers | 15 |
| MITCHELL'S Manual of Architecture | 12 |
| ———— Manual of Assaying | 13 |
| MONSELL'S Beatitudes | 15 |
| ———— His Presence not his Memory | 15 |
| ———— 'Spiritual Songs' | 15 |
| MOORE'S Irish Melodies | 18 |
| ———— Lalla Rookh | 18 |
| ———— Journal and Correspondence | 3 |
| ———— Poetical Works | 18 |
| ———— (Dr. G.) Power of the Soul over the Body | 15 |
| MORELL'S Elements of Psychology | 7 |
| MORELL'S Mental Philosophy | 7 |
| MÜLLER'S (Max) Chips from a German Workshop | 7 |
| ———— Lectures on the Science of Language | 5 |
| ———— (K. O.) Literature of Ancient Greece | 2 |
| MURCHISON on Liver Complaints | 11 |
| MURE'S Language and Literature of Greece | 2 |
| New Testament Illustrated with Wood Engravings from the Old Masters | 12 |
| NEWMAN'S History of his Religious Opinions | 4 |
| NIGHTINGALE'S Notes on Hospitals | 20 |
| NILSSON'S Scandinavia | 9 |
| NORTHCOTE'S Sanctuary of the Madonna | 14 |
| NORTHCOTT on Lathes and Turning | 12 |
| NORTON'S City of London | 16 |
| Notes on Books | 20 |
| ODLING'S Animal Chemistry | 10 |
| ———— Course of Practical Chemistry | 10 |
| ———— Manual of Chemistry | 10 |
| ———— Lectures on Carbon | 10 |
| ———— Outlines of Chemistry | 10 |
| O'FLANAGAN'S Irish Chancellors | 4 |
| Our Children's Story | 17 |
| OWEN'S Comparative Anatomy and Physiology of Vertebrate Animals | 9 |
| ———— Lectures on the Invertebrata | 9 |
| PACKE'S Guide to the Pyrenees | 16 |
| PAGET'S Lectures on Surgical Pathology | 10 |
| PEREIRA'S Manual of Materia Medica | 11 |
| PERKINS'S Italian and Tuscan Sculptors | 12 |
| PEWTNER'S Comprehensive Specifier | 20 |
| Pictures in Tyrol | 16 |
| PIESSE'S Art of Perfumery | 13 |
| ———— Chemical, Natural, and Physical Magic | 13 |
| PONTON'S Beginning | 9 |
| PRATT'S Law of Building Societies | 20 |
| PRENDERGAST'S Mastery of Languages | 6 |
| PRESCOTT'S Scripture Difficulties | 14 |
| Present-Day Thoughts, by A. K. H. B. | 6 |
| PROCTOR'S Handbook of the Stars | 8 |
| ———— Saturn | 8 |
| ———— Other Worlds than Ours | 8 |
| ———— Sun | 8 |
| RAE'S Westward by Rail | 16 |
| Recreations of a Country Parson | 6 |
| REICHEL'S See of Rome | 14 |
| REILLY'S Map of Mont Blanc | 16 |
| REIMANN on Aniline Dyes | 13 |
| REYNOLDS'S Glaphyra | 18 |
| RILEY'S Memorials of London | 16 |
| RIVERS'S Rose Amateur's Guide | 9 |
| ROBBINS'S Cavalry Catechism | 19 |
| ROGERS'S Correspondence of Greyson | 7 |
| ———— Eclipse of Faith | 7 |
| ———— Defence of Faith | 7 |
| ROGET'S Thesaurus of English Words and Phrases | 5 |
| Roma Sotterranea | 16 |

| | |
|---|---|
| Ronalds's Fly-Fisher's Entomology | 19 |
| Rose's Loyola | 14 |
| Rothschild's Israelites | 14 |
| Rowton's Debater | 5 |
| Rule's Karaite Jews | 14 |
| Russell on Government and Constitution | 1 |
| ———'s (Earl) Speeches and Despatches | 1 |
| | |
| Sandars's Justinian's Institutes | 5 |
| Scott's Lectures on the Fine Arts | 11 |
| ——— Albert Durer | 11 |
| Seebohm's Oxford Reformers of 1498 | 2 |
| Sewell's After Life | 17 |
| ——— Glimpse of the World | 17 |
| ——— History of the Early Church | 3 |
| ——— Journal of a Home Life | 17 |
| ——— Passing Thoughts on Religion | 15 |
| ——— Poems of Bygone Years | 18 |
| ——— Preparation for Communion | 15 |
| ——— Principles of Education | 15 |
| ——— Readings for Confirmation | 15 |
| ——— Readings for Lent | 15 |
| ——— Examination for Confirmation | 15 |
| ——— Stories and Tales | 17 |
| ——— Thoughts for the Age | 15 |
| ——— Thoughts for the Holy Week | 15 |
| Shakspeare's Midsummer Night's Dream, illustrated with Silhouettes | 12 |
| Shipley's Four Cardinal Virtues | 14 |
| ——— Invocation of Saints | 15 |
| Short's Church History | 3 |
| Smart's Walker's English Dictionaries | 5 |
| Smith's (Southwood) Philosophy of Health | 20 |
| ——— (J.) Paul's Voyage and Shipwreck | 14 |
| ——— (Sydney) Life and Letters | 3 |
| ——— Miscellaneous Works | 7 |
| ——— Wit and Wisdom | 7 |
| Southey's Doctor | 5 |
| ——— Poetical Works | 18 |
| Stanley's History of British Birds | 9 |
| Stebbing's Analysis of Mill's Logic | 5 |
| Stephen's Ecclesiastical Biography | 4 |
| ——— Playground of Europe | 16 |
| Stirling's Secret of Hegel | 7 |
| ——— Sir William Hamilton | 7 |
| Stonehenge on the Dog | 19 |
| ——— on the Greyhound | 19 |
| Strickland's Tudor Princesses | 4 |
| ——— Queens of England | 4 |
| Strong and Free | 7 |
| Sunday Afternoons at the Parish Church of a Scottish University City | 6 |
| | |
| Taylor's History of India | 2 |
| ——— (Jeremy) Works, edited by Eden | 15 |
| Thirlwall's History of Greece | 2 |
| Thomson's Conspectus | 11 |
| ——— Laws of Thought | 5 |
| Three Weddings | 17 |
| | |
| Todd (A.) on Parliamentary Government | 1 |
| ——— and Bowman's Anatomy and Physiology of Man | 11 |
| Trench's Ierne | 17 |
| ——— Realities of Irish Life | 2 |
| Trollope's Barchester Towers | 17 |
| ——— Warden | 17 |
| Twiss's Law of Nations | 19 |
| Tyndall's Diamagnetism | 8 |
| ——— Faraday as a Discoverer | 4 |
| ——— Lectures on Electricity | 9 |
| ——— Lectures on Light | 8 |
| ——— Lectures on Sound | 8 |
| ——— Heat a Mode of Motion | 8 |
| ——— Essays on the Imagination in Science | 9 |
| Uncle Peter's Fairy Tale | 18 |
| Ure's Dictionary of Arts, Manufactures, and Mines | 12 |
| | |
| Van Der Hoeven's Handbook of Zoology | 9 |
| Visit to my Discontented Cousin | 17 |
| | |
| Warburton's Hunting Songs | 18 |
| Watson's Principles and Practice of Physic | 10 |
| Watts's Dictionary of Chemistry | 10 |
| Webb's Objects for Common Telescopes | 8 |
| Webster & Wilkinson's Greek Testament | 14 |
| Wellington's Life, by Gleig | 4 |
| West on Children's Diseases | 10 |
| ——— on Nursing Children | 20 |
| Whately's English Synonymes | 5 |
| ——— Logic | 5 |
| ——— Rhetoric | 5 |
| White and Riddle's Latin Dictionaries | 6 |
| Wilcocks's Sea Fisherman | 19 |
| Williams's Aristotle's Ethics | 5 |
| ——— History of Wales | 1 |
| Williams on Climate of South of France | 10 |
| ——— Consumption | 11 |
| Willich's Popular Tables | 20 |
| Willis's Principles of Mechanism | 12 |
| Winslow on Light | 8 |
| Wood's (J. G.) Bible Animals | 9 |
| ——— Homes without Hands | 9 |
| ——— (T.) Chemical Notes | 10 |
| Woodward and Cater's Encyclopædia | 3 |
| | |
| Yardley's Poetical Works | 18 |
| Yonge's History of England | 1 |
| ——— English-Greek Lexicons | 6 |
| ——— Two Editions of Horace | 18 |
| Youatt on the Dog | 19 |
| ——— on the Horse | 19 |
| | |
| Zeller's Socrates | 3 |
| ——— Stoics, Epicureans, and Sceptics | 3 |
| Zigzagging amongst Dolomites | 16 |

www.ingramcontent.com/pod-product-compliance
Lightning Source LLC
Chambersburg PA
CBHW022042230426
43672CB00008B/1048